The RELUCTANT MOTHER

A Story No One Wants to Tell

ZEHRA NAQVI

HAY HOUSE

HAY HOUSE INDIA

New Delhi • London • Sydney
Carlsbad, California • New York City

Hay House Publishers (India) Pvt Ltd
Muskaan Complex, Plot No. 3, B-2, Vasant Kunj, New Delhi – 110070, India

Hay House LLC, P.O. Box 5100, Carlsbad, CA 92018-5100, USA
Hay House UK Ltd, The Sixth Floor, Watson House, 54 Baker Street, London W1U 7BU, UK
Hay House Australia Publishing Pty Ltd, 18/36 Ralph St., Alexandria NSW 2015, Australia

Email: contact@hayhouse.co.in
Website: www.hayhouse.co.in

First published by Hay House India, 2021
Reprint, 2025
12 11 10 9 8 7 6 5 4 3

ISBN 978-93-91067-20-5
ISBN 978-93-91067-21-2 (e-book)

Printed at Repro India Limited

FSC www.fsc.org MIX Paper from responsible sources FSC® C047271

Hay House is committed to a sustainable future for our business, our readers and our planet. This book is made from Forest Stewardship Council® certified paper.

Zehra Naqvi is a hands-on mother and a journalist who has spent a decade writing on literature, gender, and socio-political issues. She has written for various national and international publications such as the *Indian Express, Reader's Digest, The Hindu, Financial Chronicle, The Quint, Child* magazine, and *Women's Web*. Zehra is a quadruple gold medallist in journalism from Aligarh Muslim University. This is her first book.

Praise for *The Reluctant Mother*

'Honest, humorous, and heartwarming.'

—Milan Vohra,
author

'Is it my voice? Is it her voice? Or is it our voice? Zehra Naqvi speaks for every woman in *The Reluctant Mother*. Not everything is hunky-dory after the pregnancy test or pink and blue balloons and booties after motherdom. There's reluctance to become a mother in the event of an unplanned pregnancy and post-partum depression after birth. Every relationship is tested, trying to adjust and adapt to the little one. All this and much more is captured by Naqvi, and I could feel my tears well up at many places remembering my own days as a new mother and the trials and joys it brought.'

—Rana Safvi,
historian and author

'An immensely honest and emotional take on relationships and parenting. It doesn't take the clichéd route of self-help books, yet the layered narrative helps you to understand the complexity and beauty of a man-woman relationship.

Not just for women, Zehra Naqvi's emotional and moving storytelling is an essential read for men, too.'

—Yasser Usman,
TV journalist and author

'. . . A fresh new voice, brimful with life and real, lived experiences, redolent with the joys and sorrows of a young woman's life, a life that is a little less ordinary and a voice that is well worth listening to.'

—Dr Rakhshanda Jalil,
writer and literary historian

'Love doesn't always have to be gushy; it can be prickly and it can hurt. Zehra writes definitively about the two different loves of her life—her husband and her child—and how the line between them doesn't blur. It's refreshing to read a story of a reluctant mother, one who doesn't subscribe to motherhood as an exalted state of being. Motherhood is exhausting and life changing and not always a blessing. It takes courage to put that out into the open.'

—Andaleeb Wajid,
author

'A realistic and poignant story about a young woman's journey through the rites of passage. A tale of love, heartbreak, and redemption. Must-read!'

—Debeshi Gooptu Bakshi,
author

'This is every mother's worst nightmare and every mother's dearest moments. This is us.'

—Nazia Erum,
author

For my husband,
who embodies gentleness as strength
and loves me as few men can love

And for my son,
who blessed us both by choosing to be born to us

Contents

Introduction

This book is the story of a woman who became a young mother in her twenties. A significant period has elapsed between the writing of this book and its publication. As people grow, they change; their needs change, their dreams change, and the way they look at the world also changes. They are no longer the same person that they used to be.

In the introduction to the latest edition of his evergreen and much-adored book, *The Room on the Roof*, Ruskin Bond writes:

'What makes it "different", I think, is that it is a novel about adolescence by an adolescent, and for this reason, I have never changed a word or made any revisions. It reflects the writer as he was when he wrote it—naïve, trustful, eager for love and friendship.'

This is precisely how it is for this book, too. It reflects the writer as a young woman full of dreams and longing. A woman who was naïve, trustful, and largely unaware of the harsh realities of life.

Bond writes further, 'Yes, it was written out of the loneliness of a young person longing for love and family. It has the passion and intensity we possess only when we are in our teens, and that I think is what has kept it alive all these years.'

This book, too, was written out of the 'loneliness of a young person' who had to watch her hopes and dreams being dashed to the ground. It is a moment suspended in time and will, perhaps, remind the readers of who they were when they were young . . . passionate and full of dreams and romance.

Prologue

May 8, 2014

I lie in bed watching myself hanging from the fan. Feet dangling, neck broken, eyes bulging like a ghost.

Every night now, I see myself hanging there.

Every time I step out onto the road, I see my body—mangled and spurting blood—beneath the wheels of a passing car. I see them everywhere. Corpses of myself.

I see strange things and images inside words. The word 'slaughter' reveals to me the 'laughter' hidden inside it, flashing visions of a pile of dead, bloodied bodies and a killer with a dripping butcher's knife laughing hysterically over them.

I am a woman possessed.

Possessed by the idea of murder, of killing, of suicide.

Possessed by the idea of death, the idea of escape.

Chapter 1

The Tempest Brews

December 26, 2011

New Delhi

10:00 a.m.

I am running up a flight of a hundred steps, taking two at a time, late for office, as usual, and trying to make up in speed for what I have lost in a delayed start from home. At the top, my heartbeat quickens manifold, banging like a hammer in my ears. I have to grab the railing and catch my breath—two more minutes lost. I am lost, too, I had so far prided myself on being able to run up the stairs without a care. Time is ticking away though, and I have that metro train to catch from Jasola to Green Park.

2:00 p.m.

The three of us—Shreya, Sameer, and I—are sitting in the cafeteria with our lunchboxes, ready to trade morsels of home-cooked food. I know what I have in mine—*sabzi* of beans and potatoes with three *rotis*—I packed it myself. I am starving. But as soon as I open the box, a wave of nausea hits me with a single whiff of the food.

'Umff!' I clamp the lid shut.

'What's wrong?' Shreya looks at my green face quizzically.

'Don't know, maybe the food has gone bad . . . the smell is making me want to throw up.'

'Let me see,' Shreya takes the box from me, ever the mothering, scolding one. 'The food's perfectly alright, it's just your excuse to skip lunch again. You're going to disappear soon if you don't eat.'

I am staring at the box now and another wave of nausea hits me. 'Shreya,' I whisper dazedly, 'I think we need to get a home test kit.'

Descending from the steps of the cafeteria, I text Salman. 'I hope you know that I'm going to kill you if this turns out to be what I think it is.'

10:00 p.m.

I am reading the instructions on the kit. Salman sits next to me, sufficiently chastised. I am, however, more at peace.

'Well, after all, it's been a year since we got married, and we've had a lot of fun together. It won't be so bad.' I tell myself more than I feel I am telling him. I have always wanted more time with him, more things to do with him. It was never nearly enough.

'And anyway,' I continue, 'It is God's will. This could have happened earlier and that would have been really bad. I'm sure I can cope with it now. I'm at peace and I'll accept it with grace,' I know this is just me trying to accept the inevitable. But, on some level, I do feel calm.

Salman is silent. The way he mostly is. I know he is listening.

'Well, let's wait for the morning. Maybe it's nothing. Maybe I just have food poisoning!' I feign cheerfulness that I don't truly feel.

December 27, 2011

9:00 a.m.

I am in the washroom with Salman. I think I am at peace. With beating hearts, we watch the small rectangle of fate.

One line. The control line. Two lines.

I am pregnant.

I thought I was at peace.

I had always seen in movies that women break into tears of joy and men swing their wives up in their arms on learning that they have new life coming. I do break into tears. But they are tears of shock. Of dread. Of dismay.

And they are tears of wrath—wrath that I unleash on the man that I love the most in this world. Wrath of having my dreams washed over, having my carefully created magical universe destroyed.

And wrath at all those who had wanted this to happen.

Death.

It is supposed to be the moment when you are dying when your whole life moves before your eyes in a flash. I'm not dying. I am fully, completely alive. And I am going to bring a new life into this world. And yet, I am experiencing that moment.

I got married early, quite early—about six months past my 23rd birthday—and all because I was in love. Head over heels in love with this man whose honesty, decency, and sheer goodness of spirit bowled me over.

Getting married to him, though, was difficult enough, because a love marriage is still taboo in small-town India, an act of shame that you are supposed to hide, or your parents will be sneered at. Marrying for love is still unthinkable in parts of the country. What you should preferably marry for is your parents' happiness. Or money. Or prestige. Or to bring forth thorough-bred offspring. Or if you are a man, an acceptable reason for getting married would be to declare that you're a rather busy bachelor who is having problems feeding himself and keeping a clean house. So, naturally, this love marriage thing was no piece of cake. Everyone told me this was the wrong step to take, that we were polar opposites, that our religious approaches didn't match, nor did we match socially. Everyone told me I would regret this. But I didn't.

We had found our happily ever after, walking into the sunset hand in hand. Each morning I would wake up, watch his sleeping face and feel an overwhelming mixture of thrill and serenity all at once. I couldn't just get over the fact that I had him. Here, before me, in my arms. I had everything I wanted.

'You know it never feels like we're married,' Salman would often joke. 'It feels as if we're a live-in couple!' We had heard all the marriage jokes and none of them applied to us. Fairytales did come true sometimes.

But then, we made our fairytale come true every day, in myriad small ways. By respecting each other as individuals and never expecting the husband-wife role-related 'duties' from each other. And when we did perform them, we never took it for granted. I mean, we literally said sweet thank-yous to each other for the littlest chore done.

And so, even though I had been known as the super ambitious, super-competitive girl from the time I was 12, I still wanted nothing more than my fairy tale. Despite the fact that everybody thought I would sacrifice anything for my career—which I had chosen amid major tussle and conflict with the family, quite like how I chose my life partner. The very idea of being a journalist in a small town, civil services type family was blasphemy in itself. And the more hard-fought it got, the more determined I got about my decision. I was crazy about being a journalist. But I was equally crazy about the man in my life, and if it came down to picking one, I knew who I'd choose. But even more importantly, I'd picked a man with whom I knew I'd never have to choose.

I was living the dream here—dream man *and* dream career—and I wanted more.

More of him. More of us. Vacations around the world, romantic dinners, movies together, sharing silly jokes, long drives in the rain and making love in every corner of the house. And I was doing it. I was living the dream.

Until.

I felt my dream slip from my fingers.

December 27, 2011

9:30 a.m.

I call up Shreya.

'H-Hi,' I stutter into the cell phone. I have to tell her. I need to share this with a girl. Salman has been my best friend for so long, but right now he's not the one I want.

'Hey,' she replies cheerfully, but I know she knows why I've called her.

'It says positive,' I tell her flatly, if a little tearfully.

'Oh . . .' she takes a deep breath. 'Well, then, congratulations! Say congratulations to Salman.'

I know she's trying to turn this into a positive situation of celebration, like it is for most people. But it has the opposite effect; my tears flow freely once again.

'Hey, don't cry, it's going to be alright. I know you didn't want this right now, but it's a blessing from God. Don't cry, for heaven's sake!'

And that makes me cry all the more. Because I know I shouldn't be crying. I should be happy. I should be celebrating this the way other women do. I feel sad. Sad for the tiny life in me whom I shouldn't be treating this way.

And I feel a little abnormal.

'*Yaar* . . . I don't know why I'm so upset. I ought to be happy, right? I mean, Bella never wanted anything except for Edward, but when she became pregnant, she was really happy and wanted to be a mother . . . so why can't I be happy, too?'

Shreya bursts out laughing.

'Are you nuts? That's a story! You're not Bella! And you don't have to feel anything that anybody else feels. It's okay, you weren't expecting this. It's a shock for you and so you're responding that way. It'll be fine in some time.'

Will it, though?

December 28, 2011

Have you held someone's life in your hands?

Have you?

Held a gun in your hand and felt terrified about pulling the trigger?

Looked at the bug crawling near your bed and thought about squishing it? And then felt awful for wanting to kill it?

There are times when we do hold someone's life in our hands, even if it is as tiny as a bug's.

There was a time when I held someone's life in my hands. And that someone was my own baby.

11:00 a.m.

My regular gynaecologist, Dr Sunita, is out of town, so I have an appointment with Dr Richa instead. She's a happy-looking, friendly woman in specs and a saree.

'So, you're planning to have a baby?' she asks pleasantly.

'Well, this isn't exactly planned . . .' I tell her nervously. 'We weren't intending for this to happen so soon.'

But I had misunderstood her.

'No, I mean, you are planning to continue the pregnancy, right?'

Of course. Of course. I hear it in my mind even before I say it out loud. I cannot think of that word. I cannot think of 'removing it' just because it is too soon for me. This pregnancy is not dangerous to my life. It's not dangerous to my health. It's not detrimental to me in any way, except that it's too darn soon. For all my crying and wrath and resentment, not once have I thought about not 'continuing with it'. The thought makes me want to throw up.

And that's what makes me realise that I hold this tiny life in my hands. Its survival, its growth, its entire existence, it is all up to me. I know I can't just squish it like a bug—it is a life waiting for its place in the universe, and I can't just say no to it.

January 1, 2012

Fasten your seatbelts, please. It's going to be a long and rickety ride.

Here are the top safety instructions given to me at the beginning of my pregnancy:

1. No eating in restaurants (because I am prone to major stomach infections)
2. No road travel (because roads in India aren't exactly something to be proud of—and the first trimester is the real tricky one)
3. No lifting heavy loads (that's a no-brainer)

This short list weighs on me like a heavily rounded belly.

5:30 p.m.

I am writing an editorial—that is my daily job. I love my job. I have said that, haven't I? So, I am doing what I do, I have my eyes fixed on the screen as my fingers type with demonic speed, mind churning out one edit-worthy thought after another.

Until.

All of a sudden, my mind goes into a spin. My eyelids swoop shut. I cannot get the sleep out of my eyes. I cannot think. I complete the rest of the edit with two fingers of my left hand forcing open both the eyes, stretching up the eyelids, while the right-hand types excruciatingly slowly, unaided by its partner. Every thought takes twice as long to form itself and every sentence takes twice as long to type.

As soon as I am through with the edit, I hurriedly wrap up the page, hand it over to my boss, and ask permission to leave office immediately.

On the way home, I doze off instantly and almost fall off the auto-rickshaw twice!

January 6, 2012

11:30 a.m.

The Jaipur Literature Fest is a much-awaited event in the world of bibliophiles. For the first time in my life, I am going to be attending it. Correction, I am going to be covering it in my capacity as a journalist. I am overjoyed.

My time to go places is going full throttle!

I have been on professional trips before this, both domestic and international, but this one is special, because it mirrors my love for the world of books. I would be face to face with so many of the authors whose voices I had only heard in their narratives, whose worlds I had lived in through their pages—I have lived in those worlds much more than I have lived in my own, perhaps.

The event is just a couple of weeks away now and I'm enthusiastically trying to make train reservations when I am hit by a sickening wave of nausea. I almost faint on my desk with a sudden onset of dizziness, following which, I am hit by a sickening wave of truth.

I have this wonderful, amazing, golden opportunity in my hand, and I have to let it go.

a) There are no train tickets available; the flights are super expensive and,
b) Even if I do get there, I don't want to throw up in the middle of conducting an interview or, worse, feel my eyelids drooping shut while the author is telling me what inspired them to write!

There goes the Litfest and any other assignment that involves travelling.

My time to go places . . . screeches to a halt.

January 9, 2012

11:30 a.m.

I am still in bed. Already late for office. Too weak to get up from the bed. Salman is already off to work, having served me the usual glass of hand-squeezed orange juice and an egg—which is pretty much all I can bear to eat without throwing up.

I have to inform my boss now—that hated task of posting a leave application, especially when it is every other day. I send the message and immediately go off to sleep again.

January 20, 2012

I throw up twice in office. Have to, literally, run to the washroom from my desk. I feel so faint with weakness that I excuse myself early from work.

January 22, 2012

Two different colleagues had given birth to healthy babies after continuing to work till almost their eighth month before I even knew I was pregnant. Now, they were back in the office from their maternity leave within three months of delivery. There are women all over the world who do just this and, so, I have been reassuring myself that I can, too. Until.

Until my body grows so weak that I can't get up from the bed even if someone is continuously ringing the doorbell. Until my brain gets so fatigued that I am sleeping most of the day *and* night. Until something goes so wrong in my brain that any strain on my eyes for more than half an hour at a stretch—reading, working on the laptop, watching TV—starts giving me splitting headaches; headaches where I writhe on the bed, clutching my head and screaming in agony. Headaches where I wish for a hammer to break my head and end this once and for all.

Whoever said that pregnancy was a beautiful, wonderful, ethereal experience should definitely get their head examined. Or, maybe, they were just plain lucky.

January 25, 2012

Why is it that I am such a reluctant mother? Why is it that I have, literally, hated the whole world since I became pregnant? Is it that I never wanted to have a child at all? No, that is not true.

Whenever Salman and I would talk of getting married, we would always talk about having kids. We would have fun thinking up baby names, talking about the games we'd play with them, and imagining life with a new one amongst us.

In truth, though, I didn't want one *right now, so soon.*

What is really exasperating is that almost everyone I know equates getting married with producing children. Indians, generally, consider this the topmost among the Ten Commandments of Marriage—sacred laws set in stone, as it were—that you must get pregnant the moment you get married. If not the next day, the very next month, at least. Woe unto you if you choose otherwise.

Relatives, acquaintances, in-laws—especially the in-laws—will pulverise your brains to pulp incessantly interrogating you about the 'good news' and why it is taking 'so long'.

And when you tell them the truth, that it is taking so long because that is how you want it, they have well-meaning advice ready for you. 'If you keep delaying this, you'll regret it later. There are so many childless couples who, later, regretted their delayed family planning.'

That hurts. Terribly.

And creates deeper furrows of anger. The more they insist, the more you hate the idea of ruining your marital bliss.

Yes, I said ruining.

I find it impossible to reconcile myself to the idea that the purpose of marriage is procreation and extending the family line—or *nasl* and *khaandaan* as the relatives so love to emphasise. Marriage has to be about companionship and cherishing one another, or else we're fine on our own, thank you. Marriage is about finding that other half of yourself, the one that helps you see the world in a way you'd never seen before.

Yes, you do have children, eventually, but that is not the *purpose* of marriage. You don't have children because 'things will get better once you have a *bachcha*, just wait and watch!' or 'things get boring between a couple so you need a child', or even, 'the child makes you complete'—all platitudes underlining our society's approach to marriage. You have children when you want them, when you'd like to create a family together, when you're ready to take on the responsibility of a new life. And no, you don't necessarily *need* one to be complete—for you are already complete with each other.

And so were we, complete with each other, squeezing every drop of pleasure from our time together, before a third person came along to share every single moment with us. It had to happen at some point, but I wanted to have a big buffer before that, to enable me to look back with satisfaction and think, 'Yes, I experienced and achieved all that I wanted to. *Now* I'm ready to welcome my baby.'

But life has a habit of messing with you.

When the bombshell dropped, for some inexplicable reason, I was overcome by a feeling of defeat. I had lost and 'they' had won. All those 'well-wishers' out there who couldn't believe that a *love marriage* was not going wrong somehow, that my husband was not the restrictive, oppressing *mullah* they had imagined him to be; all those people who had been waiting for me to feel *trapped* instead of delighted with my marriage, had won. They had won. And I had lost.

And that right there is why I cannot get over my fury. It isn't that I resent this tiny, helpless being. I feel sad for her . . . or him. I feel sad for this precious little creature who ought to be in a happy mother's womb, the kind of mother who would be overjoyed and ecstatic. I do wish to give my baby that kind of a mum.

But, for the life of me, I just can't bring myself to be happy.

Chapter 2

The Reluctant Mom

January 26, 2012

9:30 a.m.

I'm at the hospital for my first ultrasound—the TVS or the Total Vaginal Scan. It is one of those countless, hugely embarrassing exercises that you are subjected to during the course of your pregnancy. But the reason this TVS merits a mention is not because of its embarrassing nature but because *this* is when I say 'hello' to my baby for the first time.

It's when I hear that sound.

Knock-knock-knock-knock-knock.

It isn't like the twin bump-bump, bump-bump of your heart that your palm feels across your chest. It is a steady thumping, like a super-fast engine rushing ahead. The sound fills my ears, it fills the room, and I am wonderstruck.

This, this precious moment, is my first *pleasant* contact with my baby. After days and days of whining, moping, crying, and swearing, this 'knocking' gives me one little moment of simple, wondrous pleasure.

'Hello, little one . . .'

My first thought is that Salman isn't here to share this with me. He is waiting outside, and I wish and wish and wish that I'd called him in. I make a mental note to ask him to come inside with me the next time. He is going to love it.

Here's what the report says:

> Early live intrauterine pregnancy of approximately 8 weeks. Heartbeat: 144 beats per minute.
>
> That's one helluva speed for that teeny-tiny heart, little one! I can see you're in a great hurry to be here.

February 14, 2012

It is our second Valentine's Day after the wedding. Normally I'm the super-enthusiastic, let's-do-this-let's-go-there kind of person, but when you're throwing up at least six times a day and feeling dizzy for the most part, all you want to do is lie back on the bed and groan. The hospital where I'm getting all my tests done holds a pregnancy workshop every two months and at the very first workshop I discover that I am the *only* one, among a group of 40 first-time moms, who is experiencing such severe nausea, fatigue, and headaches. Hallelujah.

So, nowadays, I have to be dragged from bed to go anywhere. But here is the silver lining: we've just crossed the first trimester and I can now eat at restaurants! And, funnily enough, even though the smallest amount of home-cooked food comes back up my food pipe instantaneously, now every time we go out to a restaurant, my appetite returns. Thank heavens for small mercies.

We decide to celebrate Valentine's Day by gorging on *golgappas* together. Not at some roadside stall, though—that's forbidden for me for now—we are at the food court of The Great India Place Mall, Noida.

'Hey! *Chunnu* is having *golgappas* for the first time!' Salman grins at me.

'Yeah,' I grin back. 'I think she likes 'em.'

Chunnu. It is a gender-neutral term for the little one and that is what we've always called our baby, even before I got pregnant. But this is a new ritual that just formed itself: now, every time I eat something, Salman exclaims delightedly over how *chunnu* is trying new things. And, every time I watch an animated movie (which I do lots and lots of) he asks me whether the baby likes it.

So, I'm quite sure my *chunnu* likes *golgappas*. I mean, who doesn't?

For my V-Day gift, Salman gets me a fluffy, feathery, heart-shaped pillow that reads 'I Love You'.

I know, it is no diamond ring. But diamond rings are far too overrated and I would much rather have something cute and lovable, than something necessarily expensive. If it has to be an expensive gift at all, I would much rather he took me on a vacation with all the magic of a living world. Who needs another stone?

Plus, this pillow has become my very best pregnancy-friend. It helps me sleep comfortably on my side, as sleeping on my back has become a distant dream. I have been plagued by acute backache, already, even before the bulge has started becoming prominent. God alone knows what would happen once my body balloons up and the load on my back weighs me down. Ah, yes, the pillow's going to be an even better friend then. On the bright side, though, Salman exclaims, 'Hey, *Chunnu* has already started using a pillow!'

March 1, 2012

4:00 p.m.

I am taking a walk outside my house (thank goodness I finally have the strength for it). It is spring and the balmy air envelops me in an embrace that speaks of a beloved lost and found again. The sun doesn't sting yet and newborn flowers peek out in curiosity all around the premises. I have just finished the light exercises advised by my doctor and

I sit on a raised step, watching the squirrels scamper on the buildings. The scene reminds me of how my sister was amazed every time a squirrel climbed the concrete walls. I guess that is an adaptation for you.

I look around happily at this spring-city landscape laid out before me, and I wish my little one turns out to be a nature lover, too.

I place a hand on my belly. 'See that little furry thing scampering about with its tail in the air? That's a squirrel. Oh, this tall brown scaly thing with green frills all over? This is a tree. And those pink soft dewy little clusters? Those are flowers. Aren't they pretty? Oh, darling, you're going to love it here.'

March 5, 2012

11:30 a.m.

I miss my office. I miss going to work every day. I hate having to sit at home with nothing to do.

I don't want to watch movies . . . I don't want to read books . . . I miss my work friends, our conversations. I am so . . . lonely.

Why, oh why am I surrounded only by people whose only topics of discussion centre around how irregular the help is, or how clean their cupboards are, or what's going on in Tulsi, Parvati, Ichcha, and Tapasya's fictional lives, or how much *zeera*, *adrak*, and *lehsun* to put in a dish. Aagghh!

I don't care about any of this. All I want to do is to be able to go back to work, write editorials on what is important in the country currently or, simply, write my regular features on literature, art, history, and travel. Can't I please just go back to work without throwing up half a dozen times a day? God, pleeaassee!

March 10, 2012

It is not going to be so bad. Children are nice . . . at least, mine won't be like that bawling kid across the block.

My neighbour's anniversary celebrations were ruined by her tantrum-throwing child. Nope, mine won't be that way.

My husband's cousin says that the first two years are terrible. Nope, mine will be an angel. A calm, well-mannered ball of love.

Kids can be nice, right? Not all kids turn out to be total brats, right?

RIGHT?

March 15, 2012

1:00 p.m.

Dr Sunita is the best gynaecologist I have ever met. She is my saviour. Here's why:

'I am not able to eat anything again, you know,' I complain to her as she carries out her routine checks. 'Just tomato soup, and, at times, bread and butter . . . I haven't had a single *roti* in 5 days. Nothing goes down. No rice. No vegetables. No *dal*. Maybe some home-made *aloo tikki* sometimes.'

'That's fine. You're getting enough nutrition. You don't have to worry,' she murmurs, going through my reports.

That is not really what I want to tell her. I'm on the verge of tears, actually. Today is one of those days again.

'You know all this stuff about great glorified motherhood? I think it's utter crap.'

I have her attention now.

'Why?'

'I don't know . . . I just feel angry all the time. Like I want to get a punching bag and keep at it the whole day. I don't have the energy to feel happy about anything. I don't think I love my baby just yet. What is wrong with me? I feel like crying all the time.'

'That is just because you're not keeping well,' she says gently. 'You're having nausea, fatigue, and all these other problems. They are making you weak and extremely irritable. Once this phase passes, you will be fine and you *will* love your baby.' She smiles.

'I hope so.'

'In the meantime, you can just fight with your husband and make him your punching bag!' Her eyes twinkle.

I grin. Poor Salman!

April 20, 2012

I am sitting in the waiting lounge of Sitaram Bhartia Institute of Science and Research for my routine check-up. Out of the blue, there is something like a pulse inside my stomach. I am jolted to attention—what is happening? There! There it is, again!

Realisation dawns. I just felt my baby's very first movements.

Wow.

And this is not the ecstatic, overjoyed kind of 'wow!' It is the awed and overwhelmed, eyes-wide-with-astonishment kind of feeling . . . the 'wow' whispered to yourself at the sheer magnificence and enormity of it all.

I just felt my baby move. Wow.

I feel myself slowly smiling.

It is the exact same feeling that I had when I received the report of my first-trimester ultrasound. That was when I saw the shape of a slowly forming human being: a rounded head, a tiny forehead and—wonder of wonders—the nose!

The black images showed me a teeny, tiny nose with the report that said: Nasal bone, measuring 3.1mm.

A 3.1 mm nose. I can see you, baby. I can see your nose.

And, now, I can feel you move.

May 14, 2012

We are in Aligarh. Salman is sitting before me on the bed. We'd been away from each other for about 15 days because I came here to meet my mom. He hasn't felt his baby's movements yet; when I was with him, they were too light to be felt on the outside. He has his hand on my belly as his eyes search my face with anticipation.

BUMP!

That was a huge one!

I am delighted to see the wondrous, childlike grin on my husband's face. He laughs out loud. He is amazed. It is a moment we'll cherish forever.

June 15, 2012

This baby is going to be really naughty. Lord knows how she/he manages to do it, but every so often I feel 4 simultaneous kicks at 4 different places in my tummy! There's hardly a moment when this little one lies still.

My sister Farina says that she can actually see her/him 'swimming around' in my tummy. I know what she means; the bulge often seems to 'glide' from one end to another. Dr Sunita says these movements are so visible on the outside because I'm still so thin and that there's been no fat increase on other parts of my body. To quote Farina, I present the literal image of an egg on a stick.

June 25, 2012

New Delhi

Salman and I are out for our daily post-dinner walk around the park. These walks with him are perhaps the best part of my day, the simplest of joys in the homeliest of surroundings. Hand in hand amid the lush green, swaying to the symphony of the wind in the trees. In a way, it is a good thing that

I've taken time off from work. The music of the wind is best heard unhurriedly.

July 14, 2012

It is raining hard. Monsoon has arrived in all its glory. Salman just came back from the office a few minutes ago. He takes my hand now.

'Care for a drive in the rain?' he smiles at me.

Yes. Of course. Would I ever say no?

He is reversing the car right to the door so I don't get wet. Our neighbour comes out of his house. 'Coming from somewhere?' he asks over the loud rumble of the rain.

'No, going for a drive!' I giggle.

'In such rain!'

I nodded, 'In such rain!'

Lost in our fancies we had forgotten that we're in Delhi, not the Garden of Eden, and rains here spell out traffic jams like nothing else. But I have Michael Schumacher for a husband, and I could trust him to zigzag through it all.

I have never loved rain so much. And him.

July 21, 2012

12:00 a.m.

We are having dinner at Comesum, the all-night restaurant near Nizamuddin Railway Station. I hadn't even heard about this place before today. To be honest, Salman had never suggested dining out at midnight before today. He is trying hard to make this right for me, to assure me that nothing is going to change between us.

Perhaps it won't. Perhaps it will. But what won't change is what happiness is.

Happiness is us. Whether it is the both of us, or the three of us. It is always us.

August 20, 2012

One a penny, two a penny, hot cross buns; 'May you have no daughters, only bear sons.'

This is an undisputed truth that every unborn child in India is always a boy. Nobody hopes for a girl, unless they already have a boy to 'carry on the family name'. And if you have two girls, well, the third one will mostly be finished off in the womb.

I may be generalising it a bit too much. Educated people may not kill the baby. But they do heave a sigh of despair, receiving condolences instead of congratulations from visiting guests: 'Don't be disheartened, next time, God be willing!'

It made me furious during my teen years, but now, now when I might just be at the receiving end of it, I feel a surge of power. Power that I can change, at least in my minuscule portion of the universe, how I react to the arrival of this unborn creature—and how I allow others to react to it, at least in my presence.

And yet, one thought confounds me.

All cultures value the love of parents above everything else. It is supposed to be the purest because it is unconditional. So why is it that everyone wants a son? Because he might provide for them in old age or be a source of security while a daughter will only be a liability? If parental love is indeed unconditional, why would you prefer to have a child who brings you more benefits (supposedly)? That sounds a lot like a transaction to me.

Even now, even in the age of 'daughters are not lesser than sons', the point still remains pertinent. The 'unconditional' love of parenthood isn't all that it is cracked up to be if the only cause for celebrating your child's birth is the future benefits the child would bring.

So, it has been that even before I became pregnant, I was deluged with blessings from a whole bunch of elders to bear a son. Try as I might, with a fake smile and gritted teeth, to brush those 'well-meaning' blessings away I couldn't help but point out to them that I don't give tuppence about the sex of the child.

Faizan, my husband's cousin, is staying with us right now, and he is a real Godsend for I have someone to talk to while Salman is at work. I give him very strict instructions:

'Listen, bro, I am going to buy a chart paper and a permanent marker. If I give birth to a baby girl, this is what I want you to write out in bold and then stick outside my hospital room: *"If you are coming to console us instead of congratulating us, please turn back right now. We are busy celebrating."*'

Every time I think of the whole *'beta'* scenario, I can't help but recall this beautiful thing I once heard in a religious lecture back home:

Moses asked the Lord what he does when he is happy. God said: 'I make it rain upon the earth.'

Moses asked again, 'What do you do when you are happier?'

'I send guests to people's homes.' Because guests bring blessings with them as they enter.

'And what do you do when you are the happiest, Lord?'

God smiled. 'I create daughters.'

I am looking forward to having a daughter. But then again, I'd be equally happy if it were a son. As long as she/he is healthy, happy, and sweet-tempered.

I am not going to choose. God will choose for me. Because you cannot—and should not—be picky about gifts. Especially when they are coming from heaven.

Chapter 3
'Normal' Delivery?

September 1, 2012

3:00 a.m.

I am woken up in the wee hours of the morning by a terrible backache. Oh no, it must be because of that pregnancy yoga. Maybe I stretched a little too far this time.

I don't know how to define labour pain. Some women say it is like a bolt that moves from top to bottom in your abdomen. But that is not how it is for me. All that I keep feeling is a terrible, terrible pain in my lower back and thighs that throbs and throbs and returns like spasms from time to time.

It is actually not so bad as to make me scream. But bad enough to make me hyperventilate. And a weird kind of shivering takes control of my legs every time the spasms come. I think I might just start running in circles like a mad dog.

However, my mum had defined labour pains as 'someone sticking a knife in your stomach repeatedly'. (What the hell!) I don't feel quite that way *yet* so I've been saving my screaming for then.

I've always wanted a normal birth. No painkillers, no epidural, and certainly not a C-section—which has become the norm in India now, with people actually asking for it. Dr Sunita was pleasantly surprised at my insistence on the natural way.

I did everything advised by my doctor (and my mom-in-law)—exercises, walks, balanced nutrition, extra prayers, and anything else anybody cared to suggest, just so I could have a normal delivery. I wasn't scared of the labour pains; I had chosen this option. However, choosing it doesn't mean you're prepared for it.

8:00 a.m.

We're inside the labour room at the hospital. The pains are getting terrible. Walking around helps. But then you have to be strapped down so that the baby's heartbeat can be monitored and that increases the pains manifold. It is like an earthquake that begins in my belly and goes right down to the thighs, splitting my body in half . . . aaaggghhh!

My thighs shiver violently. The doctor says it is because I am so thin—gained only 5 kg during the entire nine months.

(Still not screaming, though. Feel proud.)

1:30 p.m.

Normal.

An adjective defined by the Merriam-Webster Dictionary as 'usual or ordinary; not strange.'

What the hell?!

Who on earth came up with this bright idea of calling a vaginal birth a 'normal delivery'? Will the stone-hearted brute/bird-brained idiot please stand up?

Mother Nature has indeed chosen this horrendous, ghastly, third-degree torture of a path to bring babies into this world, so I understand 'natural' delivery. But even 'natural' has a gentle feel to it, like something tender—which does not come remotely close to the terrifying process that childbirth is.

But normal? NORMAL, for Christ's sake?

It makes it sound so ordinary, so commonplace. Nothing worth fretting about. Just the usual.

Talk about adding insult to injury. Literally.

It's been more than 10 hours since the pains started. I am strapped down on the bed and writhing in agony in the middle of my most horrendous nightmare, and I can't even wake up. I cannot make sense of anything anymore. Dr Sunita sternly orders me to let go of her collar. I look at her blankly; I don't know what on earth she is talking about.

'Let go of my clothes,' she points out. I realise dazedly that I have her clothing in my fist and I'm violently pulling her. At which point I let her go and promptly catch hold of the nurse in exactly the same manner.

'Hold this railing,' Sunita orders me again. It's good that she is being stern. Nothing short of that would get my attention right now.

They keep asking me if I want water, which I don't—I just want this to be over with—so, they just keep wiping my face which is encased in sweat. So is everyone else's in the room, since I've demanded that the air conditioner be turned off. The cold air was making me shiver and shake far more, and the heat, surprisingly, feels welcoming to my skinny body.

I lose track of what is happening around me, surrendering to the searing torment and the quakes reverberating in each pore, mind overcome by images moving in such a frenzy that they reduce the present moment to a blur. Amid shouts of 'Push! Push! Push!' from the two doctors and several nurses in the room, there are only two things that I will forever remember about my birthing experience.

One: the man I love was by my side during this most torturous, petrifying time, holding my hand. This wouldn't be such a novelty if not for my small-town origins, where people are astounded to know that in Delhi, one family member—*any family member*—forget husband (at which mention their eyes might pop out of their heads) is allowed inside the labour room during delivery. So, this is unimaginably unforgettable and unique for me.

Two: The *SNAP!* I heard as I jolted my head back in one piercing, agonised wail as the doctor performed an episiotomy—basically cut me open down there—so that my baby could be safely born.

Normal . . .?

You gotta be kidding me.

September 1, 2012

2:00 p.m.

'It's a boy!' Sunita announces as I grow aware of the fact that I've managed to 'do it' and they didn't have to ultimately perform a C-section. I did it. I gave birth to a healthy baby, the natural way.

I drop down, exhausted beyond belief. The other doctor, Dr Manu, is removing the placenta now. More pain.

'Please. Pleeaase don't do this . . .' I beg her.

'*Arrey*! You've tolerated so much pain, what is this compared to that?'

What is this compared to that? It is a needle being stuck in and moved round and round in your skin—after you've been sawed through.

That's what it is. But they've got to do what they've got to do.

The placenta is out. The pain subsides. Relief.

I am aware that Salman is still holding my hand. 'I love you,' I whisper. He holds up my hand and kisses the back of it.

'I did it,' I tell him. I can't get over that feeling of extraordinary achievement over this 'normal' delivery. 'I was thinking I wouldn't be able to do it. I was thinking they'd just move me to the operation theatre anytime now . . . but I've done it.' I manage to smile at him.

He is stroking my hair, I think. Not easy to focus at the moment.

Dr Sunita and Dr Manu are stitching me up, chatting like it is an everyday chore. Which it is—for them, of course.

'God, how hard is this baby crying!' Dr Sunita exclaims suddenly.

It is then that I grow aware of a bawling baby somewhere in the room. In truth, I had not even registered his cries.

Dr Sunita is right. The bawling is strong and insistent, unlike the mewling newborn sounds that you sort of expect.

'Don't all babies cry this way?'

I can't believe I'm chatting with my doctor even as she is stitching me up.

'They do, but not so much!' she laughs. 'This one's just going on and on!'

'I suppose he takes after his mother,' I say this to Salman, not the doctor, with a weak smile. 'His mother is such a crybaby!'

'Not at all!' Dr Manu cuts in unexpectedly. 'You are a wonderful patient. You took the pains so well, without a complaint. You should just see the tantrums we get to witness here! You asked for nothing at all, and no screaming either. A little towards the end, yes, but that is completely natural,' she beams.

That one is going to rank high-up in my list of the most memorable compliments ever!

The baby is *still* bawling. It is then that I turn my face to the right and see my newborn son, lying in a glass rectangle under a bright white light. I see him wailing for attention. I see his body, his face—just the side profile—mouth wide open, eyes shut tight.

'*Kya hua, kyun ro rahe ho*?' I call out to him.

What's the matter, why are you crying?

The crying stops immediately. Instantly. The baby opens his eyes. I see him opening his eyes.

And I have witnesses to prove this.

There is a strange, soft, cotton-candy kind of pleasure in making a baby's cries stop with the mere sound of your voice. It is a pleasure that you never, ever forget.

I have actually given birth to a baby. A baby that stops crying at the sound of my voice.

September 1, 2012

2:15 p.m.

I am too exhausted with the effort of giving birth. I can hardly hold up my hand when Dr Sunita congratulates me. And, then, this tiny creature is brought before me, wrapped in a cloth whose colour is blurred in my memory. This, now, is the moment when the world is supposed to change.

I look at him.

Nothing.

I feel nothing. No urge to take him in my arms. No desire to hold him. I hold up a weak, shaky hand and touch his cheek lightly . . . more for the benefit of everyone else in the room, perhaps, than from any deep motherly feeling.

I watch his face. He is very fair. But . . . but . . . he is nothing like the baby I imagined.

I have to say this with a lot of shame, but here is the truth: to every mother, her baby is the most beautiful in the world. However, I look at my baby and think, 'Lord, he is not good looking at all.'

I've always known in the back of my mind that care does not equal love. People prove their love by telling you how much they care about your well-being. Yes, you cannot love without care. But you can care without love.

Having a baby filled me with a deep, overwhelming sense of responsibility. I was immediately attuned to every need of his, I was greatly aware of every duty I had towards him—I was the one who was going to protect, nurture, and cherish him. During those nine months of carrying him in my belly, I followed the doctor's instructions to the last detail, did nothing that would ever, ever harm this little one, even if it meant having to give up things I never thought I could do without. I fought with my own mother over what was best for the baby.

And yet, all of this care did not automatically translate to love.

Because caregivers can be professional, too. They can fulfil all your needs, but they can't smother you in that inexplicable blanket of security and comfort that is love.

Love is when you think of that person and it makes you smile. Love is when you see their face and your heart leaps. When you swear to stop talking to them but never keep that oath. You are in love when you know you are.

Yes, you care about them and their needs. But most importantly, when you look at them you *know* what it is to love.

So, here is the most horrible confession of my life: when my baby was born, I was filled with concern. I was filled with care. I was filled with protectiveness. But love . . .?

September 1, 2012

3:00 p.m.

Pain comes in many forms.

Everybody emphasises, over and over, the important fact that as soon as the baby is born the most terrible part of the pain is over.

But.

Nobody tells you what comes after.

I've been stitched up and cleaned and covered. I am still in the labour room; exhausted, shaken, and lifeless. Salman is holding up a glass of juice and I am sipping it with a straw. It is a tad uncomfortable drinking this way and I want to scoot up a bit, in more of a sitting position (the bed is already inclined to support my back). I try and then it hits me like a bullet.

Moving my back—and my hips—even a quarter of an inch creates waves of screaming pain inside me. I cannot move a muscle without grimacing in the most horrible way imaginable. The entire portion is numb, but not numb as in 'without sensation'. Numb as in 'heavy as lead, impossible to move without the greatest effort but with an indescribable, tear-inducing agony'. The mere act of sitting up is now petrifying.

I wish there were more synonyms for pain, more words to describe a sensation that is as much mental as physical. But words can only reflect so much and no more.

The events after this are somewhat jumbled up in my mind. My mom is in the room. So is my mom-in-law. My brother-in-law has just arrived. I feel happy to see him, that he rushed over from another city at such short notice. But the in-laws have started calling up people in a mad frenzy and spreading the good news like I just won an Olympic gold—which is what it feels like to them, I suppose, what with the baby being a boy, a *ladka*.

This doesn't really make me happy, though. It takes away attention from me when I want it the most. When I am at my weakest and shittiest. It takes away my man on totally unnecessary phone calls, which adds to my sullenness.

But this is just the small stuff.

About an hour—and a half?—later, after the room's been cleared of everyone but my mom, they bring my baby back in to be fed. Lord knows how eager I had been about feeding my baby, having resolved to go the whole 'six-months exclusive breastfeeding' way with no formula feeds whatsoever.

But right now?

Do I really have to do it now?

I can't even get up. All I want to do is sleep. As a matter of fact, I kept dozing off in between the 5-minute gaps of labour pain, perhaps on account of sheer exhaustion. Sleep, sleep, sleep. The urge is almost painful.

Okay. Turns out I have to. Right now.

Great, he won't latch on. I am not holding him correctly. The lactation counsellor shows me how.

Now, I am feeding my baby for the first time. This ought to be a wonderful, tender moment—except it isn't. I am acutely aware of the pains shooting through my bottom, thanks to the episiotomy. And the sleep is clogging my brain.

But then, just after he is finished, he nuzzles my skin with his face, almost clutching me with his fists, and goes back to sleep. There is a gooey, warm feeling, like a little closed fist that wraps itself on my weary heart—my heart that thaws just a little more.

However, there is no time for joy.

Another nurse arrives and asks me to stand up, walk to the toilet and take a leak. I look at her as if she has just landed from outer space.

Get *UP*?!

WALK to the toilet?!

Have you freakin' lost your mind, lady?

Of course, my ever-loving mother protests and asks for a bedpan; anyone could see I was in no condition to get up. Although I had been told beforehand in the pre-natal workshops that the sooner I did the get-up-and-take-a-leak thing, the faster I would heal. However, listening is one thing and doing it is quite another.

But the nurses haven't been trained for nothing.

'Oh, okay,' she says, coolly. 'Guess we'll just have to insert a catheter to pass the urine.'

Now, a catheter is a tube that is inserted right inside you to get the waste liquid out, and it is not a thin tube either.

I had seen my grandad use it for years. Yes, years. And one can quite imagine where they stuck it in his body.

I had just pushed out a 3.5 kg baby out of my tender parts. Nothing, absolutely nothing is going to be pushed *in* now. I grit my teeth.

'NO! Please, no. Just help me up and support my weight, please. *Of course*, I can go to the toilet. That is going to aid the healing, isn't it? Of course, I'll go.'

It's a wonder what a little incentive can do.

Turns out, the getting up isn't the hardest bit.

Not since potty-training in childhood did I have so much fear of the toilet seat. I shakily murmur ten different prayers and hold my breath the entire while, like a person stepping across a field full of landmines. Only, here, *I* am the landmine.

For many days after that, trips to the toilet become trips to purgatory. Feared. Hated. Terrifying. Tear-inducing. An act of courage, almost.

But now, as I am being wheeled out of the labour room into my room for the next two days, I have just one thing on my mind. I have spoken to a lot of women about their childbirth experience and almost everyone said they had absolutely no sexual desire for the first few months after. Well. Not me.

I am panic-stricken, with the most alarming thoughts rushing through my brain.

'Oh, GAWD! This is all so terrible. I have terrible stitches and injuries . . . oh no, no, no—I will never ever be able to DO IT again! Oh how, how, how am I going to HAVE IT now? How?' Mental sob.

Then I remember. People just don't stop having kids after *one*. They have more. Many more. Which means, of course . . .

And then it dawns.

Uh oh.

More kids? More? MORE?

Never, ever. Never ever is this birthing process going to be repeated, I swear.

Never. Ever.

September 1, 2012

Day One at the Hospital

It may be the post-partum depression (does it really kick in so soon?) or it may just be the blinding pain. But now, as dusk falls, my mum, sitting beside me, asks, 'Why so glum, dear?' and I just start to cry. I cry and I cry and I cry and I cry.

'It hurts, mummy. It hurts too much. There is SO much pain . . .' Pain of the kind that steadily chokes, not the spiking waves and spasms that you can drown in screams. Pain that everyone had promised would be long gone.

And furthermore, it is not just the pain. It is the images and memory of pain as well. I had watched in movies that when heroines had nightmares, they would wake with a jolt, eyes flying open in a horrified flash. Breaking news: it happens in real life, too.

Every time I try to close my eyes and get some rest, the entire labour room, complete with the doctors' faces swims before my eyes, ending in the SNAP of me being cut open. The intolerable, unbelievable agony of that moment. And my eyes fly open in horror. This is not a literary description or an exaggeration. It really is happening. And I can't seem to stop it.

And then there is the toilet-terror.

It is when you are in mortal fear of your own body, ever mindful of taking a step too big and ripping yourself apart at the seams.

When the moment you touch yourself you feel like bursting into tears. 'Good Lord, my body is completely deformed! Am I permanently deformed? Will it always be like this?'

When feeling your stitches gives you a weird light-headed feeling, giddy and slightly nauseated, like a merry-go-round-ride gone awry.

You are terrified of your own body.

Day Two at the Hospital

Three hours of sleep after 24 hours of torture is pitiful compensation, but beggars can't be choosers. However, there is one thing that brightens me up—the food! One of the great blessings of having a normal delivery is that you get to eat normal food right away. The first bite of the vegetable sandwich tastes like heaven! To be fair, the first bite of anything edible post-childbirth would taste great. But the chocolate milk and the *poha* and the noodles and more sandwiches, I devour them all like I've never been given food before. Mealtimes become my new silver linings of the day!

The pain is still there, but it's got a blunt edge. When I have visitors, I forget all about it. I talk and laugh like my usual self, particularly when Shreya and Ankita—my friends from office—enter with a smile and a hug, having had to leave their big bouquet of flowers outside the hospital. But whenever someone asks me, 'So, how was the experience?' this is my standard reply: 'I do NOT want to talk about it.'

Day Three at the Hospital

If someone were to tell you that there is a solid connection between breasts and great chunks of plutonium, you probably wouldn't believe them, right? Well, ask any lactating mother.

On my third day at the hospital, I wake up with a strange, very uncomfortable feeling of rocks being loaded onto my chest. Uncomfortable does not even come close to defining it; it is sheer torment. Turns out, the third day is when the 'real milk' is produced, as opposed to the yellowy colostrum earlier. This is a great 'mother' thing, of course, but as far the 'person' inside the mother is concerned . . . not so much.

I am reminded of a Russian fairytale I read in childhood where the female protagonist is dumped into a river with a load of rocks tied to her chest. Of course, unlike the story, I can't be rescued. I just have to get used to being drowned with rocks crushing the breath out of me, and the feeling of water flaming savagely in and out of my lungs.

A few days later, I would be found crying desperately, sobbing into my husband's chest because I couldn't get any rest. Every time I try to turn on my side, the solid plutonium bores into my flesh, causing searing pain through my body. So much for pain ending with the baby being born.

But, before that, rewind to the day I get to leave the hospital. I get dressed, bidding farewell to the green and white striped nighties I had been donning for the past three days. Just the act of getting dressed feels like normalcy being restored. However, the agonising walk, merely from the room to the car, erases all such ideas.

With shaking baby steps, I get into the car. The ride, as I am well aware, has only just begun.

Chapter 4

Enter the Dragon

Hamza was born in 2012, the Chinese Year of the Dragon. My mom got really furious whenever I referred to the hyperactive baby in my belly as the 'little dragon'. You see, dragons aren't considered to be good creatures. They are monsters to be feared. (I could never understand all the fuss. I mean, tigers are ferocious, too, and yet people love to be called a tiger.) According to the Chinese tradition though, the dragon is majestic, powerful, successful, and fearless—with a noble heart.

It is true that I didn't fall in love with my boy when I saw him for the first time. But long before he was born, deep in my heart, a tiny, almost indiscernible space had been carved out by him as he tumbled around in my womb. A dragon-shaped space with little wings. A home for a fearless little dragon.

September 3, 2012

I bring the tiny creature home.

He doesn't resemble me at all. This is disappointing. He doesn't seem to resemble his father either, though everyone else says he does. The way I see it, he is a determined little person with a face all of his own.

Hamza was born with a good weight of 3.5 kg, but he never looked like the chubby little babies you see on TV. Long wiry limbs, with fingers that weren't clenched shut but spread apart in a perpetual gesture of surprise. Thoughtful, pensive eyes that seemed to contemplate the deepest philosophies of life, like he was deep in thought from the moment he entered this world; solving an existential mystery that had followed him here from the dark home in the womb.

He'd often put one of those tiny outstretched fingers awkwardly on his cheek, the perfect touch to complete his look of a contemplating philosopher.

My scatter-brained, forever joking mother takes to calling him *tidda*— grasshopper—for his long, thin body, much to the chagrin of his doting father. It makes me laugh to see how possessive and protective Salman is. He is so much more of a mother in this sense than I am! His company gives employees a one-week paternity leave, and, so, Salman is having a blast playing the hands-on dad. Changing nappies, bathing the baby, taking turns with soothing the baby to let me get some sleep. And the burping, of course, is his sole domain, accompanied by much merriment and mirth! I suppose I do understand now why women find baby-loving men attractive.

I *almost* forget the myriad pains in my body during those quiet moments when we both talk with little Hamza and he listens to us intently with the same contemplative gaze. He has his father's eyes, I can see now; the loveliest, most sincere eyes ever.

I think I do love this little philosopher, the one of the shiny thoughtful eyes and the outstretched wiry limbs. Happy little grasshopper. The wise, noble dragon.

Amid all the pandemonium that descends on your life post the new baby, there are tiny, ever memorable islands of peace.

I am greeted with a traditional welcome by my mother-in-law when I get back home. She is sweet and high on the traditional things in life, which becomes a big boon for me during the post-pregnancy days. She knows all about the herbs and the dishes that are given to a new mom to help her body get back its strength and shape. The best part of all the pampering I receive is, undoubtedly, the herbal baths she gives me in the first week post-childbirth—equal parts exciting and embarrassing. Exciting, because a warm, comforting concoction of herbs is poured upon your limbs and joints with much fanfare, so much like the *maharanis* of yore! But embarrassing because, well, just like your newborn, you are also being bathed by others! I'd be dead with mortification if it weren't for the heavenly feeling of warm elixirs flowing down my limbs, decidedly bringing me alive.

Traditions have their flipside, too, and some of the horrid ones are common to the country across regions and religions. Tradition says that the woman has to be confined in the house for 40 days. It was so she can get enough time to recuperate. But am I glad that this is not being enforced! Not that I'd have given in.

Another decadent and terrible tradition inflicted is the one where the husband and wife are not allowed to sleep in the same room for 40 days. It was, of course, meant to prevent insensitive (read psychopath) husbands of yore from torturing their 'injured' wives. Forcing them into sex while their body parts were mauled beyond recognition.

I, however, might have murdered someone if they dared try to enforce this rule.

Sleeping beside Salman is perhaps the most blissful part of my life right now, my greatest source of comfort and peace in these days that vacillate between acceptance and anguish. Even if the 'sleep' consists of two-hour bursts, or just two hours in one whole night. What matters more, though, is that there is someone beside me whom I can wake up at any time and in whose arms I can sob unrestrained in the dead of the night.

My mother proves to be a lifesaver. Hamza is one of those myriad babies who just would not sleep at night. At all. He wants me to sit there with him in my lap, cooing to him unceasingly. The moment I put him down, he lets out a long, deep-throated wail reminiscent of his insistent bawling at the hospital. This is one strong-willed boy. Good for him, but not good for me right now, for his wailing makes me burst into tears—tears of helplessness and fatigue, tears of a woman struggling to find her way inside the maze of motherhood. That is when my poor darling mother takes it upon herself to keep him in her lap for three-four hours at a time, after which he would start bawling for milk. But for those precious three hours, I could, wonder of wonders, sleep.

In all such times when you are tumbling downwards, it is the hands of people who love you that hold you up and pull you out.

September 4, 2012

You never see the air. Never see the stars or
the moon when the sun shines bright.
Never see your own brain. Nor the heart that
beats inside.
Seeing is believing—or is believing seeing?
There's so much more to see
If only you'd believe.

I have just fed Hamza and he lies peacefully in my arms, quiet yet wide awake, gazing right into my eyes. A wondrous, rare moment of silent communication.

Suddenly, he amazes me beyond words by stretching his tiny lips into a split-second smile! I do a double-take and peer closely into his face to check if he is smiling in his sleep, by any chance. Nope, he is wide awake.

Slowly, I count the days. 1, 2, 3, 4.

4-day-olds don't smile! No way! But there is no mistaking what I saw. That was one definite smile.

My 4-day-old just smiled at me. For a split-second. I stare at him in a state of disbelief—and also of elation. Then I rush out to my mother in the other room.

'Mummy! Hamza just smiled at me!'

My mother looks at me for a moment. And smiles. But it is a different kind of smile. The oh-no-you-must-be mistaken kind.

'Honey, that's not possible. He must be sleeping.'

'But he wasn't. I checked.'

'Then you must be mistaken. The "social smile" doesn't appear until at least a month.'

'Oh.'

I really must be mistaken then . . . I guess.

September 7, 2012

Salman and I are off to see the gynaecologist for a routine visit. It is my first outing from home after the delivery. Since we'd be back within two hours, we are not taking Hamza with us. Mummy will be keeping him company.

Two hours later

As we enter the house, we are greeted by an ecstatic voice.

It is my mom.

'You were right! He smiled! He smiled today! It is unbelievable! Well . . . it was really for a split-second, but he did smile.'

She can't contain her excitement. The house help that she has brought with her all the way from Aligarh beams almost as much; she was actually the one whom Hamza had really smiled at.

'Didn't I tell you?' I'm grinning from ear to ear.

'Yes! I didn't believe you then, but now I've seen it for myself.'

There's so much more to see if only you'd believe.

September 7, 2012

Heroine.

A word we're all familiar with, and yet not in the way that it was originally intended. The dictionary says that a 'heroine' is a woman who displays some sort of heroism—an act of courage, noble qualities, or outstanding achievements. But we don't mean that when we call someone a heroine.

Our daily understanding of the word equates it to an actress. So, when someone calls you a 'heroine', what they are saying is that you look as gorgeous as their favourite celluloid Goddess.

Flattering, I know.

6:30 p.m.

My first outing after the birth of my son, and it is no big deal since it is just a routine visit to the gynaecologist. But it is a big deal for me because I can wear something nice after 6 months of breathable loose-fitting attire followed by 7 days of feeding gowns.

Of course, all the nice dresses I wear are worn underneath my abaya and hijab, which is second skin to me now after almost a decade of having adopted it. Friends wonder what good are all these dresses if nobody can see them. My friends can see them, though, when I am at home without my abaya. My husband can see them and tell me, 'What did I do to deserve a stunner like you?' But, most importantly, when I get dressed, I can see my glorious self in the mirror, and tell myself like Kareena Kapoor aka Poo from *Kabhi Khushi Kabhie Gham*: '*Tumhein koi haq nahi ki tum itni khubsurat lago!*'

Ain't that what we call self-love? (Or narcissism, if you like.)

There is a new maxi dress my mom brought for me, a body-hugging pink-and-white one that I couldn't wear during pregnancy because it wouldn't fit over my belly, and pink leggings to go with it. This is what I am going to wear now, underneath my favourite maroon abaya. I slip the dress over my head.

Et voila! It is a great feeling to be able to get back in the clothes you like. And the best part is, I don't look like a stick-insect anymore; the curves are all in the right places!

And then Salman barges into the room because it is always his job to ensure we're not late for our appointments. Whatever he is about to say dies on his lips for, with a sparkle in his eye and a broad, delighted grin, this bursts out instead:

'Meri heroine!'

This man has always incurred my wrath for his lack of compliments to his wife, his stinginess with admiring statements. In one fell swoop, he has made up for all of that. I am his *heroine*!

Life suddenly feels reassuringly normal.

Chapter 5

Love in the Time of Nappies and Yowls

My home in Delhi was a delightful little haven, a real-life version of a poem I wrote as a teenager. It was cosy, compact, surrounded by open spaces and greenery, and flowing with bird song in the mornings. Full of light and air, and, most importantly, peace and love.

And then I had to let it go.

October 2, 2012

A month after the birth of our son, we pack up every single belonging so lovingly placed in our home and head into a life that would test us to the hilt.

It wasn't like everything happened overnight. We had known for the past six months that we would have to vacate this house and look for another one. What we hadn't realised, however, was how different things would be with the arrival of the baby, especially in terms of finance. Money had seemed so trivial before parenthood.

Nevertheless, we had been looking for another apartment in Delhi. But fate had other plans. Salman got an offer from Oman and, to cut a long story short, he would be moving there in a couple of months' time.

I am supposed to stay in Aligarh until then, after which I will be joining him in Oman—at least, that is what they've promised.

Doesn't sound so bad, does it?

October 5, 2012

3:00 a.m.

I am at my in-laws' house in Aligarh. Hamza is on my lap. Every time I try to put him down, he bawls his head off and I can't understand why. I had, in the past month, trained him to sleep at least for two hours at a stretch so I could also sleep in two-hour bursts. But moving from his home seems to have derailed him, too. I don't get a single wink all night, even as the entire household sleeps peacefully.

I resent that.

I hate it. I hate that I am the only one awake here with this awful nuisance while the whole damn house snores. I hate that this baby goes to sleep during the day when I just *can't* because of the incessant stream of visitors all day who just don't give a fig that this is the only time I can catch up on some sleep.

And, most of all, I hate it when *some* people, who had pulverised my brains to pulp while lecturing me to have a baby, smugly watch me when I cuddle my child and declare:

'There, now! See? You should hand me an award. Wasn't I right in telling you to have a baby straightaway? See how much you love him? Didn't I tell you that you'd instantly love him?'

As if. As if I wouldn't have loved him had he been born a couple of years later. As if I could do anything but love my son. As if not loving him was even an option.

As if loving him could erase the pain of being separated from every little thing I had ever dreamt of—my dream man, my dream house, my dream job.

The fact that I did love my son didn't obviate the fact that I was an unwilling martyr. I wouldn't say that I was willingly doing it all for my son. I hated, positively hated the sacrifices

I had to make for him. And here, all they cared about was that they were right. That once you become a mother, nothing else matters.

Sorry, it does matter. Very much.

November 5, 2012

For practicing Muslims in India or any other part of the world, circumcision is an absolute must for the male child. The earlier, the better because we believe that a boy who is born to Muslim parents will not be a Muslim until he is circumcised.

One may reason that male circumcision has many benefits—lowering the chances of contracting STD or urinary infection, among others, but ultimately it boils down to personal belief and cultural tradition.

Now, there are close to zero boys in my family. I have one sibling who is a girl, my father's brother has two girls, and two of his three sisters have two girls each. His youngest sister has two boys and a girl, but they've lived in the US all their lives. So, I have no experience whatsoever of how boys are brought up. *Especially* not how they are circumcised.

My mother's only sibling does have a boy, but he was circumcised in a hospital. My boy wasn't. In hindsight, my boy ought to have been operated upon at a hospital, too. But I was inexperienced and unsure, and therefore not very vocal about this. Plus, I was assured by the elders that 'this was how it had always been done', and I couldn't really argue.

So, the local *jarrah* who is apparently a circumcision-specialist comes to the house and performs the process without any anaesthesia. I think I would have died had I known beforehand what it really entailed. I actually thought that it would be like his vaccination—he'd cry, I'd soothe him, and everything would be fine in ten minutes. In hindsight, this would be funny if it weren't so . . . horrifying.

The only silver lining in the entire day was the fact that Salman rushed over from Delhi to be with his wife and son, to not leave them alone to deal with this. He surprised us all by arriving at the crack of dawn, despite having spent over 10 hours working the night shift at the multinational company where he was employed. He probably started driving towards Aligarh right when he left the office building.

It was Salman who soothed his tiny son throughout the day, rocking the baby gently in his arms and speaking to him earnestly. Little Hamza would immediately stop crying and gaze at his father with rapt attention, as if understanding every word. And in those precious moments, the baby seemed to forget his pain.

Later, my mother's sister-in-law narrated her son's experience and told me that even if I got it done at the hospital, it would still be equally painful once the anaesthesia wore out. And, the younger the boy, the faster the healing, she added. The pain was certainly gone after the first day, but if I ever decide to have another baby, and if it happens to be a boy again, I am certainly putting my foot down about the at-home procedure. For good reason.

I can never, ever forget my tiny son's scream from the other room, and I will never forget bursting into tears at that sound. Not because I was angry or frustrated. I just wanted his pain to disappear.

I will never forget weeping listening to his wails, and earnestly pleading to the Lord, 'Please, please, dear God, just take his pain away and give it to me instead. I'll take it. I will.'

That is when, I think, I understood what a mother's love is all about.

That love and hate can coexist in the same place seems such a strange thing. But truth, as they say, is stranger than fiction.

December 4, 2012

You would think that a couple of months would be enough for the body to heal from all the damage done during childbirth. But here's the thing: recovery requires rest. Loads and loads of rest, after the body has been literally transformed into a live volcano. Ironically, though, rest is the one thing you never get. The entire cycle of feeding, burping, changing the nappy repeated over and over and over again; waking, sleeping, waking, sleeping ten times a night, night after night after night, is not just too much for the body but also quite enough to numb the mind.

I have depleted my reserves of energy. The mere act of bathing my baby and then taking a bath myself exhausts me so much that I can hardly step out of the house for the rest of the day. This might sound excessive and unreal, but it is really not! Because, if you think about it, delivering a baby is as unreal a process as can be.

Unreality, thy name is motherhood.

Then, of course, I am saddled with the extra load of bringing up a baby with an absentee father. This, in fact, is my prime burden, because it turns my marriage into a farce. Can't speak on behalf of other people, but, for me, the joy of having a child is to have a real, living creature that embodies the love you share with your spouse. It is *because* you married someone and wanted a family with them that you decided to have babies, not that you wanted to have babies and bring them up, so you got married. What was I doing here with this baby anyway, when the very reason for his existence wasn't here?

There is a sinking feeling of being trapped in a role you never fancied much from the beginning. Being reduced to a bonded labourer without any life of her own, unable to do anything that I want to, unable to have a social life, unable to be with the man I love, unable to spare a moment for my own self. The more I think about it, the more I blame the baby.

There are nights when after hours and hours of unsuccessful attempts to soothe him or get him to sleep, I want to slap him hard—yes, the three-month-old—and hit him for turning my life into a living hell.

I don't, though. I don't slap my three-month-old infant.

I know he is innocent, but more than anything else I know that I can never, ever face God if I hurt a little baby for things he doesn't even know of, let alone be responsible for.

There are times when the fear of God is good for sanity. And the love of God for responsibility.

From the beginning of my pregnancy to this day, I have deeply felt my responsibility as a mother. A responsibility bestowed upon me by God. A baby given to me is not 'for me', really. He is an individual born to fulfil his own special destiny and I am just the channel. I am the person entrusted with the task of showing him how to reach the potential he was endowed with; showing him how to differentiate the good from the bad and the right from the wrong. I am the one who has to prepare him for his journey. His journey isn't mine. Nor is he mine to claim later.

Whatever I do for him, is not for him—it is the fulfilment of a task defined for me by God. I just have to do my bit, in good faith.

Faith is a wonderful anchor when you risk losing you.

December 10, 2012

Make love not war, sang John Lennon. If only.

The world abounds with scaremongers. Doomsday prophesies *a la* Nostradamus and shrieking banshees shocking the lights out of you *a la* Pan the Greek Goat-God. Everyone's ready, hands crossed across the chest, to let you know how terrible a place this world is, and how things only get worse as you get deeper into life. Have I been turning into one of those banshees? I hope not.

Perhaps I grew up on too many fairy tales, but the essence of my being is love.

My former boss—the editor—and a colleague were once discussing with me a premise that humans are all driven by the desire for immortality: if not their own selves, then their name must live on forever. We were talking about the things that are most important to people, and the editor, who was of the opinion that it is either money or family, claimed that he could guess what mine was—family.

'Nope,' I said, 'you're wrong. Close, but wrong.'

He was surprised, because he'd often heard me speaking of my mother.

'Then it must be God,' he said triumphantly, because he knew that it wasn't money.

'Wrong again,' I grinned, though I could understand why he made that assumption.

'Yourself!' exclaimed Kunal, my colleague, like he just hit the nail on the head.

'Hmm . . . close . . . you could say that,' I mused. 'But not exactly.'

'Then what is it?' Kunal insisted, exasperated. 'You must tell us!'

I smiled mysteriously.

'No, really. Tell us.'

'Okay,' I said. 'It's love.'

'*Haan*, so that's family,' the editor interjected immediately.

'No, it is not family per se. It is the man I love.'

'So, then it is children,' he insisted.

'No. Definitely not children. Just the man I love,' I repeated emphatically.

'Just you and your man?' Kunal echoed, genuinely perplexed. 'Like Adam and Eve?'

That made me laugh. 'Yes, somewhat like that. Just love. Everything else comes second.'

Cotton candy, hearts, candles, and waves against the beach. Dark clouds, sea-storm, and thunder. Conquering the world together. That is what my dreams are made of.

To not have romance in my life is to be sucked clean of blood, zombiefied into blank bitterness. But here's the thing: like all good things in life, you need to work hard for romance, too.

Before coming to Aligarh, for the first month of Hamza's life—in Delhi—this is what I used to do: when I should also have been sleeping while our baby slept, I instead found a better use for that time. Salman and I watched movies on weekend nights, just like we used to before the baby came along. It made life seem a little more continuous. I couldn't make love yet—too injured for that—so we used to talk love. And then those little things that taste like love.

Aligarh was a lot more difficult because the move upset the tiny tot, disrupted his routine, and turned life into a general nightmare, compounded by the fact that Salman and I were together for only about a day and a half every week. But thank goodness for mothers that play cupid! My mom ensured that she babysat Hamza often, especially during the weekends so we could go out together. Half the nights she would keep him in her room, rocking him in the bouncer, giving us that silver lining, the moonlight behind the clouds.

Today, for instance, Salman and I are sitting in a restaurant, talking, laughing, and holding hands. The waiter suddenly comes to us and, beckoning to a private table in a dimly-lit corner of the restaurant, asks in a low voice if we'd like to sit there. Considering that in small-town India, the only people who ever sit in dimly-lit corners of any place are college lovebirds, we are left grinning from ear to ear for this compliment!

Over and above any of this, though, we realise now what makes love work when there is three of you—you take the baby inside the two curves of the heart.

You make caring for him an act of bonding; you make kissing him and cuddling him an extension of your love. The burps and gurgles become a reason to look at each other with joy.

We take Hamza along on our outings. When he was a month old, we took him along to see the Qutub Minar on a weekend Delhi trip. Little Hamza was tucked securely in a 'baby basket', photographed by all tourists in the complex!

Our baby isn't an intrusion on our exclusivity; he just turns our love a richer shade of red. Yes, we do have to work harder to keep the colour from fading, but, as Jim's dad tells Michelle in *American Wedding*, 'It's called making love 'cause you have to make love work.'

Chapter 6

Dr Jekylletta and Mrs Hyde

How would you know if you had multiple personality disorder? You wouldn't. Like Norman Bates, Alfred Hitchcock's famous Psycho, you'd just believe you 'wouldn't even hurt a fly'.

December 15, 2012

All parenting websites declare that your baby's sleep problems—and hence your own—would be over by the time he is four months old. But, as sure as the world goes around, harried and impatient mothers get blessed with the most exaspera . . . uhh . . . challenging. . . children. I fit perfectly into that mould.

My son goes to sleep with me while I pat him gently, persistently for about 40 minutes. It makes me feel warm and fuzzy inside that he seeks me out every so often, seeking the feel of my skin to reassure himself. But just about an hour later, the bawling starts.

No, it is not a wet diaper.

No, it is not colic.

No, it is not hunger.

He just wants to sleep in mamma's lap.

I have a bawler in my bed.

Bright idea #1:

I try to get him to sleep inside the bouncer, rocking him every now and then when the wailing begins. All is fine, at first, except that now he expects mom to rock him all night.

Woe unto me if my hand falls limp in a state of drop-dead sleep. And so, my hand moves of its own accord.

Bright idea #2:

Enter the pacifier.

My good ol' country-dwellin', traditional medicine lovin', all-righteous in-laws abhor pacifiers. Oh, and generally all modern child-rearing practices. Normally, I find their advice useful; it is pretty comforting homey stuff that helps build the child's (and the mother's) immunity without over-dependence on antibiotics and doctors. But the barbs about the pacifier are never-ending:

You're exposing your son to an addiction.

It is a lazy mother's crutch.

And, the best of all: '*Our* kids never needed these contraptions to fall asleep!'

My mom has been watching me struggle for the past four months. She has suggested the pacifier several times, but I've been resisting, primarily with my in-laws' advice in mind. But the wailing echoes ceaselessly, and so I cave in.

When I was six, my then young-adult uncle had a poster on his wall, where Dennis the Menace declared:

'If at first you don't succeed, try, try again.

Then give up. It's no use being a fool about it.'

Meanwhile . . .

Me: What's the news about your visa?

Salman: The company is facing some paperwork issues. They say next month for sure.

Next Month

Me: Any news?

Salman: The X, Y, Z has not been cleared (some new problem cooked up by the employer). Just about a fortnight more.

A Fortnight Later

Salman: Some more legal hassles. Next month, I am positive.

Me: Let's rent a house in Delhi again and just drop the idea.

Salman: We're so close, it is just a month. Just one more month, sweetheart, please.

He visits every weekend, arriving Friday nights and leaving Monday mornings. A strange behavioural pattern emerges in a mostly consistent form: instead of feeling lighter and happier in anticipation of him arriving on Friday, by Thursday I find myself completely spiralling into derangement. Boiling over at the drop of a hat, erupting at the slightest provocation, and looking at the baby with hatred and loathing—the projected self-loathing of an unhappy woman.

Then the weekend comes and Mrs Hyde disappears, leaving behind a grinning, civilised, loving Dr Jekylletta.

January 18, 2013

3:00 a.m.

We are in the little room to one side of the backyard, a cosy sanctum for lovers—a place where virtually no sound would carry from the main house and vice versa.

My mother got this room constructed when her brother got married and brought his new bride into the house. My mother is quite the patron saint of romance; she would have done St Valentine proud. It was her desire for her brother and his wife to have the utmost privacy from us two intruding kids—my sister and I—that led to this room being constructed.

I suppose my mother's great sensitivity to lovers is where I get my own romantic inclination from, and I wonder if her becoming a widow at 34 subconsciously fuels my frenzied longing to make every second count.

So, we are snuggled into the folds of our super heavy quilts on a teeth-chattering winter night. The room has served its purpose well; we are sated and relaxed.

Salman is fast asleep, but I just can't be. And there is a definite reason for my insomnia.

'Hey,' I nudge him. 'Hey, I can't sleep.'

'Mmmm . . . ?' he mumbles. 'What's the matter?'

'It's been three hours.'

'Huh?'

'It's been over three hours since I fed the baby. He must be hungry.' The room is pitch dark and there is no way to know the time.

'Has it? Been that long? It couldn't be—the baby isn't crying, or mummy would have called us on the phone to come and get him.'

Our occasional arrangement with mummy works this way: she keeps Hamza until he gets hungry and starts crying, and then she wakes us to come and fetch him across the courtyard.

This is in the dead of winter when we beat the biting cold wrapped in layers of thermal inners and sweaters and socks. So, we carry the baby through the open, windy courtyard, wrapping his bouncer tightly in several layers of quilt. Several thick layers below the baby and several thick layers above.

'It's been over three hours. I am telling you my baby is hungry. I know it. I just can't sleep. I tried . . . but I keep getting this . . . feeling.'

'Maa . . . maa . . . maa . . .' chants Salman, sighing, smiling and getting up to go fetch Hamza.

Mother, mother, mother. A mother can't sleep when her baby is hungry.

Truth be told, I recoil from this sudden 'Mother India' characterisation of myself. I hate being a martyr. Or a saint.

Nevertheless, the baby's needs do take precedence.

Dr Jekylletta at your service.

January 22, 2013

Aamir, my friend from college, an idea machine and eternally red-bull-charged, calls me up:

'Hey, wassup?'

'Same ol', Aamir, same ol'. A hateful life of feeding, soothing, changing diapers. Ugh.'

'Come on, Zehra, it's been a long time now. You can't still be in that phase—four months already!'

And then, in his characteristic wisecrack style he says, 'In case you hadn't noticed, people around the globe have babies but then get on with their lives!'

There has been many a moment in college when I felt the urge to box this guy's ears. We are not in college anymore and the urge has resurfaced.

'So? I am not people. I thought you knew that.'

'My dear girl, there was a time when we debated politics, religion, international affairs. When we bounced ideas off each other. And now all one can get out of you is this never-ending rant about having had a baby.'

'It is hard work, Aamir. It is SO hard.'

'Oh, come on! Who keeps sulking for so long after? Throw out these emotions of feeling like a victim.'

'I wish I could just throw out the baby.'

'Umm, what!'

And that is Mrs Hyde.

January 30, 2013

When Pandora's curiosity got the better of her, setting free heaps of troubles upon this world, by great good fortune the worst of the lot managed to remain locked up—foreboding. Knowledge of future events, mostly the ones you would really not like to know about.

There is a good reason people can't see the future—it would make you believe you can change it, when you actually can't. But then again, if you could see your future, perhaps you really could change it. Who knows?

Most of us don't consider the future as given, no matter what our beliefs and value systems. Most people are obstinate in thinking they can change the track of their lives and lead better ones than those who came before them. But sometimes, just sometimes, you wish that hope wouldn't be so darn tenacious; that you would know when the right moment was to let go. You wish you wouldn't keep holding on for far too long. But that, precisely, is what we have been doing.

From the time I shifted to Aligarh three months ago, month after month has passed with the Omani company holding our little family on tenterhooks with no visa in sight. Several times I urge Salman to just get us back to Delhi so we can go back to living like we were, and we can move to Oman when the time comes. But here's the thing: they never postpone the date by more than a fortnight or a week, so we are prevented from planning ahead. Each time I remind Salman of getting a house, he reminds me back that a rent agreement would legally require us to stay in Delhi for at least a year. And then what would we do when the time came to move?

To be fair, though, he isn't the only one to blame for this. Mea Culpa as well.

I, too, have been so eager to taste the pure, fresh air of a distant land, a country with better roads, better houses, better facilities, stronger currency, and all the promise of a better life. Most of all, since this offer came, I have been holding my breath to set foot on the port town of Muscat, which I imagined would be my home for the next several years. The sea speaks to my soul like nothing else and to spend every weekend by the sea is a glorious dream that seemed just about to come true. To top it all, Muscat is a city with pleasures galore—turtle beaches, whale watching, partially submerged caves, ancient forts, hot water springs . . . who wouldn't want to be there? And then again, that seldom mentioned but all-important reason: distant lands mean heavenly distance from pokey, nosey relatives. That is a definite plus point.

Whatever the reason, the dream has been dangling right in front of our noses for months now, just a little beyond reach—not far enough to make us forget it and not close enough to grab. Meanwhile, the carefully woven tapestry of our marriage keeps unravelling, one thread at a time.

Sometimes, I wonder if letting foreboding escape might not have been such a bad idea after all. Then, at least, you would know when it was time to let go.

Chapter 7
Babe in the Woods

Rock a bye baby
On the tiger's trail.
When the baby's upset,
The baby will wail.
Silence in the jungle,
But baby will bawl
And down will come Mommy,
Daddy and all.

June 10, 2013

Jim Corbett National Park

The Nirvana Wilds Resort is set in serene, sigh-inducing surroundings; quaint, spacious stone cottages dotting the outer edge of the hill atop which it sits gazing thoughtfully, chin in palm, at the lazily swaying, brown-with-mud river Ramganga and the emerald-forested hills that lock hands round the snaking bends like uniformed sentries. A handful of cattle cross the bridge connecting the banks of the Ramganga while polished white stones from the dry bed gleam softly in the moonlight.

This is where we'd be spending the next two days, at the far end of the park zone beyond Mohaan village; actually quite far from the core park area itself. It takes a long, winding drive across the forest periphery to reach Nirvana Wilds, nestled as it is within the hills on the outer edge of Corbett National Park. We chose the place precisely for its picturesque location, but even then, it was our second choice. The first choice for any visitor to the Tiger reserve will always be the forest lodges owned by the government, sitting smack in the middle of the wild Dhikala zone, offering 'just the bare necessities', as *The Jungle Book*'s Baloo would say, but satiating you with howls and growls and snarls and roars all night long. Here's the catch, though: you can't pre-book them in any way. They are allotted mainly on a first come first serve basis, and too bad if you arrived late. With a nine-month-old in tow, we didn't want to take that chance, so we booked the next best alternative.

So, here we are. Our third vacation since our marriage, but this one is a throwback to my singlehood because my mom and sis are accompanying us. Correction. It is the other way round. It is Salman and I who are accompanying my mother and sister, because this is primarily their holiday. The summer holiday is a long-standing tradition between us three women. Post-marriage, though, I had a separate life and, so, separate vacations, and our girl band had disintegrated. But the unexpected turn of events in the past one year has brought us together again. This time, our trio is joined by two guys—one bearded and thirty, the other a diapered baby.

Corbett is really my mom's choice since she is the ultimate wildlife buff. Till the time that my father was alive, her vacation choices always centred around national parks and wildlife sanctuaries. We still have pictures of her 'hunger strike' protesting my dad's apathy towards the long overdue trip. I remember him laughing as he clicked pictures of her grumpy face.

Now, almost two decades later, she has made the same choice. And that, I suppose, is because we now have a 'man in the family' to 'depend upon'. The man, though, isn't very keen on Corbett; his ancestral home is a farmhouse and trips to nearby forests were a commonplace childhood feature. So, we negotiate with him, and he agrees to join us in return for another two days in Nainital, the hill station that gets its name from the lake it nestles within. I have been there thrice already, but I keep my mouth shut for the sake of successful negotiations.

Peace prevails.

And we are here.

June 11, 2013

Lots of rain on our parade.

The core Dhikala area is supposed to stay open till June 15, but the rains arrived early this year. So, on the very day that we had planned our jeep safari, Dhikala closes down for the season by order of the District Forest Officer. My mom, the erstwhile government officer's wife and now an officer herself for nearly two decades, had dashed off the previous evening to meet the DFO to try to wheedle out some 'official' concessions for us. It didn't work, though, because no concessions could be given where public safety was concerned. We must, therefore, content ourselves with a morning safari in the peripheral zone.

It isn't so bad—we do get an eyeful of the spotted deer and the barking deer, along with a golden-throated martin. But that is about all. I mean, everyone who goes to Corbett wants nothing less than a tiger striding majestically across the road. Here, at Nirvana, our neighbouring cottage was occupied by a man who had been coming back every year for the last ten years, determined to spot a tiger through endless safaris both in the night and day, with zero, absolutely zero success. Talk about persistence.

Amid all this, Hamza has been surprisingly well behaved. Well, by his standards, of course. My initial fears were put to rest by my mother who took him off my hands the entire seven hours it took us from Aligarh to Ramnagar. The fact that he is bottle-fed now is an added advantage. She even took him into her cottage last night, and I snuggled into my king size downy bed with Salman, feeling blissfully calm and all in the mood. Of course, that is when my son put his tiny little foot down. No more tricking him out of his parents' company.

In the middle of a deliciously quiet jungle night in a wonderfully romantic old-world cottage, the air is ripped apart by ear-splitting screams emanating from the wall adjoining ours.

I rush to the other cottage to find Farina, my sister, vigorously wheeling the pram back and forth with all the gentleness of an earthquake, trying helplessly to quiet him down and get him to sleep. While it may look like my sister lacks technique, the truth is that the more vigorous the rocking, the faster my little monarch nods off. Not this time, though, of course not. Never when you really want him to. I sigh, take him in my arms and bundle him back to our bed, where, as sure as daylight, he promptly falls asleep.

All in the job description, darling. All in the job description.

June 12, 2013

Fools walk in where angels fear to tread.
Welcome to the All Fools' Family.

Since there isn't much to do now that the core reserve area of Dhikala has been closed, we scrounge around for options. Turns out there is still an interesting activity available in the buffer zone forest of Durga Devi—follow the tiger's trail on elephant back. I had done this many, many years ago with papa when I was 8, and we had spotted a glorious, majestic orange tigress that time.

But that ride had been in Dhikala, a 'proper' forest, the kind you see on the Discovery Channel and Animal Planet, with golden-green grassland flaunting herds and herds of thousands of chital shifting around as one big, hazy golden-brown-and-white spotted cloud, and a reservoir with the *ghariyal*—native alligators—lazing around tricking you into taking them for slow creatures until one of them zips into the water. Monkey shrieks rip the air and wild boars appear right on the mud track. What wondrous scenes spring back in my mind from my childhood: watching langurs fall splat-splat-splat from trees, a sign that the tiger is nearby; swaying in tune to the elephant's gait as we approach the little clearing, watching the orange and black-striped tigress stand up warningly and gaze directly into our eyes. What a moment of pure awe and elation! A little guttural growl warns us off from treading too close into the territory of the Queen.

But the queen definitely has competition from another species in the award for the Most Menacing Mammal of the jungle. Tuskers—wild Asian bull elephants—are arguably the most hot-headed mafia of the forest, deceptively calm from a distance. You can enjoy the sight of a tiger from close quarters in the safety of your closed jeep, but if the tusker spies you staring at his kin, you'd better make tracks or watch your vehicle turn to pulp, with yourself inside it.

Years ago, my mom almost didn't make it back in one piece. She and half the vacationing party had taken the jeep to the river. I was with my father and the other half of the party, who had chosen to go in search of the tiger again. My mom and her friends had been watching, from a safe distance, an elephant herd frolicking in the water. When they had had their fill of jungle sights and turned to leave, they found the path blocked by a very irate tusker, deliberately stopping their jeep from escaping. Since I wasn't inside that jeep, I can only imagine what state the occupants of the vehicle must have been in. Chanting their prayers? Imagining last words left unsaid and wills left unmade?

They managed to get out of the situation alive though, thanks to the driver who knew his way around the jungle as good as any animal; he zipped away in reverse—tyres screeching—out-manoeuvring *colonel hathi* and found an alternate route out.

But all of this is the distant, thrilling past.

Right now, my mother, sister, husband, nine-month-old son, and I are all set on the back of a tamed she-elephant who will take us inside the jungle of the Durga Devi buffer zone.

We have two bottles of water tucked under our arms, baby tucked securely in his baba's lap, pacifier firmly inside the baby's mouth. Radha, the elephant, takes off into the wild, as the mahout chooses a horrible, uneven path through a shallow, uncovered drain-cum-trench, near the homes of the tribes that live on the national park's periphery. He points to a dog-like creature sitting around—a jackal that has partly been domesticated and now has a litter of three pups playing with the village kids.

I am unimpressed. One, the memory of this morning's rather fruitless jeep ride weighs heavily on my mind and two, I have done a little too much online research and found warnings saying that the mahouts will rip you off or fool you into believing you saw something that you really didn't.

In due course, we cross the disgusting drain and arrive at the river bed. The elephant moves right into the river, with the water nearly reaching the beast's belly. Goodness, that snaking brown sludge of a river has shed years off her age! She's a gushing little enchantress here, and the view on both sides is gloriously spectacular. Hills to the left, frothing river to the right, lean-muscled young boys with shiny brown skin swimming joyously around, and us perched atop Radha.

Radha decides she can't resist the water, and as we are her guests, after all, she ensures we don't miss the fun. So, we are almost treated to the luxury of a priceless elephant-trunk-bath as she begins to spray water cheerfully over herself. One cracking order from her master, with a sharp nudge of his feet, and the lady is back on duty.

As soon as we cross into the jungle, it is clear that this one is different. Not the Animal Planet variety, but *Jurassic Park*. Ferns and moss and huge grass, not golden but tropical green, grow haphazardly and eerily, covering every inch of space. The vegetation is sparser at the edges where we spot our first animals: spotted deer. Farther ahead, there is a pair of sambar—larger sized, unspotted species of deer in these parts.

My mother, who would probably live in a jungle given a chance, is happily clicking away pictures. The other one clicking away, to my surprise, is Silent Salman. He wasn't very keen on the whole wildlife thing, but now he is having a blast. I am still unmoved, though. Just goes to show that too much research isn't always good.

'Keep your eyes open; I tell you there's a tiger in here. It's been dragging off cattle for a couple of days now. I guarantee it. You'll get your tiger here,' the mahout keeps assuring us.

Yeah right, I think, rolling my eyes. *Sure* there is.

The elephant turns left, heading deeper into the jungle, and suddenly, underneath a bush, we see it—the half-eaten carcass of a cow.

Holy cow!

There really is a tiger in here, and it really has been dragging cattle away.

Now we are all very alert, little shivers of excitement running down our spines. We move deeper and deeper. The bushes get greener, thicker, higher and the trees clumpier until we are being attacked by the jungle—tree branches coming at us from every possible angle, forcing us to stretch out our arms in defence as they try their best to whack us to the ground.

Salman and I hold Hamza with an arm each crossed around him, because we need our other arms to defend him against the branches. The mood between Salman and me is a little tense . . . he is feeling increasingly protective towards Hamza and beginning to regret bringing our little one here. Since he can do nothing about it now, he gets grumpier and grumpier.

And then it happens.

The baby's pacifier falls out of his mouth and onto the forest floor.

All four of us gaze at each other in dismay and horror. Who the heck is now going to climb down to retrieve it?

'Stoppp,' we shout in unison to the mahout.

'What? What is it?'

'*Bachche ki chusni gir gayi, bhaiya*.' The baby has dropped his soother, I whine stupidly.

'Oh, *itni si baat*?' Is that all? 'Watch my Radha here,' he says proudly, and making a sound like 'hek, hek', nudges her with his foot and presto! The elephant holds out Hamza's pacifier, neatly folded in the hollow end of her trunk.

Unbelievable!

Now we just have one more problem. This is an elephant holding the pacifier in her trunk full of germs and dirt and what-have-you, and this pacifier is supposed to go inside the mouth of my nine-month-old. And no, we have no sanitiser, no soap—nothing except a bottle of mineral water, with which my mom proceeds to 'thoroughly' and 'diligently' wash the thing.

Super.

'I can't put this inside his mouth!' I gaze at the others, appalled. 'The ELEPHANT held it, for goodness' sake!'

'But, baby, I've washed it really properly,' my mom attempts to placate me.

'Seriously, mummy, this is not going to happen!'

'Oh yes, it will!' My mom flares up now. 'You will jolly

well put the darn thing in his mouth before he begins to scream his head off!'

Silent Salman is horrified and disgusted, but he seems to think it better to keep Hamza's mouth shut, if only to keep him from drawing the attention of wild animals.

So, the pacifier goes into the baby's mouth.

This is disgusting, irresponsible, totally insane! I'm a terrible mother! I should have just hung the soother around his neck with a piece of ribbon. How could I not? I should have carried a sanitiser. How could I not? And how could we let him suck that thing?

Well, we did.

The elephant resumes its trail. We find what looks like a little tortoise in a water-filled ditch, and the mahout stops for us to take a picture. I peer at it closely, because, from my perch on the top of the elephant's back, it looks a lot like just a stone. I am still wondering if he is making a fool of us when he suddenly swivels the elephant in a semi-circle and moves to the right.

'He's here! The tiger is here!' The elephant circles another bush. The mahout goads her on. But this time Radha refuses to comply. She is scared. (At least, it appears to be the case—you have to assume that in the absence of knowing elephant-ese).

The mahout shouts at it, '*Arre kya ho gaya? Pagla gayi hai kya*?' What's wrong with you, you crazy wench?

Several things happen at once:

Hamza begins to cry. Salman and I desperately begin shushing him. 'Make him quiet!' orders the mahout. 'Be quiet!' he throws in for our benefit, then gives Radha several blows with his wooden stick. Abruptly, he draws out an iron goading hook—a *bhaala*—and brings it down sharply on her back.

'Arrreee *#@##@**, chal CHAL!' Move MOVE, you bloody sister-f*****!

A monkey suddenly comes crashing down in fear from

the trees above. A sure sign of a tiger being around. Mummy and Farina cry out in unison, 'There, move there! That's where the tiger is!'

'Oh be quiet everyone!' Salman almost hollers uncharacteristically, making my eyes pop.

The mahout, instead of taking the elephant in the direction of the monkey, turns her completely around.

'What? We're going back? Why? WHY??'

'He was here. He's gone now. You were making too much noise,' he declares decisively.

'But the tiger is there—in that direction! Why won't you take us there?'

The mahout remains obstinate. That's that.

My mom is livid. 'It's the baby! You couldn't shut the baby up!'

'What! It was both of you who started screaming! The baby had stopped crying before that!' I furiously defended my little one.

A sullen silence accompanies us as we slowly rock back to the edge of the forest. As we cross the river again, it gradually dawns on us how close we were to becoming tiger dinner—with a nine-month-old side dish thrown in for good measure. Shudder.

With an animal like the tiger, you can easily transform from being a pursuer to being pursued in the wink of an eye. Several YouTube videos reveal how. A tiger can also jump high enough to take off the hand of a mahout sitting atop a huge elephant—another video that bears proof.

So, is it foolish to go looking for tigers on elephant back? Well . . . not really. It is all about the thrill, and where there's a thrill there's a way. But is it a foolish thing to take ready-to-bawl nine-month-olds on a tiger hunt in a dense Jurassic-esque forest? You shouldn't have to ask.

Fools most definitely walk in where elephants fear to tread.

Chapter 8

All Aboard: Nightmare to Nainital

June 13, 2013

2:00 p.m.

Off to the Lake City.

Ideally, we ought to have left several hours ago, but Hamza is showing signs of an upset stomach and this, coupled with my mom's sudden desire to take the hotel staff to task over the wrongly charged price of several platefuls of sandwiches, has delayed us quite a bit—and annoyed us even more. After extracting due apologies and the rightful amount from the management, mom is finally ready to be herded into the car. We are all a little flustered by now, but the subsequent drive through the hills, alive with gorgeous forests, soothes our nerves and brings us back in holiday mode.

Starting late means fighting long-drawn-out battles with the traffic in all its honking, zig-zagging glory. It takes two hours for us just to get past the Kosi Barrage of Uttarakhand—which would be a nice enough spot for a picnic and drinking in some sights if not for the endless traffic snailing ahead.

After we've got through to the other side, braving a painstakingly long queue of cars, we stop at the nearest ATM as we have all but run out of cash. I stick my hand under the seat to extract my handbag and pull out my debit card. My hand flails in the empty space: no bag underneath. I look around: no bag between Salman and me, none between mummy and Farina, not under the back seats, none over or around all the other pieces of luggage. Then it hits home: no bag at all.

After having travelled over two hours, well into the second leg of the journey, I realise I have left my handbag containing all the remaining cash, sundry debit cards, and multiple IDs (including my PAN card and driver's licence) back at Nirvana Wilds Resort.

Forgetfulness is a remarkable trait we three Naqvis share ungrudgingly—along with the rather delightful propensity of erupting at the smallest inconvenience. And so, we erupt, turning the car into a steaming bowl of lava-on-wheels: squabbling, bickering, blaming. Salman Abbas Zaidi is normally the voice of sanity in all arguments, but it seems the volcano effect is beginning to rub off on him, too. All four of us are absorbed in a hodge-podge game of blame-flinging and self-saving arguments which obviously serve us no good because there is nothing to be done but turn back all the way to retrieve the bag.

7:00 p.m.

The bag is successfully retrieved. We have moved to the lower edges of Ramnagar, but now it is too dark to take on the journey in the hilly terrain, and we must look for a hotel nearby to spend the night and rest after a long day of such high emotions.

June 14, 2015

Finally, off to Nainital. Corbett Falls is a short stop on the way—nothing spectacular, but with a little bit of imagination and effort, it could easily be rendered picturesque. The walk from the gates to the fall is a pleasant experience, amid the ferns and the banyan trees with hanging roots, and the little natural puddles appearing now and then on the sides could be turned into faerie pools if only someone had the inclination. Also, you wish everyone had enough civic sense around places of scenic beauty to not destroy them with wrappers and bits of garbage. What a pity.

Entry into Nainital in peak tourist season is another traffic disaster. There is an endless stretch of bumper to bumper traffic and hours and hours of waiting just to enter the city. Admittedly, the drive offers many a pretty sight with clouds hanging low and terraced hillsides basking in the sun, but the wait is too much.

Unlike Corbett, our hotel here isn't booked in advance. There are many reasons for that, including our hurried programme and the lack of unanimity in vacation choices. So, here we are, smack in the middle of a sea of tourists with tariffs shooting through the roof and touts having a field day all around us. A combination of poor planning, stretched resources, and unbelievable over-crowding has landed us at the Moon Hotel, which is a decent joint for a short stay. But we have been idiotic enough to opt for the lowest category of rooms, and we are now not-so-comfortably lodged in the budget rooms of a two-star hotel; absolutely not my preferred style for spending a precious annual vacation.

Oh well, it is only for two nights. And right now, we are focussed on visiting the beautiful lake ahead.

4:00 p.m.

I have probably never disliked rain so much. A light drizzle has transformed into loud patters. If it were not for the little monkey clinging to us, Salman and I would have loved the Mallital-Tallital walk. But, it is cold enough already and getting the baby wet wouldn't be helpful at all. We decide to split up: shopping for mummy and Farina, and sitting-on-the-bench-with-an-umbrella-and-a-baby for Salman and me. With Hamza in one set of arms and a positively enormous bag of baby supplies in the other, we sit under two precariously-held umbrellas with our backs to the lake, hoping for it to stop soon so that we can go boating or try something else that is fun. Something to remember this place by.

Little did we anticipate that this was destined to be an unforgettable holiday in the way that most nightmares are.

7:00 p.m.

May you live in interesting times.

This is a very famous Chinese curse—famous everywhere except in China. On account of the common practice of quoting 'China' on sundry issues, for it carries a mystic and mysterious air.

So, three hours later, here we are, decidedly distressed—barely shielded by an umbrella that seems flimsy as a leaf under the relentless rain thundering down with palpable anger. Standing by a traffic-clogged road, we are waiting for the driver to pick us up, all the while bouncing an increasingly cranky baby. Mummy and Farina are nowhere to be seen.

Another half-hour later, the taxi is here. Hamza has managed to fall asleep in his baba's arms, soothed at last by his mumma's lullabies. Perhaps that is the reason he had been so irritable all this while; he was sleepy. But a mother's instinct is telling me there is something else. A sleepy baby wouldn't cry for one hour before dozing off, comforted by rocking arms and lullabies. A sleepy baby wouldn't refuse to take the milk bottle. The reason becomes clear when we reach the hotel. Hamza has a major—and I mean major—nappy rash, owing to a severely runny stomach. The incessant crying was probably on account of a stomach ache.

The rain is still pouring down mercilessly. The heavens have flooded, water crashing over from the edges upon the mortal world. Just this corner of the world, that is. Heaven tipped to a side with all that weight.

It is well past 9 p.m. now. The rain shows no sign of abating and we have no clue where to locate a doctor or a chemist. I call up Hamza's paediatrician in Delhi but she doesn't pick up. There is a mild probiotic that I have brought with me but that is no match for the severe infection that he seems to have picked up. In hindsight, he was showing signs of a mildly upset stomach even when we had arrived in Corbett, but it wasn't very prominent and I am more the stay-away-from-antibiotics kind of mom. Well, so much for that.

2:00 a.m.

The baby is in great pain. It is the worst rash I have ever seen. A sleepless night is bad in itself, but the worst thing ever is to see your helpless infant suffer agonisingly. Am I a bad mother? Could I have tackled it differently? Was it because of the elephant-soother episode? Was I neglectful? Should I have acted upon the very first signs?

Experience is only gained through the worst episodes.

June 15, 2016

The final day of our doomed vacation. And the rain still crashes down angrily.

The heavens have truly ripped apart.

We depart for Aligarh around noon. Hamza seems a little better, though Salman and I are more the worse for wear. We have over eight hours of road journey ahead, but with the persistent rain it would take us longer.

7:30 p.m.

An otherwise drab journey suddenly turns eventful as the rain-soaked universe stops us midway. This potholed road passing through a village is nearly flooded and we see a bulky white Scorpio stuck in the water. A ditch? Probably. Dead engine? Perhaps. No one can make out from the water-logged road. Our driver is apprehensive of venturing into the large muddy pool. But we can't keep waiting in the middle of nowhere forever—and forever is what the rain gods seem to have in mind.

Mummy's lips start fervently moving with inaudible Quranic verses. She is the most devout of us all, the first to break into prayer at the slightest provocation. I suppose Salman gets the distinction of being the sticking-to-the-rule-book type of person, but when it comes to impromptu prayers from the heart, mom beats us all hands down. Well, here we are, engines revved up and sloshing through the murky water, with the odds stacked high in favour of us getting stranded right here.

But.

We beat the odds!

And reach Aligarh around 10 p.m. Sigh of relief acquires a whole new meaning.

June 16, 2016

Salman leaves for Delhi the next morning as we resume our weekends-only marriage. Mom, too, gets back to the office. I am left to nurse an extremely unwell baby alone. And bizarrely, it is raining in Aligarh, too.

My grandmother, who lives with my mom, swears she has never heard a baby scream quite so excruciatingly—and she has brought up two of her own along with two of my mom's. The paediatrician from Delhi refuses to prescribe antibiotics until the stool test reports are available, which basically means two more days of agony.

Hamza's cries are ripping my heart apart.

Panic.

Lots of panic.

I rush to the local paediatrician, shielding Hamza from the unbelievably obstinate rain.

But the doctor is out of town. There is a substitute doctor who prescribes an antibiotic along with a high-potency ointment for local application.

Every time the ointment makes contact with Hamza's little bum, he lets out a heart-wrenching, ear-splitting wail. The next day I take him to our family homoeopath.

Turns out, the painful skin-burning ointment was actually a treatment for piles. How wonderful.

When it rains, it pours.

June 17, 2013

This downpour is phenomenal. The entire mountains of Uttarakhand have been devastated by the flood of the century—India's worst natural disaster since the Tsunami of 2004. The North India Flood of June 2013, attributed to a cloudburst and to the piling up of debris from the building of dams upstream, which caused rivers to block up and overflow.

'Breaking News: From 14th to 17th June 2013, the Indian state of Uttarakhand and adjoining areas have received heavy rainfall, about 375 per cent more than the benchmark in a normal monsoon.'

Don't I know it.

'The worst day of the flood was 16th June 2013.'

Exactly one day after we departed from the ill-fated Uttarakhand mountains.

For days the newspapers and news channels are deluged with reports of over a hundred thousand tourists trapped in the hill stations, as well as pilgrims trapped at the three Chhota Char Dhams in the lower Himalayan ranges.

Houses collapsed. Bridges uprooted. Humans and cattle washed away. The Indian Army, Air Force, and paramilitary deploy their might to evacuate the stranded. India is besieged!

My entire family and I pray for the victims as well as the armed forces at namaz time every day. And I, the petty mortal that I am, can't help thinking over and over that we had been there just two days ago. My mother, my husband, my sister, my son. The sum total of my entire life. Escaped by the skin of their teeth the ire of the great North India flood.

Interesting times, indeed. No wonder they call it a curse.

Chapter 9

The Ghost of George Bernard Shaw

'There are two tragedies in life: One is to lose your heart's desire. The other is to gain it.'
—George Bernard Shaw

July 14, 2013

I had read this quote in the unlikeliest of places, when I was about 12 years old—in an Archie comic. For some reason, the line haunted me all those years like a symphony that makes you cry for no reason at all. Perhaps, in a cosmic irony of sorts, it was a portent of things to come.

It has almost been a year now that Salman and I have been leading separated lives. Weeks slipping into fortnights, days creeping into months.

A popular post on Facebook goes like this: if you want to know the value of nine months, ask an expecting mother. I had been every bit through those tedious nine months, but I can solemnly swear that these ten were worse.

Ten months of uncertainty, of standing still or oscillating like a pendulum, of not knowing whither your life is headed. Of the myriad horrible conditions to be in, perhaps one of the worst is having to wait.

Wait, at the mercy of another. Wait, without an action plan. No matter how terrible your condition, as long as you are battling it—strategising and waging war—you know you can make things better. Somehow. But this—this waiting without moving, waiting without knowing, waiting without a decision. . . It is not something I had ever done, not something I was ever used to. I had always planned my life far in advance.

Until.

At some point in your life, there will always come an 'until'. That will, perhaps, be the day that you wake up to the hand of destiny. In more ways than one.

As it does now. After ten long months of agony, everything falls into place. Salman gets his visa. The relief washing over me is palpable.

As I wave goodbye to the love of my life at the Indira Gandhi International Airport, I have none of the nervous sinking in my stomach that accompanies lovers bidding farewell. My heart is at ease with the deepest conviction that in a couple of months I will be there with him. And a sissy I never was.

My father-in-law would later remark that I had been *daler* about this. Fearless. Intrepid. Not batting an eyelid. No teary goodbyes and no vacant silences. I was my usual, cheerful self.

One of my relatives works abroad and his wife wanted to know how I could be so cool about Salman's departure. I didn't want her to feel bad—she had been separated from her man just three months after marriage, and that, too, when she was pregnant. I choose my words carefully, deciding not to talk of my hopes for the future. 'I am going to pretend I am still single,' I tell her. My newspaper columns, my personal blog, all those books that demand reading plus shopping, parties, weddings, and hanging out with friends—there is a lot to be done! And then she asks me the question. That question.

'But what about Hamza?'

'Ah, Hamza!' I am still cock-a-whoop, such is the levitating power of fresh hope. 'Well I am going to pretend he is my brother! I can look after a baby brother, can't I, and still be single!'

Yes, I actually said that.

When people are happy, joyful, hopeful, they can dream up the craziest scenarios.

And I am happy. Really happy. It is not just the promise of finally being together in a few months. It is also the promise of uncovering new secrets together and discovering new joys. This has always been our 'thing'. It is what we are best at.

Every couple has this little 'thing' with each other, the little thing that is their glue. This is ours. We are not Romeo and Juliet, Laila and Majnu—or even Raj and Simran from *Dilwale Dulhania Le Jayenge*, though Lord alone knows the tonnes of labour Salman put for the *ladki wale* (the bride's side of the family) during our wedding. We are hardly any of those eternal, evergreen couples because Salman is mostly the guy who would start cracking jokes during a romantic moment. In fact, you can trust him to spoil it with his corny sense of humour.

Nope, the maximum supply of romance here is definitely from my side.

What Salman brings to this relationship is far greater than candies, hearts, and roses. He brings a childlike quality to 'us'. Like two children playing, sharing, jostling, bickering, whining, and getting along all the same. We are not the best lovers, perhaps, but we are the best of friends.

I know every girl wishes for Prince Charming. I did, too. But it is sort of lucky, in a weird way, if you end up with Peter Pan. He is never going to grow old.

And, so, skippity-hop, hoppity-skip, this is what defines our relationship. Doing stuff together. Exploring. Imagining. Creating. Experiencing. We are a team.

Like Lisbon and Jane. Teresa Lisbon and Patrick Jane. Salman is the one who got me hooked onto *The Mentalist*.

But then he has had me hooked onto a zillion things—I don't know how, but he knows exactly where to find my 'hook'. During the early days of our relationship, we used to trade with each other; I picked out books for him to read and he picked out movies for me to watch—Hollywood movies. I was a total Bollywood buff, and the handful of Hollywood movies I had seen were *Jurassic Park* and *The Lion King* kind of movies—baby stuff. The hand-picked selections clicked for the both of us. *The Mentalist* falls into that very category.

From the start, Patrick Jane reminded me of Salman.

They are actually not the least bit similar. Salman isn't glib like Patrick, nor is he the smooth-talking ex-imposter. He is not defiant or rebellious. But right from Season One, Patrick Jane reminded me of my man. Why? Well, for one, beneath the cheery exterior the core of Patrick's character is his undying, obsessive commitment to his wife even after her death, his refusal to take off that wedding ring or to move past his little daughter, long passed on from this world, until he brought to justice the man responsible for their murder. Also, his compassion for the weak, his solidarity to his team—all of which remind me of Salman—and, most of all, the way he treats Teresa Lisbon. He drives her mad, defies her, breaks every rule and, yet, there is something about the two of them that makes them great together. He really, truly cares for her more than anything else in the world. (And don't forget the exasperating sense of humour.)

It's in the way she knows he's incorrigible—and indulges him, nonetheless. What cosmic coincidence is it that for the first ten years of our relationship, my guy's number was saved in my cell phone as *Incorrigible Salman*?

We're a team, he and I. When we are together, we do things better.

That is why I am so happy about Salman going to Oman—I already have visions of my new home in an enchanting new country. Irresistible, unknown lands for us to discover. A couple more months to go and we would be celebrating Hamza's first birthday together.

I hadn't accounted for George Bernard Shaw, though, who chose this most inopportune moment to demonstrate his words from so, so long ago. There are, indeed, two tragedies in life. The first is to not get what you desire for so long. The other, of course, is to get it.

Sigh.

Chapter 10
LABOUR OF LOVE

One of the major casualties of 'motherdom' has been my work. The work that didn't just mean money and prestige for me, it meant the world. Because it was my passion—an affaire de coeur. I don't write just because I get paid for it, I write because it is essential to my existence. Like breathing. Like blinking. Or even like taking a leak—because if you are forced to hold it in for far too long, you might just die. Prisoners have actually been tortured to death that way: 'holding it in'.

This is exactly the same. I can't hold it in. I would die. I write because once a thought, an idea has its hold on my mind, I can neither eat nor sleep until I have committed it to pen and paper—or laptop, as is the case now. I remember sleeping beside my mom, huddled inside a quilt with a torch in the left hand, writing down poems that would snatch at my sleep and wouldn't let go, like unruly sylphs, well past midnight. This was when I was 12.

Now, imagine loving something so entirely, so naturally, and then being paid to do it. Like a chocolate addict being paid to taste chocolates. But that is not even the best part. The best part is that unlike writing privately in your diary, you write in a newspaper—a medium that is being read and absorbed by hundreds of thousands. You have your name marked on top of what you write, smartly etched out in print, made eternal and exhibited for the world to see. The feeling is indescribable.

Like the rush of falling in love, every single day.

And then to have this love wrenched out of your grasp.

When I had to let go of my job around the time that I was three months pregnant, it took a pretty big toll on my mental well-being. A job like mine wasn't just a paycheque. It meant eight hours of doing something just for your own satisfaction, eight hours of time spent with like-minded people. It meant going out of the house every day, seeing the world and its minute changes every passing morrow. Meeting diverse people from diverse disciplines, not to mention star achievers in their respective fields, and acquiring new knowledge every day. Travelling far and wide on official trips, seeing the world without spending a dime. It also, emphatically, meant having other people to have a good time with than just your husband.

Having no job means being cooped up at home, which puts unnecessary strain on your relationship with your partner. You begin clamouring desperately for his attention, which can't be entirely reciprocated because he has a job and other occupations of the mind. The only company you have around is the people whose conversations centre around either daily soaps or the daily help—none of which are remotely interesting to the thinking woman. I was utterly and completely alone during those months of pregnancy, and then I realised I had to be involved in something constructive to stop myself from slipping into depression. One of my friends suggested joining an MPhil programme at Jamia Milia Islamia, which was then a 15-minute drive from my place. But the near-constant retching and throwing up had left me in absolutely no condition to go anywhere on a daily basis. Then I remembered the thing called the National Eligibility Test. If you qualify the NET, you are eligible to be selected as a lecturer in any central university. When I had completed my Masters in Mass Communication, I had been advised about a hundred times by well-meaning people to take that test, but that is not because they thought it would be a great and fitting career option; it was because of the age-old belief that 'teaching is the best profession for women'. And then, too, not because it is a noble and honourable choice, but because it is a 'safe profession' with 'undemanding timings'—basically being a woman you ought not venture into anything too adventurous.

No offence to educators and academicians anywhere in the world, but here is the thing: teaching can be the best profession for *anyone*—not just women—only if they have the aptitude and the inclination for it, not to mention the skill set. It can't be a career choice based only on your gender.

When I had interviewed Margaret Atwood, she had mentioned how during her time there were only about five career choices open to women: nurse, secretary, airline flight attendant, school teacher, and home economist. She said she opted for the secretarial sciences because, in her cryptically witty manner, 'I thought that if I had to have a job I didn't want to have, it should be the one that pays the most.'

I remember musing then, how far we had gotten from her times in terms of choices available—but not so very far in terms of mental mathematics, all things considered. The safest, staidest choices were still considered ideal for women—and, of course, the best job for anyone had to be the one that paid the most. Aptitude and passion be damned.

I refused to toe the line. I hadn't the slightest inclination towards teaching nor was I bothered in the least by social norms or what people thought of me. I had decided to be a journalist and that is what I eventually became. But in this period of absolute indecision, where obscurity fogged out the future, I grasped at the one straw in my sight—teaching—which was safe for all occasions, and which, I thought, would certainly save me from the fatal boredom and mental vegetation that accompanies a lonesome woman at home. It would occupy me in the pursuit of knowledge rather than brooding over the turn of my fortunes. And so, just to keep myself constructively occupied, I sat for the NET during the seventh month of my pregnancy. The results were announced six months later. I had not only qualified the NET but was also selected for Junior Research Fellowship (JRF) offered to the top scorers. This would get me into Aligarh Muslim University's research programme easily, without a written test.

The JRF-NET is a big deal in the world of academics, especially in a small town which has at its very centre a historic 150-year-old University. Small wonder then that every one of my family, friends, acquaintances, and former teachers hailed my success. A jubilation that I could not feel myself, because this wasn't something I loved.

To me, the difference between journalism and teaching was the difference between a love marriage and a marriage of convenience. You might get a match that is, for all practical purposes, a source of envy for everyone around you. You might get beauty, wealth, and resources beyond your imagination. But there is one little thing on which it all depends. The 'salt' of life: love. Love alone brings elation. You cannot settle for something and feel elated about it. This wasn't my love. I could scarcely revel in it.

In any case, I couldn't join the research programme that year because the dates had already passed by when the results were declared. That was just as well, for my baby was far too small and helpless. I had one more year to decide which way to go. I could join the next year or even the year after, since the JRF is valid for two years after the announcement of the result. But I didn't care much either way—we were far more focused at that point on Salman getting his visa and moving to Oman, after which, so would I.

And now that Salman had finally got his visa, I didn't want to end up stranded in Aligarh with a research programme to complete, while the life I wanted slipped farther and farther away—a continental shift, so to speak.

I have always been pretty clear about what I want and when. What I want more than anything right now is to recreate my cosy little nest, for us to be reunited. I do not need any fresh entanglements here. All I want is to join my man in Oman, to pick up the broken pieces of that dream we shared and make a luminous new rainbow for us. Redesign those rose-tinted glasses to view the world with, so that we see only beauty. Experience only joy. Three glasses this time—an additional smaller, rosier one. Yes, that is what I would be doing, and that is where I would be going.

Soon, very soon now.

Chapter 11

Mothering, Nannies, and Olympic Babies

July 19, 2013

I have been told by so many parents, both new and old, that the hardest part of bringing up a child is the three-month period after giving birth, before the baby learns to sleep all night through. My own experience, though, proved that there are other parts of parenting that are even more excruciating. Like helping the toddler learn how to walk. It has to be the most hair-raising part of the child's development chart, especially when you live in a home like mine, which must certainly be featured in the *Good Homes Magazine*—just to warn everyone else what their home must *never* look like.

The state of my maternal home has to do with my family's undying belief that everything must be within arm's length of wherever you are. So, for instance, you don't have to walk all the way to a water cooler or jug or the fridge to quench your thirst; every room has its own permanently stationed jugs and water coolers. And first aid kits, and little boxes for spices, and little boxes for extra sugar, and salt and pepper shakers, and so on and so forth. And we still hold onto every little bit of furniture and home décor, broken or otherwise, since our father's time. Before that fateful car accident took him away from us forever.

My mother has a bit of a Miss Havisham affliction—you know, that lady from Charles Dickens's Great Expectations.

Like the eccentric Miss Havisham, my mom refuses to part with old broken things, setting them up as reminders of an age long gone, an age she refuses to let go, clutching it desperately to her heart. Falling apart herself, even as it all falls apart, too. It is chaos of the most heartbreaking, carefully curated kind, the kind that you can't change or set right, because someone's heartbeat connects to it. Because what seems like junk to you are the salvaged pieces of someone's once-glorious, now-shattered love story.

But now, place a baby inside this chaos, a toddler learning to walk who is curious about everything that seems so new and amazing—not to mention, delicious, for toddlers do have a habit of putting the most inedible things in their mouths—and you have a sure-shot recipe for disaster. So, I spend my days running from table to table, thing to thing, trying to keep my son from wrecking the house, or himself. At night, he hollers for milk, and because milk is the one thing you can't keep inside the room, I have to rush out to the fridge to get it. By the time I begin measuring it out for rewarming, Hamza is already crawling out of bed and, standing with the support of mesh-doors that open and shut through a spring, is attempting to come out. He can't yet handle a spring door; he manages to push it open but doesn't know how to rush out before it bangs in his face. Which it inevitably does. This results in me rushing to pick him up before he gets to the door. Then rewarming the milk, measuring it, and pouring it in his feeder—all with one hand, while the other hand balances him firmly on my hip. At this rate, I could soon perform in a circus.

For a while, I consider putting him in a crib, to keep him from rushing after me. After a couple of attempts, though, Hamza's crib has to be put away for his own good. Even though he can't yet walk without support, Hamza manages to hoist himself to his full height holding the crib rails, stands en pointe on his toes like a ballet dancer, and through some marvellous feat of gymnastics, launches himself straight over the edge—landing face down on the ground.

So that is the story behind the crib being discarded.

January 9, 2013 (Six months ago)

Sitaram Bhartia Institute of Science and Research

Every three months after Hamza's birth, I used to come to Delhi for a couple of days for his check-up to be done at the hospital where he was born. During my pregnancy, we had volunteered to be a part of a research tracking the growth charts of babies over the first year. So, every three months they assessed Hamza's mental and physical development. Usually, Salman accompanied me for vaccinations and such, but this time he had an important meeting at his office, which held him back. I had to go alone with the baby, and I was perfectly okay with that. Never been a damsel in distress.

What I hadn't realised, though, was that it was one thing to be an independent woman travelling alone, and quite another to be a woman with a three-month-old travelling alone. To top it all, I was carrying Hamza with one arm and filling up and clutching the various hospital forms with the other. I forgot to bring the baby stroller. Foolish me.

Things were going pretty well until I dropped the folder while getting up from my seat and the man sitting next to me didn't even budge to pick it up. His wife, who was nursing a baby on her lap, nudged him twice but he was too busy on his cell phone. I somehow managed to balance Hamza against my shoulder, support him with one hand, and picked the folder up. The wife smiled at me apologetically. I smiled back. It wasn't her fault that her husband was a total jerk.

With Hamza's vaccination over, I needed to get a shot, too, against cervical cancer. Now, in the cold, cold month of January, getting a shot meant pulling up several layers of clothing, which can be a major task. The baby, who had been lying quietly by the side so far, decided it was time to start bawling. Amid all the pulling and the wailing, my hand smacked the folder from the tabletop, sending it spinning to the floor with all its contents splattering out. The damned folder!

Simultaneously, the door whooshed open and another woman stepped into the chamber with her baby, nanny in tow. She took one look at me and rushed to help.

'Thanks so much,' I murmured gratefully. 'It's tough handling a little one alone. You see, my husband had an important meeting today and he couldn't accompany me here . . .' I was ashamed at being so flustered and clumsy.

The woman, cool as a cucumber in her elegant dress and coiffured hair, smiled at me sagely and pronounced a line I will never forget:

'You don't need a husband, darling. You need a nanny.'

July 29, 2013

It has been about a fortnight since Salman left for Oman and now my mother has managed to arrange a nanny for my son. A live-in babysitter. A Godsend!

Respite had already reached me around the time Hamza turned 6 months old—the editor of the newspaper I was earlier working with called me up to ask if I would like to freelance.

Would a bee like honey? You wouldn't have to ask, but if somebody's asking, I guess nothing could be better. So, my *Shelf Life* column is resurrected, immersing me once again in the world of books, reviews, and author interviews. Ah, the relief! Like being submerged for so long that you are just about to give up . . . then your head breaks the surface and your lungs swell and sputter, throwing out water, as you take in gulpfuls of fresh air in sheer ecstasy. But then, writing endless columns and reading a never-ending library of books brings its own set of problems—not the least of which is a majorly attention-seeking kid. Let me elaborate.

Most mothers like to cover up with a dupatta or a piece of cloth while nursing their babies, and I have seen them comfortably chatting up other family members while the baby suckles. But not His Little Highness Hamza. He will bawl his head off if I try to cover his face while nursing, he will kick up an awful fuss if I do not maintain absolute eye contact every moment through the feeding, and he will petulantly refuse to drink altogether if I start conversing with someone else. When he feeds, I dare not engage with anyone else!

But there's more.

You cannot leave him alone for a single minute. Even when he was two months old, he would keep waking up mid-sleep and look around to ensure he wasn't alone. If he was, woe unto the entire household. Going to the loo became a luxury for me. Someone suggested a cradle with a hanging toy. But the toy held his attention for a maximum of 2 minutes. The outcome of all this was that I spent all day sitting with him, totally at the mercy of the whims of His Little Highness.

Several people advise me to let him cry for some time, letting him get used to being alone. So, I try—I go for a bath, leaving him strapped in his stroller. He cries non-stop for 20 minutes and continues to cry even after I have come out. Now, when I take a shower, I wheel his pram right into the washroom.

Some days I really hate motherhood.

So finally, when I have a chance to return to professional writing, I just can't let this baby waddle all over this as well. I try writing with him lying by my side, but now all that my belly-crawling kid desires is the laptop mommy is working on. Or the book she is reading. Or the pen she is writing with. And it has to be that very thing and no other.

And so, I am filled with a great urge to kiss Shabnam's hands the day she arrives.

Suddenly life feels so much lighter. I can read in peace, I can write in peace. I can *bathe* in peace; I can *urinate* and *defecate* in peace. I have someone to alternate the nappy changing with. Or the bottle feeding with. And most of all, when I am unwell or super tired, I have someone to call out to groggily in the middle of the night, 'Please make Hamza's bottle this time . . . I'm dead!' I can go out now with Shabnam accompanying me, sharing the caretaking of Hamza. I can visit friends without Hamza screaming for attention, I can go shopping without wondering how on earth to do it with a baby in my arms. She has taken half the load off.

That half which was supposed to be shared by the baby's father. My husband.

Somewhere in my head a voice echoes: 'You don't need a husband, darling. You need a nanny.'

Yes, yes, and yes.

And no.

Yes, you definitely need a nanny when you are managing a little kid. But you don't need a husband?

Yes, you need *only* a nanny if all you require is a load-sharing caregiver for the child. Yes, you need *only* a nanny if the child's emotional, mental, and physical well-being is not the least bit affected by the near-constant absence of one parent.

Also, if you are a heterosexual woman with a heterosexual woman's needs and desires, you most definitely need that darned husband. Or, if you do not believe in the sanctity of the institution of marriage and are not dependent on the marital bond for the fulfilment of your physical desires, then I say, thumbs up to you. Go ahead, darling, you need only a nanny.

November 18, 2013

The latest research published in a reputed American journal reveals that babies that start walking as early as nine-ten months are 90 per cent more likely than their peers to be extremely athletic, going on to win world championships and at least one medal in the Olympic Games during their lifetime.

No, of course not. This is pure drivel. But it sure does feel like the truth sometimes, considering the amount of societal pressure there is to get your baby to walk and talk earlier than everyone else does, and reach all other milestones at Olympic speed. Every mother, it seems, is all set on raising that elusive Olympic baby.

Thirteen months. Whew! Hamza is thirteen months old and still not completely able to walk without support. You would think you'd know by now all the worst parts about the child learning to walk. But you don't. After all the running, balancing, diving, and retrieving that you do day in and day out, your child still turns out to be a slow learner. And yet, that is not the worst part. It is this:

'One year old and still can't walk! What? His father was already walking without support at 10months!'

'He hasn't been given proper oil massages.'

'He hasn't been fed enough eggs.'

'What! 13 months and can't walk! His father was—' Yes! Yes! I know! How many more people will inform me about it?

I know that his father was the poster boy of The Olympic Babies Club. The kind of babies who are so smart they walk, talk, kick, jump, read, write—practically do everything so early they are sure to win an Olympic Gold in their lifetime, or at least a Nobel Prize. So why don't they?

We have become so accustomed to incentive-linked target achievement with an inflexible deadline that we treat our children in exactly the same way: targets to be met on time. But then, this isn't a recent phenomenon. This race has been on for generations. Go back farther and farther in time, and you would find it intact. The my-mothering-is-better-than-yours complex—a subtly malicious way to make a mother feel useless and inferior.

In truth, the only kind of good mothering is the one that nurtures a happy, confident child, who feels secure and protected. Aware of his parents' belief in him and with ample space to grow as slow or as fast as he likes. For a child, the world is fascinating, sparkling, jaw-droppingly awesome. The faster the train hurtles along the tracks, the faster the scenery goes crashing past, and you miss out on all the glorious details of the splendid world outside.

Why rush?

The cherub that crawls through the garden finds all the hidden treasures.

Chapter 12

Steps in Darkness

September 1, 2013

Almost every couple I have known values their first child's first birthday as one of the most important events in their lives, and it is fittingly celebrated, perhaps even a little over the top, with great pomp and show. Like the first wedding anniversary, the first birthday of your child is one of those fist-bumping, high-fiving, 'we did it!' moments that you share, revelling in the fact that you made it this far through a life-altering change and did a pretty good job of it, too.

I am, perhaps, the world's only mother who doesn't want to celebrate her first child's first birthday. At all.

I had been waiting for this day. Imagining it. Replaying it in my mind. Over and over again. 'Hamza's first birthday!' I had been thinking all this while. 'It will be so wonderful to celebrate it together in Oman.'

I had been so sure. So full of energy, full of hope. And now, slowly, reality was spreading its cold pallor over my heart. I did not want to celebrate anything, leave alone this first birthday that served as a mocking reminder of one whole year of my life just laid waste.

Hamza's *nani*, his *true* mother for all purposes, has her heart set on it, of course. She makes it a point to remind me every day: 'You're not his mother, *I* am. You're just his nanny appointed to take care of him while I'm not at home.' That statement is one of the high points of my days because it warms my heart to see my mother with this little imp of a boy. He has wound her round his little finger and has found a perfectly hilarious name for her. Not nani, nanna, nani-ammi or any of the names we address our grandmas with. He calls her 'office'. Just that. Office.

It originated thus: Hamza was all of ten months and already yakking away. (He may not have inherited his father's Olympic walking skills, but he has certainly inherited his mom's talking ones.) He began addressing his grandma with the perfectly innocuous 'nani'. During the day, when she would be at work, Hamza would knock at the bolted door of her room, and ask me questioningly, 'Nani?' And I would tell him, 'Nani office *gayi hain*,' which he interpreted not as 'Nani office gayi hain', but as 'Nani-office gayi hain'. So, from nani, she became 'nani-office' and then the 'nani' was dropped for convenience, with only 'office' remaining.

So 'office' cannot have enough of her little Noddy. He has managed to fill that gaping void, that scary black hole in her heart created first by the death of her husband, and widened by the death of her father. My grandfather passed away just this year, around the time Hamza was four months old. Sometimes I feel that the reason I am here is by the will of divine forces, who wanted this baby to be here for my mother. It isn't about me all the time—this is about her sanity, about her shattered heart. I do see that. And yet, I can't be happy about it. There is nothing exciting for me to look forward to as my mother plans my son's birthday party.

Hamza's youngest uncle—my brother-in-law—serves as a father figure during most of the birthday party, holding Hamza's hand while cutting the cake, entertaining the kids, and joking around. Hamza seems happy. He is intensely attached to his *chachu*.

And I—I am once again reminded of my childhood.

My sister and I often found, in various uncles and grandfathers, new fathers to fill our tiny hearts' yearning. It was our mother who was doomed to be alone forever.

October 9, 2013

Another month, another milestone. Tomorrow is the third anniversary of my marriage.

As the days move on, time grows heavy, leaden. Refusing to pass. Hanging heavy upon the ceiling, watching me from the rotating blades of the fan. Dark and grey upon the sky.

Hope sits quietly in a dark corner.

7:00 p.m.

My father-in-law barges into my room, all smiles, and asks Hamza and me to come outside.

'There's an amazing gift waiting for you outside!' he beams.

For one glorious moment, my spirit surges for I feel that Salman has flown down impromptu just to give me this surprise. I rush towards the door, and then a small voice in my head reminds me of all the eager anticipations of previous months that proved to be huge let-downs. I don't want to end up that way again. I take a deep breath, calm myself, and move slowly ahead, hoping to take whatever it is with equanimity, sans extreme emotion of either kind.

I open the door. And there stands Salman.

The normal me, the impetuous, impulsive me would have erupted with joy at the sight of his face. Ironically, though, I have calmed myself so well that I am indifferent. I muster a smile broad enough to make him feel I am happy. But I feel angry at myself for ruining this moment.

Sometimes we are so scared of disappointment that we shut ourselves off from extreme joy. I had read somewhere, 'It is better to have loved and lost than never to have loved at all.' It is. It is indeed. To know a joy so pure, so unadulterated, to know an emotion that springs from the depth of your heart, to have been through all of it is worth the heartbreak. When you are open to great joy, you are also vulnerable to great pain. But if you shut yourself off, you feel neither joy nor pain. And as I realise now, the joy is always worth the pain.

11:40 p.m.

'Hey, I left my laptop back in the car,' Salman says suddenly. 'Just let me get it out.'

'Okay,' I say. I suspect he has something up his sleeve.

And he does. He returns to the room with a beaming smile, a lovely bouquet in hand.

'Happy Anniversary, sweetheart,' he says.

And it is. It is.

October 10, 2013

I am wondering what Salman has planned for today. But, knowing him, I haven't kept my hopes up high. He spends the entire morning and afternoon with his parents, and I am nowhere in the picture. I mean I am in the picture, of course, but when you are meeting your husband after five months, you want more than just sitting with his parents and listening to them talk. I know they are meeting their son after five months, too. But again, I can't reconcile myself to it. Over the past one year, I have found myself resenting my in-laws more and more, and it is for no fault of theirs.

When we were in Delhi, Salman and I used to make a trip to Aligarh every fortnight. I knew that was his parent-bonding time, and for those 48 hours, we completely detached ourselves from each other. My folks live in the same city, so I used to go spend time with them, too. It was a perfect arrangement. But everything is haywire now. After five months of being away, he has come home to the both of us—his wife and parents—and we are both vying for his time. And because it is our anniversary, I sort of expect my share to be larger, just this once.

Afternoon turns to evening and I am hoping Salman will take me out for dinner. We do go out. But guess where?

To buy new upholstery fabric for the sofa in my in-laws' drawing room. Apparently, nothing is special today, it is just another day.

My mom rings me up. 'Listen, are you going out somewhere with Salman?'

'No, mummy,' I tell her briefly.

'Then I'm taking you both out to dinner. To Fazle Kareem, that new restaurant you've been wanting to try so much.' She is super enthusiastic. I feel a wave of warm feelings for my mother. And then I go and tell Salman.

He nods, but first, we need to go buy that sofa fabric. Because no other day except the anniversary of our wedding is perfectly auspicious for buying upholstery. After one hour, we have bought nothing. Because nobody could come to a consensus.

We head back home. I am waiting for Salman to inform his parents about our plans.

Nothing.

I glare at him. He is immersed in his smartphone. I nudge his foot. He looks up at me blankly and asks, 'What?' I grit my teeth. And then my mom-in-law, who has been watching this charade out of the corner of her eye, asks me what the matter is.

'Well . . .' I say hesitantly, 'mummy wants to take us out to dinner.' And then, because I am super irritated, I blurt out, 'But he won't tell you anything. He will make *me* say it every time.'

My mother-in-law laughs. She is a kind woman, generally, cool about things. 'Is that all?' she says. 'Of course, you should go. And it makes no difference whether he tells me or you tell me,' she smiles kindly at me. Yes, I know. But if you are an Indian *bahu* you know how much easier it is for your husband to communicate things to your in-laws than it is for you. Doesn't matter if they are kind, sweet, and everything. They are still unpredictable, and you never know when your words might be met with a cold silence.

We do go out and celebrate, but I am confused. I cannot fathom this man who has come all the way from another country to spend time with me, to spend with me the day that we were united body and soul, and then finds it absolutely appropriate to waste it buying sofa fabrics and getting absorbed in his smartphone. Or maybe, I am just 'being a woman', as men tend to say. Never satisfied.

October 13, 2013

Indira Gandhi National Airport, New Delhi

This is it. He is going back. Again. Without me. Without us.

For the past five days, I had been putting it off—thinking about this moment. I had been blindly telling myself that we would fly off with him this time, happily into the sunset. And now, we are here. At the airport. And he is the only one flying off yet again. My father-in-law is trying to make this a happy farewell like the last time; he is clicking photographs of the three of us together. But a lot has changed since the last time. There is none of the euphoric 'it's almost done!' feeling, none of the anticipatory glee. I can barely smile for the photographs.

Salman finally hugs his dad and his youngest brother, kisses Hamza, and for a very brief moment, looks into my eyes and holds my hand. For him to do this in front of his dad means a huge thing, since his family has impossibly strict codes about public displays of affection. You can't hold your wife's hand in the presence of elders. But he does that now, and I clutch it as tight as I can, for that one fleeting moment. And then I must let go.

I must let him go. The person who completes us, who makes me feel I am home.

I've been homeless for a year now.

We head back slowly to the car, and I can't see where I am stepping. The future has clouded over, and I blankly step into the darkness, not knowing where I am headed.

Chapter 13

The Addams Family

In the 1990s, when Cartoon Network was the rage, one of my favourite TV shows was *The Addams Family*, a quintessential horror family.

Gothic mother with an octopus-like slithering gait.
Super enthusiastic but crazy gothic father, eternally and passionately in love with his wife.
Poker-faced weird daughter and horribly annoying monster son—both with a penchant for torture.
Frankenstein-style butler.
Sneaky, explosive, shark-toothed uncle; and,
Motorcycle-riding,eerily-cackling, spell-casting granny.
Oh, and a dismembered walking hand for a pet.

Welcome, everyone, to The Addams Family.

Grandma Bazooka is the Border Security Force in my maternal household. Navy, Army, Air Force all rolled into one—no external power, no matter how strong or sneaky, can ever attack us and get away with it. She has her guns, missiles, and bombs forever directed at anyone who so much as wishes to harm a hair on our bodies, and her internal intelligence bureau is highly trained to keep an eye on all intruders.

Inside those borders, however, she can wreak major havoc. Military rule, so to speak.

Benevolent General of sorts, for you are lavished with sumptuous delicacies, spoilt with beautiful gifts, and promised the inheritance of all the gorgeous heirlooms she has lovingly preserved. But with all of that, you will also be reprimanded for every step you take, the tiniest of mistake you make, and though you will be encouraged to find your path, that path shall be strictly and unreservedly laid out for you—brick by brick, direction by direction. *If* she could have her own way, that is, which she mostly doesn't.

Ours was never an authoritarian household, so she couldn't technically be a matriarch. To be honest, there is no 'arch' in our family—patri, matri, or otherwise. We are quite close to the definition of anarchy.

It wasn't always so.

Before papa died, mom was just a sweet, loving homemaker—well-read and up to date with world affairs, but a homely woman nonetheless. I was a timid nine-year-old, brilliant in academics but quite a bit of a sissy. My sister was two, an audacious toddler with a huge obstinate streak. And my grandmother was just an external force, encountered merely on occasions like birthdays and vacations.

Then the world as we knew it was no more.

Like I have said before, our loss, though greater in absolute terms—loss of a parent—was nothing compared to the loss experienced by our mom. We could create new fathers in our uncles, grandpas, and whatever male relative that looked kindly upon us. For our mother, love was lost forever.

Without a stern patriarch to head the family, we escaped the trappings of the traditional Indian home structure, where the man's word is final and no one dare question it. So we grew up in a crazy democracy—with the right to protest and the inalienable right to freedom of speech and expression—but squabbling all the way with progress often stuck in first gear.

We are closer in the sense that we don't feel obliged to maintain a persona in front of each other, as seen so often in small-town families. But we also have significantly less peace and less direction. The best outcome of all this is that we have developed the faculty to think for ourselves and not blindly follow our forefathers and foremothers. The worst is that compromise never comes easily to us, with no semblance of sanity to our dawns and our dusks.

Into this kaleidoscope of crazies entered this man—this quiet unassuming man with his droll, Jughead-style sense of humour—like a sliver of sunlight in an unceasing storm.

There is a huge banyan tree right at the back of the auditorium in Women's College, Aligarh Muslim University, underneath which I used to sit and read out poetry on the phone to him. Rabindranath Tagore. *Gitanjali*, *Lover's Gift*, *Crossing*. Narrate to him stories of the books I was reading. *Time Machine, Chitra, The God of Small Things, The Inheritance of Loss, The Alchemist*. And sometimes, couplets from Ghalib. Or Mir. Ever wondered why trees are so often used in the backdrop of romances? Because trees are the poetry of the earth. They are the welling up and bubbling out of love from the core of the earth's heart—as shade and fruit and breath. Guardians and protectors. Preservers of love.

The weary heart always seeks refuge from the unending buffets of life. Asylum from the onslaught of accusatory screams and persistent, unresolved emotional clutter. And though I was an equally crazy member of The Addams Family, I desperately sought refuge from it, too.

This man became my refuge. Noah's Ark, with just me on it. And the promise of safer lands.

It is easier for a father to have children than for children to have a real father.

—Pope John XXIII

My father was the kind of man who delighted in being asked nonsensical questions. By me, of course. It assured him that his offspring was using her mind, probing at the world instead of taking it as a given. So, questions like, 'Why is a mango called a mango?' were never answered with, 'Well, that's just how it is.' They were answered with equally nonsensical, hilarious episodes created extempore by his fecund imagination.

'You see, when the British came to India they had no clue what a mango was,' he would begin, with a completely straight face. 'One of the senior British officials received a gift of a bushel of the best quality mangoes. His servant clumsily dropped a few while setting the bushel down, and they rolled into a far corner. Irritated at the man's clumsiness, the officer shouted at him, pointing at the fruits: Man—Go!'

He would pause, eyes twinkling, to smile at me conspiratorially.

'The servant, of course, took this as the name of the fruit,' he would grin widely, mischievously, 'and that, my dear, is why a mango is called a mango!'

I would break into squeals of delight, entirely aware of the answer being nonsense, but happily satisfied nonetheless.

Here is one of his best answers by far, in response to this query of mine: 'Why is a '*naao*' (boat) called a '*naao*'?'

'There were two friends who first made a boat to cross the river,' he replied. 'No one had ever wanted to cross the waters before, and so they never knew what the thing was called. When they reached the middle of the wide river, they were spotted by some villagers on the other side who started waving frantically at them. The villagers knew there was a storm brewing over the river and wanted to warn the men who'd be caught well before they reached the shore. So, they continued waving vigorously, shouting at the men to stay back. "Na Aao! Na Aao!" they shouted. *Don't Come Here!*

But the men didn't speak the same language, so they inferred that the thing they had made was a "Naao" and the villagers were cheering them for having created it. Since then it's been called a *Naao*!'

I dissolved into peals of laughter.

The thing about these funny little stories was that they satiated a little heart's yearning for an answer—any kind of answer, in the absence of the correct one. Far more importantly, though, they taught a curious seven-year-old that no question, no matter how strange or nonsensical, ever had to be quashed. Questions were meant to be asked. And answered.

And above all, that life is nothing without a sense of humour.

Distance makes the heart grow fonder, they say.

Not if you are running away.

Home was never home enough without my father in it. By the time I was in college, I found myself aching to be away, to cut myself off from the place that had sheltered me all those years. The cage is always safer, but the sky is irresistible.

My moment of freedom—a brief one—came for a month during my internship at one of India's leading news dailies. I remember waking up that first day in my dank hostel room and whispering a prayer of thankfulness that I was here and not back home.

Later, when I started my first regular job as a journalist,

it was always a thrill to go back to the *koel* on the neem tree, the hibiscus flowers in the spacious garden of our home in the government officers' colony, the pink walls of my room and the bookshelves lining those walls, their contents spilling out of the shelves to the floors of the room. It was a pleasure to be back with family and catching up on all that we had missed in each other's lives. Sometimes, I even ached for home, for the feeling of just flinging my shoes over with abandon. But the feeling never ran so deep as to make me wish to go back. Delhi was my destiny, my ticket to freedom.

Every time Gomti, the ever-so-dependable train to Delhi, would slow down while approaching the New Delhi Railway Station, my mind would start playing:

'Yeh Dilli hai, mere yaar . . . Bas Ishq, Mohabbat, Pyaar . . .'
(And this is Delhi, my dear. Longing, Love, Amour . . .)

And it was. Delhi was my amour.

India's most polluted city, the queen of traffic jams, the rape capital of the country—call it what you will. To millions of small-town cage-breakers like me, Delhi is the place where dreams come true. Yes, you would have heard that more often about Mumbai—the one with the glamour and star power. But Delhi is, shall we say, more inclined to the intellectual side? Of course, since I have never so much as smelt the Bombay air, I cannot really compare. But I will defend Delhi to the last of my pollution-plagued breath. Every time I sat in the women's compartment of the Delhi Metro, I couldn't help but smile incessantly, much to the astonishment of fellow commuters. But that is exactly what I was—happy for no ostensible reason except that here I was, sitting in a Delhi Metro compartment, like a stray cloud that can drift in any direction that catches its fancy.

And directions there were many—the bookshops that beckoned like Aladdin's Cave, where you could sip on a lime soda, sprawl back on the couch, and read one of those seductively beckoning paperbacks for as long as you pleased. Or just ogle at them longingly and never have your fill. You could spend endless weekends exploring themed restaurants and actually eat things like a 'Pizza-Parantha'. You could find a monument right around the corner—no matter which corner you turned, and you could sit in the gardens around India Gate doing nothing but sighing at the night sky.

I felt one with Delhi—enfolded in her embrace. The proverbial monarch of all I surveyed.

A cloud floating over the Qutub Minar.

Every day before I entered the gates of the newspaper office where I worked, songs from the adjoining music shop would gently waft their way over to me.

'Yaaron—jee bhar ke jee le pal
Lagta hai aaj kal
Daur apna aaega
Yaaron—jo khud pe ho yaqeen
Toh zindagi haseen
Tujhe kal bulaega
Hai junoon . . . hai junoon sa jeeney mein
Hai junoon . . . hai junoon sa seeney mein!'

(Hey mates! Live this moment now
For the day will be ours
And this era will bow down to us . . .
Hey mates! When you believe in yourself
The world is beautiful
And tomorrow beckons.
Let the passion rule your life!
Let the passion overflow your heart!)

It would give me infinite pleasure, as if the office building had clandestinely winked at me, as if the world were leading one grand cheer for me. It was my moment. The era that would belong to me. The *junoon* overflowed from my breast.

My mother would miss me immensely every time the song came on air, for it reminded her of me. But now, years later, as I sit here back in Aligarh with a little boy and a sinking heart, the song makes my mother weep. It makes her weep as she watches my broken, bitter self—submerged in self-pity and pining for the life I had loved. She looks helplessly at the shards of my soul sticking out at the edges, without the faintest idea what to do about it.

I was given one large slice of utopia before the pie had rudely been snatched from under my nose. Unable to cope, my mind kept reeling under the shock, dumped right back into the bickering, boiling, rancid swamp of ceaseless family drama.

I was back right where I had escaped from.

Chapter 14

Marriage, Sex, and Witches

December 15, 2013

Nobody really understands.

The advice flows thick and fast; consoling words with all the soothing quality of Dettol burning on your wound—without the disinfectant effect. You are an aberration, a freak, a phenomenon unfathomable. They cannot figure you out. Why do you pine so for your husband? You have your child, after all. Isn't that amazing?

And you cannot for a single moment understand why these are the very people who most vehemently advocate marriage. I mean, by the same logic, why was there even the need of a husband in the first place? You had your parents after all.

The idea of 'at least you have your child' is baffling. Is the child a replacement of your life partner? Is one person ever a replacement of another? Is one relationship ever a replacement of another? Each person, each relationship holds its own unique place in the carefully stacked-up pyramid of life. You cannot extricate a single one from the structure without causing all others to trip over each other and come tumbling down in a heap.

But far worse are the annoyed, accusatory voices jabbing at you from all corners.

'Why do you need to keep harping on this?'

'Distract yourself, get your mind on other stuff.'

'These things happen.'

And to quote a relative: 'Well, this is entirely *normal*. It's been happening since the Stone Age. Men go away for work and women stay at home and bring up the kids.' These aren't even the words of an old man (so you could pass them off as generation gap) but a young man about my age.

It hurts.

Your pain, your anger, your rankling hollow loneliness. All of that is normal.

Because why should love be of any importance once you are married?

I wonder, though, why we never laugh at or feel annoyed with Romeo and Juliet? Shirin and Farhad? Elizabeth Bennett and Fitzwilliam Darcy? Why does the world find joy in eternal romances, why does your heart weep for star-crossed lovers that couldn't unite?

If this were a typical, pre-marriage case of love and separation, not one person would bat an eyelid over the self-destructive obsessiveness brought on by separation. Nobody questions Devdas and Paro, nobody questions Laila and Majnu. Because we all believe it is quite alright to push the world aside and fight a desperate battle for love—as long as you are not married to that love.

Marriage is supposed to work as a sanitiser, disinfectant, anti-inflammatory, and anti-allergic all combined. Whatever was in your system ought to be cleansed by now, and you must be engaged in a power tussle: sharing lame husband/wife jokes with friends, pining for singlehood, and regretting the knot. So, of course, it becomes difficult to digest that a married couple could be immune to the anti-inflammatory shots and remain pulsating in a whirlwind of romantic happiness.

No, I cannot just 'let go and walk ahead', 'shake off the past and move into the future'. I cannot 'find something else to focus upon', to accept this as 'part of life' and just get on with it. I refuse to focus on anything that declares this as an acceptable way to live. I refuse to settle for the second-best.

I suppose I would be called obstinate. But the world needs to know that it isn't okay. That it is not what is *supposed* to be done. That this should never be done. That I won't ever consider it *normal* and buckle down to it. I would dig my heels in and refuse to budge. This is my protest.

And it almost killed me.

December 28, 2013

Books. Soul whisperers and dream-sketchers. They have kept me company when I have been the loneliest. Helen Macdonald's *H is for Hawk* is a book that has attached itself to my heart like a blob of congealed blood. As I move through the pages I read of Helen dealing with her father's death and, for the first time in two decades and a half, it feels like someone, one person at least, feels the same as I do. But I also read, mesmerised, about Helen's hawk Mabel, about the author T.H. White and his hawks, and how perfectly all of these seemingly unrelated elements come together. Then I chance upon a line, a perfectly innocuous, irrelevant line inside the pages of this Samuel Johnson Prize-winning book, and suddenly it is like a door unlocked inside me, whooshing open and letting in the answer to a question bubbling for so long in the cauldron of my mind, popping up fizz-like, every now and then.

Helen's memoir also chronicles the life of T.H. White, author of the famous Arthurian Novels, and at one place, Helen explains why White's parents' marriage went haywire. Constance Aston, Terence White's mother, married Garrick White, British District Commissioner of Police in Bombay, not out of love but to escape her own mother's jibes about how difficult it was getting, financially, to keep her with them. And then, writes Helen:

> 'The newly-weds travelled to India, and as soon as Terence was born, Constance refused to sleep with her husband any more. He took to drink and the marriage toppled into violence.'

Constance refused to sleep with her husband.

I have heard it so many times now that I'd probably have believed it, if not for the little fact that I could never identify with it.

'Women want it less.' No, make that *'Married Women* want it less'. Because the only jokes you ever hear are about *wives* who never want to have sex.

Why do women want it less? For the life of me, I cannot fathom why, because it certainly does not apply to me. I remember quite distinctly when I was being wheeled out of the labour room after giving birth to my son, my first thought was concern over how I would be able to 'do it', now that my case-relevant body parts were significantly mauled. And heavens be praised, I am not an exception. A vast number of women I know—close friends, acquaintances, neighbours, and such—complain of the unfair categorisation of women's libido. In fact, so miffed was I with this gross stereotyping of the married woman's libido, that I turned to Google to search for cases where wives wanted *more* not less, a reversal of the stereotype, and was astonished by the number of cases I found.

So, where are the wives that like to avoid getting busy in bed? In plenty of places, it would seem—a part of the answer I discovered while skimming through the internet chat groups. A man engaged in one of those discussions rather proudly declared that married life isn't all about sex, that bringing up children is the most important part of marriage, and his wife was 'cured' of her 'abnormally high' libido once she had children—after which she was okay with having sex just twice or thrice a month.

How wonderful, Mr Pathetic.

I wanted to box that jerk's ears. Buddy, did you ever give thought to the fact that child-rearing is becoming too taxing for your wife, so much so that exhaustion and frustration are *killing* her libido? Did you ever consider that you might help her in bringing up your children so she could relax a bit and get her desire back? Oh, I am sorry I forgot—you thought it was 'bad' and 'abnormal' in the first place, so you are obviously glad she got rid of it. Congratulations.

Overwork and exhaustion are definitely a part of the reason. They don't just kill a woman's libido, they kill a man's libido as well. But again, as I read that line in H is for Hawk, I realised there is another reason behind it.

'The newly-weds travelled to India, and as soon as Terence was born, Constance refused to sleep with her husband any more. He took to drink and the marriage toppled into violence.'

As soon as Terence was born.

Constance Aston might or might not have had contraceptive option around her, but I shudder to think of a world where every time you had sex, you were sure of getting pregnant. You would soon develop an increasing aversion to the former for fear of the latter. Even the highest libido would evaporate like morning dew in scorching June daylight.

No wonder then that the wives refused to have sex with their husbands, because I know I would surely be very, very sparing in partaking of the pleasures of a man, if every single portion of pleasure would mean nine months of horrendous vomiting, killing backache, thigh-aches, and splitting headaches, maybe even high blood pressure and high blood sugar, fainting spells, and a super-horrid culmination into the unspeakable torture of ripping a human being out of my body.

No. Thank. You.

And that, obviously, is why men are high on the 'stuff': they never have to worry about any of the above-mentioned consequences. Do it, forget it. Leave the woman to deal with it. True, most men have to *pay* for the child's upbringing. But not everyone does that either. And then again, a super-wealthy man could bring up, oh say, 6 kids just fine. The superwealthy woman would still have to rip them out of her body, one at a time.

I think I just need to glorify the universe for birth control right here, for we can now indulge in the pleasures of our partner without constantly worrying about increasing the family size.

But I am forgetting one very crucial aspect here—women who are actually eager for motherhood but ironically are not rooting so much for intimacy. The kind of women who don't fear pregnancy but fear the act itself. Because traditionally, women had little access to information about physical intimacy, and men weren't really taught to be considerate in bed, the entire experience could not have been anything except one-sided and unpleasant. And you wouldn't be fool enough to keep wanting something that brought either pain or vacant numbness with it, rather than mindboggling ecstasy. The whole thing about having a high libido is that you *enjoy* the act, not go through the motions just for duty's sake.

Carl Jung's analytical psychology explains how mental concepts—fear, mother, God, and such—are passed on to future generations much like inherited skin colour or hereditary disease, through the collective unconscious. So, we have entire female generations *inheriting* the fear of sex, which is only countered if they live in an environment where women's sexuality isn't frowned upon. For the most part, that kind of environment is extremely hard to come by. Good girls don't have naughty thoughts—that is what you are always taught.

The more you deny your sexuality, the better you are at being the proverbial 'good girl'. But I wouldn't want to be a good girl in my nuptial bed. That is my place to let the naughty go wild.

Married women like me, we want more. A lot more. Which is a horrible cross to bear when you are a continent away from the man you married, the one man that you desire.

'We women, when we're searching for a meaning to our lives or for the path of knowledge, always identify with one of four classic archetypes.
The Virgin (and I'm not speaking here of a sexual virgin) is the one whose search springs from her complete independence.
The Martyr finds her way to self-knowledge through pain, suffering, and surrender.
The Saint finds her true reason for living in unconditional love and in her ability to give without asking anything in return.
Finally, the Witch justifies her existence by going in search of complete and limitless pleasure.'
—Paulo Coelho, *Brida*

'The Wedding of Sir Gawain and Dame Ragnelle' is a 15th-century English poem that narrates a tale so timeless, so alluring, it has been retold a multitude of times in as many versions as the mind can imagine. Over a decade ago, 12 years to be precise, I narrated one of these versions to a boy with a serious demeanour and a crooked smile—a friend and a tease. He and I sat in the verandah of my house, conversing casually but locked in a joust of wits.

He had discovered my biggest vulnerability—my fierce solidarity with all of womankind—and he knew just how to get my goat. Keep making snide remarks against womankind in general, and sooner or later you are bound to get the mercury rising. And, my goodness, it sure did work. But after several instances of this, I had grown wiser and learnt to dish it back with a smile. And so, on one of those balmy afternoons that punctuate the month of March, I began:

'You know, you have actually no idea what a woman really wants, and that's why you keep making fun of them,' I said, grandiosely. 'Let me tell you what it is.'

King Arthur, went my version of the story, *was ambushed and held captive, but his wisdom and valour so impressed the enemy that he agreed to spare Arthur's life. There was, however, one condition: within a year, Arthur had to bring back the answer to the question: What does a woman truly want?*

As it so often happens in legends, Arthur reached the end of his year without success, but then he met a witch who proclaimed to know the answer. Of course, she had her own conditions, too—marriage to the young and most handsome knight in all of the land, Sir Gawain. Poor Arthur could not subject his loyal knight to a lifetime with the ugly, spiteful, malodorous witch with a face full of boils and the most obnoxious behaviour. Sir Gawain though, loyal to the core, agreed to marry her and she, in turn, promised to give the answer on the wedding night.

The wedding day was a perfect disaster, with the lady at her witchly best—rude to guests, cackling disgustingly. Gawain, on the other hand, resolutely remained a gentleman, ignoring her behaviour and putting guests at ease. But as night drew near, Gawain rued his fate and braced himself to enter the nuptial chamber. Imagine his great surprise, then, when he found in the bed chamber not the hideous witch he had married, but the most beautiful maiden he had ever set eyes upon.

'Who are you, fair maiden?' Gawain asked, confused.

'I'm your wife,' smiled the woman, 'the witch that you married. Your courteous behaviour today has won over my heart, and I shall grant you a favour, by transforming into a maiden wondrous fair,' she paused. 'But only half the time—either by day or by night. The choice is yours.'

Wise Gawain pondered for a moment. A wife like that would make him the envy of the land by day, but this beautiful woman at night was a sight no man could refuse. The choice was tough.

In the end, Gawain made his decision.

'Since you are the one granting this favour, I leave the choice to you,' he said.

The witch smiled broadly.

'Brave and wise, Sir Gawain! Know that this is truly the answer to your King's question. What does a woman really want? The answer is sovereignty. The power to make her own decisions. And so, dear knight, I shall be my beautiful, pleasant self at all times—day and night—for you gave me what a woman wants.'

I ended my narration and gave him a smug smile. 'Now do you get it?'

The boy smiled mischievously.

'Hmm . . .' he said, his favourite word, as I was to discover later. 'But there is another moral to this story.'

'Is there?' I grinned. 'What?'

'Inside every beautiful woman . . . hides a witch.'

I could have punched him right there, but he had scored this one.

The episode passed, but the boy never forgot the story, for he remained forever a gentleman and gifted the beautiful woman in his life the best thing a man can offer: sovereignty.

But Salman had been right, all along. Inside every woman, there does indeed hide a witch.

On the surface, I might as easily have identified with the

Virgin: 'complete independence'. But there is always that little matter of the witch lurking inside. A witch with deep, burning desires and clandestine thoughts full of sorcery. The witch that, if you believe Paulo Coelho, '*justifies her existence by perpetually being in search of complete and limitless pleasure.*'

January 10, 2014

A new year, with nothing quite new to show for itself.

Except that the witch grows stronger with every breath, feeding on unspent passion, unspoken thoughts, unremarkable days, and untouched nights. She claws my insides hungrily, egged on by a weakening exterior. The witch is strong and desperate.

Every bone that holds her in is a fossil, assaulted by relentless winds of fate.

There is a reason why witches are always depicted as ugly, gnarled, crafty creatures of hate. The world is intimidated by their unashamed acceptance of desire, their full-blooded longing, their refusal to be meek martyrs—their need to ask so much of life, and their ability to extract it as well. The sorcery of her untameable spirit scares and confuses the world, and so the pleasure-seeking ecstatic witch must necessarily be turned into a fearsome creature—villainous to the core and hideous to behold. Because ugliness, more than anything, repulses humans.

The witch inside me screams.

She screams, inaudibly, in indescribable agony. Twists each strand of yearning she finds and spins technicolour dreams in my head at night—dreams purple with passion and longing, crimson with violent lust. She bottles that which has coagulated within—unable to flow for so long—and uses it relentlessly against me, against herself, revelling in the pain; hers and mine.

’tis true. The witch is forever in search of complete and limitless pleasure.

Pleasures of flesh.

Pleasures of blood.

Pleasures of vein and bone.

A caress, an embrace, a kiss, a whispered conversation deep into the night. A choreography of ecstasy. The world around her is full of it—every image on screen, every poem on page, every note of music wafting around.

‘And the sunlight clasps the earth,
And the moonbeams kiss the sea;
What are all these kissings worth,
If thou kiss not me?’

Percy Bysshe Shelley’s lines pierce through the page.

‘Fading in, fading out, on the edge of paradise
Every inch of your skin is a holy grail I’ve got to find.
. . . So love me like you do, la-la-love me like you do
. . . Touch me like you do, ta-ta-touch me like you do . . .’

Ellie Goulding croons from the opposite ends of the earth. Curse you, Fifty Shades of Grey.

‘Lahoo munh lag gaya . . .’ smoulders Deepika Padukone in the movie *Goliyon Ki Rasleela: Ram-Leela.*

‘Soya tha nas-nas mein ab ye jag gaya . . . lahoo munh lag gaya.’

(I’ve tasted blood—it smears my lips,
Long asleep in my veins, it blazes awake.)

The witch smirks. Grimaces. And writhes.

She knows.

The taste of blood never fades. Never wanes. All it takes is one sampling.

The world around her appears submerged in pleasure and not one speck can she partake. *Blood, blood everywhere, Nor any drop to drink.*

Day passes night, night passes day, and the witch's bloodlust saturates each pore. The more she starves, the more she frenzies. Gnashes her teeth and snaps my veins. My brain clots. My vision blurs.

I've tasted blood . . . it smears my lips. Long asleep in my veins . . . it blazes awake.

Blaze, blaze, inferno. Raze me to the ground.

For surely it is the fate of the witch to be burnt forever at the stake.

Chapter 15

Lands without Lines

A line: A straight continuous extent of zero thickness, that extends infinitely in both directions.

That is what we were taught when we first learnt geometry. But the line in its pure form is always an abstraction because the human existence is bound by beginnings and endings. Infinite, limitless existences confuse the human mind. The line segment and not the line, therefore, is what suits human nature better, but given our expertise at aligning abstractions with everyday concreteness, we turn all line segments into a line. So you have telephone lines, electric lines, notebook lines, scratch lines, laugh lines, and the horrible bank lines. The humble, everyday 'line' carries no semblance of infinity whatsoever, but we refuse to add the word segment to it. Doing so makes us feel better about our own segmented existence, makes us feel infinite as a line. Despite this, the line segment is an enormously more productive entity than the limitless line itself. Because the line segment connects two specific, finite points. Hundreds and thousands and millions of line segments connecting countless points. Connection is the greatest boon of life; it turns the planet into a network of heart and breath.

Like interconnected arteries, we pump blood into each other. Disconnected, the planet is a morgue. And that is why life itself needs a line to survive—a lifeline.

January 27, 2014

The worst part about someone you love being in a separate country on the planet is that you know so little about it.

Oman, apparently, is a country that rather detests visual lines. No, not in a physical sense. From what I have seen of the pictures Salman keeps sending me, Oman has breathtaking shorelines, steep stone hill lines, and impressive historical architecture lines. What it blocks are video-calling lines. Skype, Viber, and rather ironically, Line.

Essentially, for long-distance marriages (ugh, that word!) Oman likes to severe the lifeline. We are scrounging around for life support. WhatsApp chats and pictures, and very brief international calls. It is never enough. How can it be, when you have loved, lived, breathed, and, for heaven's sake, made a baby together! Thoughts lose their tone in short messaging, time slows you down in typing—and there is always the bawling/snatching baby while you are on call. Essentially, to be able to talk 10 minutes in peace, you should be sitting in the loo, and even then, the baby screams incessantly outside the door.

That, perhaps, isn't even the biggest gulf in these conversations. There is another, greater gulf, a continental gulf—a gulf of disillusion, a dread sea, a bay of delay.

'What's the update on the family visa?'My favourite question.

'There are some . . . issues with the paperwork.' Always the same vague reply. 'And I'm still struggling with the super-tough driving test here.'

Considering that this guy has been driving cars—and I don't mean remote-controlled ones—since he was barely out of his shorts, this seems completely inconceivable.

'*You're* struggling with a driving test?'

'This isn't India! You get flunked for making the smallest wrong move. You have to change the gear precisely at the indicated speed, you have to remember who has the right of way, you cannot go slower than a certain speed, certain lanes are meant to be kept free for ambulances, certain lanes designated only for trucks, and so on and so forth. We're so used to the absence of traffic rules back in our country that the brain has to be completely reprogrammed. You have to unlearn everything you've learned.' He pauses, adding, 'And most importantly, this is a right-hand traffic country. The steering wheel is on the left.'

Uh-oh. That is bad, really bad. Completely reconfiguring your driving sense.

'Oh . . .' I chew my lip. That still doesn't explain why a driving licence is required to bring us there. I voice my doubts.

'Well,' he explains, 'Oman has very limited public transport options. To be able to get around, you most definitely need a car. And with you and Hamza here, I wouldn't want to take any chances in case there's an emergency.'

Hmm. That makes some sense, I reluctantly agree. But my Oman dreams are getting steadily replaced by apprehensions of all sorts—a land with blocked video calling, meagre public transport, and a pronounced car culture. My heart gushes afresh with love for the Delhi Metro. Forget the Delhi Metro, my heart gushes afresh with love for the humble Aligarh rickshaw, too.

Salman is quick to assuage my fears. 'No, no, you're going to love it here,' he soothes me. 'Every place I go, everything I do, I just imagine you here with me, imagine us experiencing it together. Everything here is so pure and pollution-free—I haven't experienced the slightest ill health since I came. The food is absolutely unadulterated. And you should just taste the milk!'

Now that is a clever line, because adulterated food—milk, in particular—has been a common concern for the both of us ever since Hamza was born. Additionally, since the period from October to December each year was when Salman was plagued by bouts of seasonal asthma here in India, the 'not-falling-ill' part is a masterstroke. I feel better already.

'And it's really safe out here. People put up barbecues in the middle of nowhere—completely barren hillsides, even—and there isn't the slightest danger of being mugged or robbed or, you know, women's safety concerns. I'm already dreaming of us having a barbecue once you're here.'

Easier and easier. Better and better. The man has gained serious expertise in calming me down.

February 10, 2014

Finally, the day arrives. The man just cleared his driving test. We can officially drive around in Oman when I get there. There is only one little problem though. Nobody knows when I am actually going to *get there*.

I cannot understand, for the life of me, what exactly is going on up there.

The company's project for building culverts under a highway has gone down the drain—quite literally. The *vaadi* (valley) came down in a landslide halfway through the construction. Have they ever even heard of insurance, I ask? Apparently, there is some tiny loophole in the policy that prevents it from covering this terrible setback. The company has been struck a major blow.

There is only so much communication, and no more. Broken, dotted line segments that refuse to be entirely linked. Like a drawing in a children's book that keeps asking you to join the dotted lines, without numbering them or ordering them in any way. So you keep trying and trying randomly with meaningless strokes to make sense of it and get the whole picture.

I see other long-distance couples, and they are always, *always* on the phone with each other, video calling, talking face to face. With no video calling available there, I am frustrated, unable to connect statements with expressions, unable to look him in the eye and get him down to explaining it all. I am beginning to wonder, now, if it is really even worth it. Is it really worth sitting around, like the princess locked up in the farthest room of the tallest tower, waiting to be rescued? How long can one wait for a line to be cast, a line to grab on to when you are drowning?

Isn't there some way to cast your own line?

I can take other people's advice and join research at the University, working for my PhD. But that is not the line taking me in a direction I want. It is a line that keeps me right here, just 'productively employed', but I can't even take that line, for another line pulls me in another direction. The one-year-old who is completely dependent on me. Shabnam, the Godsent nanny, has already escaped from the madhouse—and who can blame her? I have been trying for years to escape this place myself. My mom is an officer and works full time, so if I opt to work full time, too, who do I leave my son with? There is always Grandma Bazooka, but a hyper-energetic, super-attention-seeking boy is too much for a septuagenarian to cope with all day—heck, I am not even 30 and he drains the life out of me, too.

There is also another, equally important line segment, attached in another direction. My newspaper articles. I write about twelve articles every month, and when you are writing, researching is implicit. The work suits me perfectly, it fulfils me creatively, and I do not want to pursue any other thing professionally, if it means letting this go. So no, it isn't that I don't have anything 'productive' to do—though heaven knows bringing up a tiny human being is productive enough in itself. The thing is that, for me, as for countless other people in the universe, work cannot be a substitute for love. Creative fulfilment is separate from, despite being as important as, emotional fulfilment. Those who are acquainted with Abraham Maslow's Pyramid of Need know that the need for achievement is a separate part of self-actualisation than the need for affection, and the need for affection definitely comes first. The very basic needs occupy the base of the pyramid—so unless you have food, water, shelter, and safety, you cannot really dream of achievements and freedom. And so, too, unless your needs of love and belonging are met, you cannot completely rise to the phase of self-actualisation.

People who drown themselves in work and work alone often do it as a refuge from the feeling of being unloved. They seek refuge from a harsh world that perhaps refused them the love they deserved. But I? I can't ever stop seeking love.

So, amid all the line segments that keep pulling me in different directions, the one I seek is the one that most eludes me. Like the proverbial line of zero thickness stretching till infinity, the line carrying me to Oman has become an abstract geometric concept, one that can endlessly be visualised and theorised, but never morphs into an actual, tangible entity, a reality to be experienced. My present, my future, my life as I know it, has all been turned into '*Pi*'.

An 'irrational' quantity, whose 'decimal representation never ends and never settles into a permanent repeating pattern'.

Infinitesimally approximated, never exact.

Chapter 16

How to Create Happiness

Kathi Ostrom, one of my favourite bloggers, makes an incredible statement in one of her posts and in a very offhand manner:

> 'In the past, knowing I couldn't change my home, my job, my husband or my kids, I'd typically cut my hair . . . Cutting my hair might not have always been the best way to . . . shake things up but at least it felt like I'd done a little something.'

I wonder, Kathi, if it's just you and me?

February 18, 2014

In a little over a month now, I will be completing another year on this planet. No matter how indifferent you might claim to be, growing a year older—a year wiser, a year deeper into life—definitely calls for some celebration. Everyone knows by now, though, that I am in no celebratory mood.

I am getting way too predictable, aren't I? And tiring, too, because I have hit the pause button on life and there is only so much that can be said about being stuck.

And so, like Kathi, I have decided to change the one thing that I can surely change right now.

Snip-snip-snip.

And there goes the hair.

From glossy brown locks dangling at my hips all the way down my back, to merely brushing my upper arms, I have decimated my treasure by half—trading length for a fresh and fancy style. And it worked. I feel better already, newer and different somehow. Seems like a weight has been lifted off my shoulders, quite literally, and I feel happy.

Suddenly, I know what I want for my birthday. And I don't need a fairy godmother to get it.

I am going to gift myself a birthday fiesta.

In Kovalam, Kerala.

A trip to coastal Kerala has been my dream vacation for a long time now. Actually, make that one of the many, many dream vacations I keep conjuring in my travel-crazed head. In a world that seems a lifetime away now, Salman and I had been saving up for a really fancy holiday in Kerala, at the super expensive The Leela Kovalam. That dream trickled far down the garden path, though, as the world in all its wickedness tipped up and drained our savings away. But that was almost two years ago. I am earning my own money again and a quick calculation reveals that I have saved more than enough to gift myself a birthday vacation. I wanted to see the Kovalam Beach, and see it I will. With or without Salman. I can take my mom and sister with me, just the way we used to go before.

But even as I think this last thought, the smile in my head droops at the corners.

In truth, what I want more than anything is for Salman and me to do this together. But alright, I am not going to get hung up on this. If we can't be together, then I will do it for myself.

I do know though that Salman would have plans of flying over to India for my birthday. He is the kind of man, that rare species of male, who doesn't have to be reminded about birthdays and anniversaries.

'Are you coming over in March?' I ask him during one of our phone calls.

'Hmm . . . I think so,' he says slowly.

'Well, you are going to take us with you THIS time. If you can't, don't come over at all.'

There is a pause.

'Okay then . . .' slowly, sighing wearily, 'I won't come over at all.' His voice sounds far away, tired.

I sigh. It was worth a shot anyway.

'So, I have decided to go to Kerala for my birthday. You wanna come?'

'Kerala?'

'Yes—Kovalam. Like we had planned, remember? You can come with me if you want.'

I am giving him a choice. Asking. Not begging, not insisting. I want to show him I can be happy alone. Not that he was the one who wanted me to be alone in the first place. But he is the one who left me alone, and I have had enough.

'I'll pay for the trip, of course,' I add breezily, pointing out, again, that I was self-sufficient.

'Hmm.' That word again. 'I'll come.'

Despite my demonstrations of indifference, my spirit surges.

'We can split the bill, you know,' he suggests.

'Okay . . .' I chew my lip hesitantly. 'You take the airfare; I'll take the hotel tariff.' I keep the larger share for myself because the choice of a super-expensive hotel has been mine.

'Okay.'

His words are slow, quiet, not entirely . . . how shall I put it . . . enthusiastic? For years upon years, I have spent many a day and night trying to fathom this man's mind, trying to work out the complexities and contradictions residing within him, and failed a million times. For all the intimacy, the friendship, and the warmth we share, so much of him is still a stranger to me.

And they say *women* are hard to figure out.

I spend a few moments wondering about his moroseness,

recalling all the wonderful moments in the past that were ruined by his unexplained brooding where he withdrew into his shell and refused to let anyone in. Or even to let them know what it was about.

And then I make a decision. I will not let any brooding, any anger, any moroseness ruin this one. This is for me and me alone. I will go out there and enjoy myself, the whole world be damned. If this makes me selfish, so be it.

So, after a long while, I begin to feel excited again. And straightaway get to work. Planning the trip, booking the hotel, marking out activities to be done, and sights to be enjoyed. When I book our room at The Leela Kovalam, I choose the gorgeous beach-view suite, giving them special instructions to arrange for a cake on the 29th of March.

'Not a big one, of course, just for the three of us,' I request the amicable lady on the phone. 'It's my birthday.' Suddenly I am grinning ear to ear.

'Oh sure, Ma'am!' she says enthusiastically. 'We hope you have a great one.'

'Thank you,' I smile. And swear inwardly to *make* the day a great one, no matter what.

Enough with the moping. I will make my own happiness now

March 28, 2014

1:00 p.m.

Gurgaon. The name can literally be interpreted as 'jaggery village', which you could, if you are so inclined, read as 'sweet village'. Now, this sweet little village got lucky when the Gods of construction (read real estate giants) decided to look kindly upon it. And so, from simple *desi* jaggery, it went straight to doughnuts, macaroons, caramel éclairs, and truffle pastries. The place is now recognised by its imposing glass-fronted, high-rise office buildings, malls dripping with luscious labels, and swanky residences peopled with humans sporting the most perfectly straightened and artificially coloured hair and the most insanely expensive cars.

This is where I am today, and the reason I am here is that a certain flight from Oman is due to arrive in a little over an hour. Yep, I am here to receive my man at the airport. And at first light tomorrow, we will be heading to the airport again, this time to catch a flight to Thiruvananthapuram, Kerala.

I tell Hamza, all of 15 months, that we'd be seeing 'baba' now. Of course, he can say baba. All kids can say ba-ba, and mine is a born chatterer. At 15 months, he can speak rudimentary sentences that use about four words. Things like: '*Bahar jaana hai* (Want to go out)', '*Khul nahi pa raha* (Can't open it)','Baby *so rahi hai* (The baby is asleep)', and so on and so forth. So yes, of course, he can say baba. But whether he can relate the word to the actual person remains to be seen. It has been five months since he last saw his dad, which had been for only five days after another stretch of five months. And because we have had zero access to video calling, he hasn't seen the man on screen either.

3:00 p.m.

Indira Gandhi International Airport, New Delhi

From a long way off, I spot Salman in his grey, green, and coral panelled t-shirt and dark sunglasses, his neatly trimmed and smartly shaped stubble glistening in the sun. He is waiting for me outside the airport gates. I cut across the crowds, deliberately moving in from behind. I want to surprise him the way he always surprised me—stepping quietly from behind and poking a finger in my waist. It always worked. I would jump hard each time, caught off-guard, before realising who it was that had 'groped' me!

I poke a finger in his side now, and he jumps a little but swivels round and catches me quickly in the crook of his arm, pulling me briskly to his side. We laugh. 'Where's Hamza?' he asks, looking around. Hamza is just a few steps behind us, being carried by our driver.

Greedy woman that I am, I wanted this embrace to be mine first, not my son's. But now, Salman holds his arms out expectantly. I wonder what the little one is going to do. The baby has no such doubts. He wastes not a second in leaning over eagerly into his baba's arms and, once there, wraps his tiny arms around him. He remembers.

I see the smile of complete satisfaction on the young father's face, and I am struck by how little thought I have given to what this man is facing out there. It is not just me who has been left alone. He is all alone out there, too. No wife, no child. No family. He has fathered a beautiful little boy just about a year ago, and all this time he has been deprived of the chance to witness his baby crossing all the milestones. The chance to hear his baby's first word, watch his baby's first steps, hear those little squeals of delight, and laugh at his innocent mischief.

I am struck by the realisation of this loneliness. Then, I remember all those pictures of him dipping in hot water springs, walking along silver shores, feeding turtles, and riding water scooters, and I can't help but wonder why I must be the one carrying the sole responsibility of childcare, while he leads the 'bachelor life'. I feel my own loneliness more deeply, more bitterly than any other. Light fades, darkness closes in.

As the car meanders through the lanes I glance sideways at his face, and it seems to be the face of a stranger, a man I do not know.

This is when I am supposed to feel happy. What I feel now, though, is the way your tongue feels when the dentist injects anaesthesia in the gums. Numb. You can move it around but can't feel a thing.

7:00 p.m.

'Salman is unusually quiet,' observes my aunt, at whose house we are staying right now. 'No jokes, limited conversation . . . he is quite cheerful otherwise. What's wrong?'

If only. If only I could know what on earth was wrong. Even though the man is generally more of an introvert, he is unusually morose today. Not in a persistently sulking kind of way, but in an absorbed-in-thought manner, feigning cheerfulness when asked. After all these years I have come to associate this with 'something on his mind, but he will never tell you what'. Sigh.

What is it with husbands and their absolute fear of transparency? You never share your actual problems with your wife because you don't want to 'burden' her or make her 'worry', when in truth she would be more than happy to lend you a sympathetic ear and more than eager to help out in whatever way possible. What worries her more, ironically, is that you don't trust the relationship enough to be frank and open about your problems, that you don't consider her competent enough to support you or help you out. Most husbands think they are protecting their wives this way, when in truth they are just isolating them.

If only. If only it were this easy to explain.

There is a pattern to this pre-occupied, intermittent gloom. He is trying. He is trying very hard to stay cheerful, and often succeeds because, after all, he is back where he belongs. But then, there are those tell-tale intervals of vacant, abrupt silences. Most markedly, the complete absence of his trademark corny humour, his dry wit, and the crazy imagination. All those quirks, the most endearing of his qualities, are missing. There is no roughness in his demeanour; he is more tender and loving than ever. But there is a pensive edge to it all, like he can see something profoundly sad that you cannot see, and because you can't see it, he can't tell you what it is.

A terrible burden to bear alone.

But he is not the only one with a burden. The piling up of days and nights has left me with more frayed edges than tolerable, and I am beginning to unravel at the seams. Inevitably, the eruption occurs.

10:30 p.m.

I am in the guest room, putting our son to bed. Salman is upstairs, conversing with my uncle, and I stay awake a long time, waiting for him to come down. I can't leave Hamza alone, for this room is two floors down, and if he wakes up and cries, we won't be able to hear him. The clock ticks steadily. I wait. And wait. The magma rises.

After five long months, we finally have alone time together, and all this man wants is casual chit-chat. The magma rises higher.

I pick up the sleeping kid (who promptly wakes up), march up two flights of stairs, barge into the room, and blurt out something curt and snappish. My uncle is appalled and clueless. Salman looks blank and baffled. He has no idea what I am going on about. The reason is simple: Earlier in the day, it had been decided that we would be sleeping in the room on the second floor, but after dinner, the ground floor guest room had been cleared for us. My husband had somehow missed the post-dinner development and, as I waited for him downstairs, he was actually waiting for me to get back upstairs.

Within a minute my uncle realises what is actually going on, and speaks to me kindly, soothingly, at which point I just burst into tears.

Tears are cathartic. The rest of the night proceeds in peace.

March 29, 2014

8:00 a.m.

It is my birthday and we are at the airport, all set to fly off to the coast.

As we walk in through the glass gates, there is a palpable change in the air. It gets lighter, fresher, and easier to breathe, with a load of emotional lava suddenly cooling, crusting up, and falling off our shoulders. We have left the world, the real world with its punches and whiplashes somewhere behind, and entered a happier sphere of airplanes and sandy beaches and lighthouses and cliff-top resorts. A sphere with just the three of us, a happy little soap bubble so fragile yet so glorious with its kaleidoscopic shimmers. We hold each other's hand and savour the bubble.

Sometimes, that is how you create happiness. Purposefully, when it is not naturally abundant.

That is just one of the ways.

Chapter 17

Happy Birthday, Girl

We are on the flight to Thiruvananthapuram, and it is a very long one. Six hours. After the wearing off of the initial excitement at being in a new place with ever newer things to experience, Hamza has dozed off. The first two hours have been mostly peaceful, but now he wakes. We still have two more hours to go before we switch flights in Mumbai, and then two more hours from there to our destination.

I had come prepared for this. The baby bag is filled with new toys and picture books to be sprung as surprises at the right moment. What I hadn't come prepared for is the level of possessiveness my baby has inherited from me. Not for the toys. For his father.

Boys are usually seen to be more attached to their mums. My boy is an exception. Much before he set his tiny foot in this world, much before his tiny eyes opened to perceive his father's face, my boy was responding to the sound of his father's voice.

Scientifically speaking, babies in the womb begin to hear and respond to sounds as early as the second trimester. Initially, they only detect low-pitched sounds, so the earliest sounds your little one recognises are the grumbling in your belly, the whooshing of air in and out of your lungs and, yes, your heartbeat. There is something so warm and gooey about learning that the first thing your baby can recognise is the sound of his momma's beating heart. By the time the little one reaches the third trimester, he can already recognise your voice and begin listening to things you say, read, and sing to him. (Hence the recommendations to read out verses from the Holy Book.) But, equally important, is the fact that he can hear other sounds from the environment around, too, particularly the ones that are loud and clear. Studies of newborn behaviour have shown that babies get used to the sounds they hear often while in the womb and, once born, respond more alertly and attentively to those.

But I can solemnly swear that my baby has responded to voices other than mine even before he was born.

Ever since we started feeling the movements in my belly, Salman and I noticed how hyperactive the kid was, kicking away with aplomb. Sometimes I would feel four simultaneous kicks at once and we would wonder how he was managing to bang on the 'walls' with both hands and feet. Salman would chuckle and wonder if he was 'constructing something' inside. Over time, though, I began to sense a strange pattern to the hyperactivity. It would occur mostly in the presence of his dad. The little guy's movements would be steady and rhythmic throughout the day, but come evening and as soon as the big guy entered and greeted me with his deep, gruff baritone, the movements would go into joyous overdrive. Like a playful puppy frisking around happily, Little Hamza In The Womb would, literally, turn summersaults at the sound of his father's voice.

I do suspect that my own excessive, obsessive attachment to his dad played a small role in this development. But one way or another, Little Hamza In The Womb developed an umbilical connect not just with his mumma but with his baba, too. A connect that only grew stronger out of the womb and enthralled and fascinated me.

And, later, came to irritate me, too.

Right now on our plane to Kerala, every time I try to get comfortable and snuggle into his baba's shoulder, he pushes my head off. When I give up the shoulder approach and content myself with holding his baba's hand, he pushes my hand away, too! We are amazed, at first, and then infinitely amused.

Somewhere in my heart, I know where he gets this from.

Parents hardly ever realise the things they pass on to their kids. Not just hair colour, eye colour, height, or build, not even the susceptibility to hereditary diseases. Parents pass on, inherently, unknowingly, traits they wouldn't even acknowledge in themselves. Perhaps, a bit of strongheadedness, a bit of over-attachment. A bit of greedy loving, with attention-seeking thrown in for good measure.

He may look like his baba, but his stubbornness is all mine.

Ultimately, though, there is only so much amusement to be had in being prevented from holding your *own* husband's hand on a holiday that *you* created, for your *own* benefit. But you sure can't reason with a fifteen-month-old, and I sigh and let him have his baba all to himself, busying myself with gazing out the window. Thirty minutes later, Hamza has decided aeroplane time is over. He reaches over to the window, begins feeling it around with his little fingers and suddenly demands:

'Darwaza kholo! Baahar jana hai!'

We chuckle. As do people sitting around us. For the poor kid, though, the situation is far from humorous, and he repeats his plea with increased urgency.

Open the door! Want to go out!

We try in vain to explain slowly that we are way up in the sky—showing him clouds up ahead, and trees down below—explaining the concept of flying from one place to the other. Yes, he is only fifteen-months for goodness sake, but you need to try, right? In desperate times, you try anything and everything. Doesn't mean it always works.

The next two hours until we reach Mumbai, and then another two hours till we reach Trivandrum, are peppered with frequent remonstrations and tantrums to open the 'door' followed by frenetic efforts to involve him in picture books and musical toys. It takes quite an effort to remember, as we finally descend from the airplane onto the tarmac, that we are here on holiday. Seems like a battle mission instead, where you end up dropping dead from sheer exhaustion.

4:30 p.m.

Exhaustion makes way for elation as we descend from the Mercedes minibus that carried all of our hotel's guests from the airport, and make a grand entry into coastal opulence.

The Leela Kovalam, here we are.

I have experienced a handful of extremely gorgeous five-star hotels and coastal resorts in my life, among them the Marriott at Dead Sea, Jordan, Mövenpick Resort at Aqaba, Jordan, the Trident at Jaipur, and The Leela's own luxuriant property at Goa. And yet, I fell for The Leela Kovalam at first sight, and fell hard. The resort possesses all the quaint charm of a mermaid home atop a cliff, elevated from its surroundings and wreathed in the ocean's embrace.

Our first glimpse of Kerala's coastline had been on the way to the hotel when the ocean suddenly burst into sight with a simple left turn and welcomed us with rows upon rows of fishing boats rocking gently along the shore.

The ocean is a symphony to my soul. Passionate, unruly waves pull me towards them with all the enigmatic power of a lover from a previous incarnation. Every time I face the ocean, its roar reverberates in every pore of my body, creating an inexplicable urge to walk straight ahead into the depths, savouring the feeling of being slowly submerged until I am no more separate from it. Don't read too deeply, there is nothing suicidal about this. It is an ancient, primaeval mating urge, the desire to be destroyed only to unite with your lover—what the Sufi would term 'fana'.

The ocean accompanies us all the way to the hotel and inside it, because the hotel's most fascinating trait is its ability to bring the outside in. From the lobby to the restaurant, the infinity pool, and everything in between, everywhere you look, the ocean is there for you to behold. You can't step around in here without being conscious of the ocean's massive embrace, and, to top it all, our accommodation is the gorgeous Beach View Suite with its spectacular view, framed by blooming bougainvillea around the balcony.

One look outside and I have forgotten the annoyance of the past six hours. Most literary descriptions of Heaven and Eden depict mountains, fruit orchards, and flowing rivers. But if ever there is going to be a Paradise for me, it would surely feature an ocean.

7:00 p.m.

After the calm, the storm.

Back in battle. The son decides to get back to being the displeased monarch, within 30 minutes of arriving in the room. Tantrums accompanied by non-stop wailing stretch on for the next hour or so and, of course, woe betide the woman that dares come close to his father! Had I not had my haircut right before this vacation, I think I might have pulled it all out in sheer desperation.

My sister-in-law calls to wish me, and I am beside myself with indignation. Happy birthday, indeed!

'Oh, come on!' I rant into the phone. 'It's been a six-hour flight with non-stop wailing, and a lot more of it since we arrived. I think I've just laid a whole lot of my hard-earned money to waste.'

She laughs at the state of affairs while my attention is briefly diverted by the sound of the doorbell. Salman opens the door. Just as I open my mouth to rant further into the phone, a brilliant bouquet of blooming red roses appears before my eyes. Followed by a tantalising, glazed black truffle cake.

All worries vaporise.

I had booked the cake in advance, but the roses are unexpected. I have just been given a birthday surprise by the hotel staff. Now that's a first! I wrap up the call pronto, and we are ready to celebrate.

The sight of the flowers and cake have calmed the kid and he watches, fascinated, as his baba lights up the candles. And then we all bask in its warm glow together.

8:00 p.m.

Time to head to the restaurant for dinner. As we step out from the elevator, an incredible sight awaits us: the entire lobby shimmers in whispering fairy light. All artificial lights have been switched off, as the corridors, corners, niches all shimmer with floating candles casting glorious shadows, making you want to talk in hushed tones or just sit and sigh.

In a minute, we find out the reason for the hotel's innovative lighting: they are observing Earth Hour tonight. By delightful cosmic coincidence, on my birth night.

We walk to the restaurant and take our seats next to the pool, overlooking the ocean beyond, bathed in the darkness of the night sky. It is an unbelievably lovely night.

I am ravenous. Just as we are about to begin eating, the displeased monarch decides he would rather stand in the lobby watching the candles flicker. No problem, we tell him, go watch the candles, and we are watching you from here. But wouldn't you just know it, mumma, too, *must* stand there with him, he insists. I stand there for a few minutes in the dancing shadows. But this can't go on endlessly, which is precisely what the little boy has decided. So he unleashes his determined wail, throwing yet another tantrum for mumma to stay with him, watching candles for as long as he desires.

After an entire day of non-stop tantrums, I have reached the edge of my patience. Here I am, all the way from Aligarh, sitting beside a glorious pool in a splendid hotel, with the most scrumptious spread awaiting me in the most romantic ambience I can dream of. And beyond that, much beyond that, I have a chance to share this blissful evening that I have fantasised about all my life, with the man I have so desperately yearned for all these months. And it is being completely ruined.

Salman has been trying to assuage the little one in vain, and now he takes one look at my clenched teeth, scarfs down whatever is on his plate, swoops up the howling boy in his arms, and takes him away from the table. They hang around in the lobby for a while, then turn a corner and disappear. I am left at the table to finish my dinner in peace. At least, I am sure that is what Salman had in mind by taking the boy away from here. But all of a sudden, every morsel turns bitter and my mouth is filled with an acrid taste.

I am alone again. After all these months of loneliness, bitterness, and coping with a headstrong child, every new second tests my patience, every new moment spent alone pulls at my anger strings. I am suddenly reminded of all the reasons why I didn't want a baby so soon. I am reminded of our neighbour whose anniversary dinner was ruined by her tantrum-throwing son. The bitter Mrs Hyde in me simmers dangerously close to the surface.

I gaze at the candle flickering on my table, at the faintly glimmering pool, and beyond that, at the ocean as black as the sky, flecked with slivers of moonlight. Suddenly I remember the promise I made to myself: I will make this day fabulous, no matter what.

And I have. I made this day fabulous by deciding to come here. I made it fabulous by bringing my family here—here, beside the ocean, here, amid the candles. And Salman, he made it fabulous, too. He made it fabulous by his very presence. The universe itself has made this fabulous, by soaking everything in the radiance of a thousand flames dancing together.

No, I will not ruin this by my anger, by the months of negativity piling up inside. If I am dining alone, I will be happy alone.

I tilt back my head on the chair, close my eyes, take a deep breath. And smile—if a tad forcibly.

'Happy birthday, girl,' I tell myself. 'You did it.'

9:45 p.m.

Just as I am winding up my dinner alone by the pool, something makes me look up. The guys are back—the big one and the little one, with the latter looking decidedly chastised. Salman comes and takes his seat beside me.

'What happened?' I ask, looking from one to the other, for they are both rather sombre.

'Well,' says Salman, 'Hamza and I had a long chat about how his behaviour was completely unacceptable and why it is very, very bad to keep irritating mummy like that.' He looks sternly, meaningfully at the little boy who hangs his head in shame.

My mouth falls open in amazement and I gape at both of them, father and son. Has he really been having this stern 'long chat' with this 15-month old boy, and has the boy actually understood? By the looks of it, it seems he has! But then they have always shared this bond. When Hamza was only a month or two old, Salman would take the crying baby in his arms and speak to him directly, looking him in the eye. He would speak to him, not coochie-cooing like people usually do with babies, but speak gently, wisely, like you explain something important to another person. And the baby would stop crying and gape at his father, wide-eyed at first, and then with rapt attention. They really do understand each other.

So, finally, we finish our meal in peace, together at last, all three of us—sans tantrums, sans annoyance, sans bitterness. A moment of beauty is a joy forever.

10:30 p.m.

We are back at the suite and the little one is now asleep. Standing on the terrace, I take in the silver-tinged waves in a frame of swaying palm trees, and I am hit by an idea: why don't we take a night stroll on the beach? Why wait till the morning?

True, we have had a tough and tiring day; true, we need to get some rest. But hey, it isn't every day that you come to Kerala, do you? And we have just two more days here.

'What are we going to do with Hamza, though?' Salman looks at the boy sleeping on the bed.

'We're going to put him in the baby stroller and wheel him all the way to the beach.' I smile triumphantly.

There is a direct path just below our suite leading to the hotel's private stretch of the beach, a sloping paved route on which we now push the stroller. Well, 'we' wouldn't be the correct term, actually, because I queen it all the way to the beach and Salman obliges like a gentleman. Hamza sleeps peacefully, blissfully unaware of his surroundings—blissfully for us, that is!

A gateway leads to the shack-style beachside sea-food restaurant at the hotel, The Tides, and beyond that, the beach. We slip off our footwear and leave them at the edge of the sand. But now we have a little problem. It is impossible to drag the baby stroller over sand. My plan just backfired. Nonplussed, I wrack my brains for a solution; we have come this far, we are not going to just sit at the edge and watch from a distance. There is a whole ocean waiting out there. Then I spot the hotel guard standing nearby, and I have another idea. Walking over, I ask him if he could keep an eye on our baby while we dip our feet in the sea for a bit. He smiles. No problem at all.

At last, the ocean! Dark, mysterious, foaming at the edges, and stretching as far as the eye can see. We stroll over to the edge and let the water cover our feet. Feels like heaven already. A bit of sand gives way from underneath our feet with each wave, shifting and shimmering like silk. We walk in farther until the water swirls around our calves—the waves are boisterous and splash right up to our waists. The shore is absolutely calm except for the ocean's incessant sighs.

Slowly we walk back over the sand and park ourselves on the beach chairs. The stars peer at us from every direction. We sit there, taking in the scents and the sounds, and savour the feeling of reclining in silence, side by side. Silence that marks the ease of togetherness, silence that doesn't hang heavy in the air. And yet, some part of him feels far away, some part that I can't really pinpoint. I just hold his hand and ask him nothing. We all need our spaces and our silences.

Hamza is still asleep when we walk over to his stroller. We thank the guard. Casting our gazes back at the shore one last time, we begin the climb uphill. It is almost midnight. I look once again at the ocean and make a wish before the clock strikes twelve. Before the magic ends.

All I ever wanted is right here before me. The only thing I want is for this to last forever.

Chapter 18

THE WORRY BILL

March 30, 2014

Breakfast at The Leela Kovalam is an elaborate, sumptuous affair, their buffet tables absolutely loaded with all kinds of delicacies, making you feel like Asterix and Obelix feasting in their Gaul village. And you, of course, are not Asterix but Obelix, stuffing yourself silly. Now, I have been known for being a picky eater—a trait I annoyingly passed on to my son—but hotel buffet breakfasts trigger a metamorphosis of sorts. So here I am, combining South Indian idli-dosa-sambhar-vada and regular potato wedges with completely non-Indian croissants, muffins, gingerbread cakes, and Danish pastries, with some mango yoghurt thrown in for good measure. All of this finds its way to my plate, and no, I waste none of it. If I could have such a breakfast every day, I would be twice my current size.

As for the husband, he, at one point, used to be a lot more cautious in his food choices. Now he is more open to experimentation, not least because he invariably finds himself at the receiving end of the exotic dishes I order on our vacations, like the *halabi* kebabs in a Lebanese restaurant on our honeymoon in Malaysia (which he never lets me forget), dishes that I push aside after little more than two morsels. Being the kind of guy who can't stand to waste food, he plies through them with utmost perseverance (and a fairly murderous look).

Buffets are perfect in this regard. You can sample whatever catches your fancy without having to cope with platefuls of delicacies whose taste entirely belies their looks. But the buffet table is not the only thing that takes our breath away. The morning light has drawn back the curtains from what the night had concealed. An endless stretch of the bluest blue, the sea merging with the sky, waves twinkling merrily with sun-sparkle and the occasional speedboat weaving patterns of white foam on azure fabric. We are not just having breakfast here; we are having an entire ocean for breakfast.

For the first time since we arrived in Kerala, we are having an utterly peaceful meal without interruptions and tantrums. The little monarch is still asleep. We have wheeled him to the restaurant in the stroller. (This stroller has proved to be the best investment of my life!) Once he is awake though, we will be back in the eye of the storm. All things said and done, it is not amusing to have a moral policeman accompanying you on vacation, putting his stern little foot down at each and every display of affection. Oh, forget displays in public, this little policeman restricts you right inside your bedroom, for heaven's sake! Talk about inheriting absolute *desi* genes from his father's side.

Something needs to be done about this, and pronto.

Meanwhile, there are other 'pressing concerns' that need our attention. It is time for us to head out for sightseeing, but we have both stuffed ourselves so full that we are overcome by the same feeling one might observe in an overfed, pampered tabby cat—curl up, purr, and snooze like there is no tomorrow. The idyllic, all-blue setting doesn't help. It lulls the senses into a hypnotic calm, where the world slows down and pauses, where nothing exists except the whispering sound of waves swaying somewhere far below.

Oh well, we are on holiday—we get to decide what we would like to do. Cuddling up in the middle of the day in a super-soft, super-squishy bed with fluffy, downy pillows and a heavenly view of the shoreline is a pretty tantalising option, so we decide to take it. But that brings us back to problem number one: the anti-cupid who is now awake and won't let us snuggle or cuddle or get comfy at all.

Suddenly, just like that, we have a lightbulb moment. We pull the little one close to us. With one hand, we hold his hand, and with the other, we hold each other's. Mumma loves Hamza, and mumma loves baba, too. Baba loves Hamza, and baba loves mumma, too. And Hamza loves both mumma and baba. 'We are family,' we tell him slowly, smilingly. And then, very deliberately, we proceed to hug each other—a group hug, like a sportsmen's huddle. The little one takes to it instantly, and we are treated to excited, delighted little shrieks and gurgles as he discovers the joys of everyone hugging each other. This is the moment when we all laugh together. It is also the moment when I realise, painfully, that this little boy has had so few moments with his small family, that he needs to be shown what it is like—how we can love several people at the same time, in different ways, and it would not take away from our love for each other.

Children have an infinite, unfathomable ability to understand abstract concepts; all they need is to see the context. When they see it, they know it. They see a hug and they understand love, they see you offer a biscuit and they understand sharing. They see you smile and they understand joy, they see your face crumple and they know that is grief. When they see you hit and shout, they understand violence and when they see you put out seeds for birds, they understand kindness.

Little Hamza was only a year old when he understood what 'brave' meant: it is to get up when you fall down and not worry about a small bruise. And now little Hamza has to slowly understand what 'family' means: it means more than just one person to love, more than just one person to hug. It means that love can be shared among everyone in a family, and it wouldn't divide—only multiply.

And I, I have learnt something, too. I have learnt that when you are two, you cuddle. But when you are three, you huddle.

Sometimes, the best way to solve a problem is not to go through it, but around. *Literally.*

March 30, 2014

4:00 p.m.

The Kovalam beach in daylight is very different from the Kovalam beach of the night past. Past the resort guards, the beach is bustling with activity and brimming with the typical flavour of South Kerala. Rows upon rows of catamarans with fishing nets dangling from them, young boys lolloping in the water at a distance, and families strolling along, skimming the waves. Speedboats lined up, awaiting passengers. It is a cheerful slice of everyday life—not everyday life for us, though, and we take it all in gleefully. It is the speedboats that are the most tempting. The owner of the nearest one notices my longing gaze and comes over to give us the pitch. Since he has already seen us wandering over from the resort side, he quotes a price that seems double, if not triple, the usual amount.

Negotiating prices is sort of my Achilles heel—I am terrible at bargaining. Worse, if I really like something, I am willing to be ripped off just to get my hands on it. Call it impatience or gullibility or both. Salman is a lot better at it, and he tries to use his skills. But the speedboat owner has far greater skills for he has seen the look on my face and he, like all men, knows the power wives exercise on their husbands. Nope, he refuses flatly. Take it or leave it.

Fine, we leave it, says my guy coolly, and turns his back

on the speedboat. Oh no, we don't—I put my sulky face on, draw him to the side and tell him: 'I've never skimmed the ocean waves on a speedboat before and I don't know when I ever will again. It'll be sunset soon and then we'll lose all chance of doing this!' I hiss from between clenched teeth.

'Just give it five minutes! He'll come around, I'm sure of that,' Salman tries to reason.

'I don't care!'And suddenly, 'You've been on all those water scooters and jet skis in Oman so you couldn't care less for this speedboat ride. I'm the one who is going to miss it.' Darkness clouds my mind again, bringing back the reality of our situation—so easily obscured in this paradise. I cannot see reason. I go cold. 'We were splitting the bill, remember? I'm paying for this. Just say yes to the man.'

I see it again. I see the Silent Salman face come back on, and I know he is miffed. I ignore him and walk over to the speedboat guy myself, quoting a slightly lower price. Take it or leave it, I tell him. And he agrees.

As we are strapping on our lifejackets, we realise there is no lifejacket for the baby with us. The owner is the most apologetic, he says that they don't have lifejackets for children this small. Salman and I exchange glances. His glance says: I don't think we should do this. Mine says: Oh no. Oh no. Oh no.

The driver looks from one face to another, watches his prospects dwindling, and immediately assures us that he would go very carefully and slowly and that we needn't worry at all; people with kids do it all the time. I am desperate. I am hanging onto life with this vacation—outside these golden sands and swirling waters I see nothing but bleakness. Salman sighs. 'I'll hold him tightly,' he offers, giving up. We position the kid between us, each with an arm around him, and I have a sense of déjà vu from the time we did that elephant ride in Jim Corbett National Park. Our boy has grown up since. Nevertheless, I utter a silent prayer that this does not turn into a disaster like the last time.

The boat takes off.

There is something unimaginably enthralling about the sea, about whipping across untamed waves, about your hair—or scarf—billowing in the wind, about bouncing wildly from one wave to another like a dolphin gone somewhat crazy. With each bounce that the boat whacks the water, our bottoms also smack on the hard seats! But I am whooping with joy, open-mouthed and screaming, clutching at my scarf as the wind tries her best to snatch it off. I glance at Salman, then, and although he is enjoying himself, he looks uncomfortable and a little strung up.

'What's the matter, are you okay?'

'Yes, fine. The boat's bouncing too much. I'm worried for Hamza.'

And he is. He is clutching the boy tightly to his side, his attention focused on keeping him safe. The boy himself isn't scared, he is enjoying the ride. But I feel a surge of warm feeling for this father-son duo once again. The fact that Salman is worried about Hamza isn't just about this speedboat ride. It is a small, largely unnoticeable detail that the 'worrying' has been taken over from me, if only temporarily. After a year-and-a-half of single-handed parenting, I have just been given a break. From the moment we began this journey, this man has made it his job to do the worrying (with my responsibility being just the feeding). Perhaps that is the reason why I feel so much at ease, so free, so devoid of cares. In his own unspoken manner, Salman hasn't just split the money bill with me, but the worry bill, too. The bill that counts as much, if not more.

Almost as if on cue, the speedboat slows down. We round a cliff and come to the famous Lighthouse Beach with the lighthouse perched atop a rocky outcrop. Beyond that is the

Hawa Beach, peppered with large fishing boats of all shapes and sizes.

The boat finally turns and speeds off back across the open sea, slowing down parallel to the crimson ball of fire sinking in the horizon. Salman is visibly relaxed once we reach the edge and his darling is safely out of the water's reach. We frolic in the gentle waves, long past the sunset. This holiday is paying off far more than I had expected. Once again, I remember my promise to myself, the promise that brought us here and created this little patch of happiness. But today, the moment in the speedboat brought home a simple truth.

You can create happiness for yourself, perhaps, but to make it truly last, you need something more.

You can surround yourself with objects that signify happiness, you can create situations conducive for happiness, choose locations that perhaps deliver happiness. But happiness only arises in people willing to be happy. It only arises in people willing to bend a little for each other, in people wanting to make each other happy. Splitting the bill together—the money bill and the worry bill—and making space for each other.

Because even for something as simple as a hug, you need to curve your arms, loosen your body, and make space for another to fit in.

Chapter 19

IF LIFE WERE MADE OF MOMENTS

March 31, 2014

Another day of lazing in the beach view suite and feasting on the irresistible buffets. Our travel, though, is being thoroughly affected by the lack of foresight in planning. We have booked all three meals at the resort: buffet breakfast, buffet lunch, and buffet dinner. So, by the time we are through with breakfast and think of stepping out for sightseeing, we start worrying about getting back in time for lunch. I mean, my man here starts worrying about it. The intriguing part is, he is not even one of those food-obsessed guys that give their wives a tough time on a daily basis—we have never ever had 'food issues' at home. But every time we finish breakfast and I talk about us getting out of the resort and exploring Kovalam and its periphery, I am greeted by the same reply, 'But we won't be able to come back in time for lunch then!' And when we finish lunch, it is pretty much the same argument.

I am beginning to suspect this has less to do with his overflowing love for the resort buffet than it has to do with his general weary, morose, dampened mood that I have been observing for the past 3 days. Although he is trying to be the good husband in every way possible, he still feels distant, closed. I am trying not to create a fuss about it but I am aware that something is wrong. There is a huge build-up of stress inside him. Mental fatigue that transfers to his body and makes him want to just relax and do nothing—to find some semblance of peace and calm.

So, it is the beach again for us, and I really can't complain.

The waves are incredible today—far bigger than last evening. I wade into the shallows and sink down to my knees, letting the water embrace me. Wave after wave pummels me, sometimes going over my head.

Hamza sits on a beach chair, gazing at us nonplussed—mumma being buffeted by the waves and baba clicking away happily. The little one isn't so keen on the ocean himself; though he loves water, he is not familiar with this strange kind: alive and thrashing around. It scares him. But I don't want him to be scared, I want him to get closer to the ocean, to touch and feel and smell and explore it. It is that parental instinct to have your children love the things that you love—they might not eventually take to them, but you at least want to try.

I walk over to my little boy and pick him up. Propping him on my hip, I get back into the waves. Since I am standing with him in my arms, he can feel the ocean at a safe distance: surrounded but not engulfed. He is still not quite excited, but at least he is interested and not bawling to get back to the shore. By and by, I put him down on the beach at the edge of the waves. He is still wary of what perhaps seems to him a monster, so I try to distract him with the sand. He is intrigued. Scoops up a fistful and stares at it with a frown of concentration.

Salman joins us, and soon we are all making little sand hills. It is a moment I couldn't let slip away, and I pick up the camera to preserve it forever—this moment of father-son bonding so precious to me and so utterly gratifying.

Sitting at the shore reminds you how much the moments of your life resemble grains of sand. You can gather them in your fists or build little hills, but sure as daylight they will slip away. The tides of life reclaim them, leaving a blank canvas behind, just so you don't stay caught up in one, just so you can create another.

Like the baker's wife sings in *Into The Woods*:

'. . . Let the moment go
Don't forget it for a moment though
Just remembering you've had an "and"
When you're back to "or"
Makes the "or" mean more
Than it did before . . .'

After lunch, we go up to the Skybar, which is just an open terrace during the day, and gaze down at the azure water that turns an emerald green just where the cliffs jut out. Oh, the cliffs! They are an amazing sight, and you can just picture the mermaids coming up at night to sing their ocean songs. We stay there a long time, watching the waves crash over the cliffs, the rays of the sun lighting up the vast blue beyond, and the odd speedboat creating gullies of foam. I peer out to the right and notice a path straight from the beach to a few more rocky outcrops that we can climb. 'Hey, let's go there!' I point enthusiastically. 'It's not far, and we could take a lovely walk all the way along the beach.'

'But the sun's already inclining westward and by the time we reach the spot, it will almost be sunset. We won't be able to take any decent pictures,' Salman protests.

I am beginning to get irritated. 'Oh, drat those pictures!' I fume, but then mellow down the next second. 'Honey, who cares? Even if we don't get one decent photo, we'd at least have seen that beautiful place, we'd have experienced a magnificent sunset, we'd have been on those cliffs for real, instead of just watching them from afar. I don't care one bit about the pictures—let's just take some memories instead.'

'Hmm . . .' he says, and that's all. We go along with my plan anyway.

The sun goes down into the sea as Salman, Hamza, and I sit atop the huge rocks and the waves crash all around us. As the light wanes, the tide rises. We head back reluctantly, walking along the water but avoiding the now boisterous waves. The farther we inch away, the more the waves reach out to touch us. I laugh in delight. 'Hey, look!' I tell Salman. 'The sea loves me as much as I love her! Every time I move my feet away from her, she leaps out to catch them again.'

Salman smiles a little. 'Hmm . . .' he says again.

Not for the first time, I feel a sharp stab of annoyance at this extreme taciturnity.

I won't get angry, I remind myself for the umpteenth time this vacation. I will not spend my time fighting. I will just be happy about the fact that we are here—all three of us.

I slip my hand into his and he holds it tightly. Perhaps some things just have to be understood without being said.

April 1, 2014

The day of departure dawns. And in the manner of all things that hit you hard only when they have reached a crisis point, I am gripped by the realisation that we have spent three days in Kerala without so much as a glimpse of the famed backwaters! Who goes to Paris and returns without visiting the Eiffel Tower? Who goes to Egypt and doesn't see the Pyramids? Who returns from India without a sight of the Taj Mahal? Only the stupidest and laziest of travellers, like the ones that visit Kerala and return without experiencing the backwaters. Nope, I certainly wasn't going to be one of them.

And so, after three days of lazing around the beach and the suite, I decide I am not leaving without a backwater cruise. As soon as we are dressed, I go up to the concierge and ask them about the many backwater cruises. A cruise generally takes about two hours, but we don't have enough time. If we set off at 10 a.m., we will reach the backwaters by 11 a.m., which leaves us with just enough time for a one-hour cruise so we can get back to the hotel by 1 p.m. and reach the airport by 1:30. Our flight departs at 3 p.m. Unsurprisingly, Salman isn't charged up at all. He says that that is cutting it too close. But I am adamant. Of all things that I am guilty of being in my life, a lazy traveller I will never be.

So here we are in the backwaters of Poovar—aboard a small, shaded motorboat in the greenest of canals fenced in by lush, tall coconut palm and banana trees.

As the boat chugs slowly across the mangroves into increasingly narrower streams, even the sunlight turns emerald green, slipping in through the sieve of dense green foliage and reflected by the mysterious, somewhat intimidating murky green of the water. Fishing boats rest moored along the banks, and a coconut-selling catamaran passes us by. We take a left turn and enter a very narrow gully, hemmed in by emerald shrubs on both sides, the foliage almost cutting off the sunlight. The boatman abruptly cuts the motor, indicating that it is the perfect spot for pictures.

I am rather fed up though, of this constant touristy fixation with clicking. We are not there, it seems, to look and feel and drink it all in; everyone just appears to be travelling for the sole purpose of clicking pictures.

Nope, not me. We just get one customary click, and then ask the boatman to stay put. What we would like more is to revel in the thrills of nature.

Complete silence envelops us except for the incessant cawing of crows and the calls of birds we can't recognise. It is a scene straight out of a Discovery Channel documentary. Electric currents run up and down my spine because I feel exactly like an explorer of the wild. Eyes wide with wonder and mouth agape in fascination, I drink in my surroundings.

Then my gaze falls on the man beside me, and for once, I am utterly satisfied.

Salman is as fascinated and mesmerised by it all as I am. Being too much of a'man' though, his mouth isn't open in amazement—but you can see he is relishing it to the core.

'Isn't this exactly like a documentary of the Amazon? Perhaps there is an Anaconda slinking in the foliage,' I whisper conspiratorially to him. 'Or maybe a huge croc lurking under the boat . . .' I narrow my eyes dramatically for effect.

'Don't you hold out your hand to touch the water then!' he replies with a wicked grin, playing along. We laugh.

The boatman turns the engine on again and the boat purrs out into a wider stream. That is where we spot a snake bird and a brahminy kite, and I regret not bringing along a bird watching guide. These backwaters are a definite bird paradise.

The stream widens, the boat turns, and suddenly we are into an estuary, where fresh water merges with salty waves. Up ahead, the wide shoreline comes into view—we have reached another beach: The Golden Sands Beach. True to its name, the sand here is an arresting, scintillating gold. But even more arresting are the absolutely gigantic waves smashing upon the shore. This is one beach with no gradual undulation into the depths; the earth just sinks abruptly into the ocean's arms, like the exhausted lover seeking the comfort of familiar embrace. The dance of the ocean is an absolute delight to watch and although we are standing far off to be very safe for our little one, the waves close the distance with just one mighty leap. The foam swirls around my ankles.

I could just stay here forever.

However, my very pragmatic husband reminds me that we have a flight due in a couple of hours, so I must quit thinking of forever. Sigh.

We head back to the motorboat. The boatman takes us a little further and presents us with a scene that can only be described as a microcosmic representation of the cultural and spiritual beauty of India. Up ahead is a statue of Jesus & Mary, standing majestically upon a cliff. And just a little beyond that stands what is called the Elephant Rock, a natural rock jutting out of the estuary, looking remarkably like the outline of an elephant, a revered and sacred animal among the Hindus of South India. Jesus and Mary, in the company of the Elephant Rock—in an estuary—beautifully mirror the ethos of India. In a divinely beautiful spot on earth, where salt water and fresh water mix with ease, we find these symbols of the confluence of cultures and subcultures, religions and quests of faith. Can it get any more poetic than that?

'We have another hour of sights ahead of us. But I was instructed to take you back after the first hour. Do you want to move ahead, or would you like to turn back?' the boatman enquires.

I can't believe how foolish I have been to wait for the last day before booking this cruise. Who knows what sights lay ahead of us? Who knows what paradise awaits us? But then, something is better than nothing, I suppose. And if I hadn't been this stubborn, we would never have seen this little slice of heaven either. I feel pretty contented as we head back taking a different route, as the boatman points out floating resort cabins at a distance and several floating restaurants. How I long to have lunch one day in one of those!

Finally, we head back to the Leela in the resort's Mercedes, cutting across the unbelievably green tropical paradise that is South Kerala. Rows upon rows of palm trees with their fringed tops frame the sky and all you can do is sit back and sigh or gape in pure delight. On the way, we stop at a souvenir shop and I find something perfect for my mantelpiece back home—a model of a typical Snake Boat, which is a paddled war canoe used in the famous canoe boat races of Kerala, complete with tiny rowers all ready to zip to the finish line.

The rest of the hours slip by in mad frenzy as we race to make it in time for the flight, with a very annoyed and vexed man beside me, who detests nothing more in this world than being late. As our flight from Thiruvananthapuram takes off, we catch our last glimpse of the palm trees spreading out in a frilly green carpet beneath us, and a little off to the side, the foamy blue of the Arabian Sea. God's Own Country, as the tagline goes.

Now, everything is obscured under a layer of clouds tinged golden with sunlight.

Ascent, descent. Isn't life always like a plane journey? For a moment you are soaring in the sky and, before you know it, you are back on earth. We have been soaring high for the past three days, between the sand and the sky, in a shimmering bubble of rapture. And the time for descent has come at last. Time to return to the solid ground of everyday life. Time to tread the earth complete with its rocks and thorns. But the fact that we have had these moments, that we experienced this bit of untrammelled bliss, lends a beam of light to whatever darkness that may lie ahead. It presents images of joy to relish and hold onto, in all those moments when the mind clouds over with doubt, grief, and despair.

'Oh, if life were made of moments
Even now and then a bad one!
But if life were only moments
Then you'd never know you had one . . .
. . . Let the moment go
Don't forget it for a moment though
Just remembering you've had an "and"
When you're back to "or"
Makes the "or" mean more
Than it did before . . .'

Chapter 20

The Making and Unmaking of Lists

April 10, 2014

To the moon and back. We have been out of the stronghold of gravity, floating around in our obscure little patch of space, and now we are back to the heavy zone, weighed down by the mass of our desires and fears—pulled down by the gravity of facts.

Salman is back to the country that has laid claim upon him, and I—I am back to my state of inertia. Tagged to the end of this inertia, though, is a fresh promise: the visit visa. It is a consolation prize of sorts, to make up for the dearth of actual victories. Instead of the family visa for all of us to live together in the Promised Land, this would be a two-month passageway to happiness. The next best thing. For two months, his son and wife would get a chance to stay with him in the country that now hosted him. It isn't exactly what we had been trying to get all this while, but it is something. Something to hold on to.

It is just so doable, there isn't the faintest doubt attached. Salman is very sure of this—one more month of waiting and this time I will be with him in Oman. Briefly, yes, but I will be there. And so, despite having sworn myself off it, I start making a list. Now, I am a compulsive list maker. And I have made quite a few lists in the past two years. The first time: when there were no plans to move abroad and we were simply looking at another house to move into. I made an elaborate list of all the furniture and home appliances we would be buying because our first home had been a fully furnished one.

Oh, what joy lies in the making of lists! A little bit of order in the disorderly world, or perhaps just a scatterbrain's feeble attempt at putting things in one place. That it never bodes well for me is a different matter altogether.

We did actually find the perfect house to rent, but right after I made my list, the home-owner changed his mind and sold off the house instead. The second time I made my list was when my husband got his visa for Oman, and because I was blinded with optimism and expected to join him there in no more than two months—four months tops—I made a list very joyously of all the things I would be needing to take along with me. I should have just heeded the signs from the previous instance, though.

But after the second time, I had sworn to myself that I would never make a list again. And yet, ten months later, here I am, making another list. A small one, fit for a two-month visit. A cheerful list that speaks of hopes rising again, despite themselves, like winged seeds rising enthusiastically with the wind, despite knowing well that it is not they who can fly.

And because there is no stopping me once I get going, I make another list, of all the places we would visit in Muscat during those two months. Wadi Shab, Shatti Beach, Turtle Beach, Muttrah Corniche, Muttrah Souq, Sultan Qaboos Grand Mosque . . . the attractions seem endless and choosing is quite a task. A deliciously thrilling task that reminds me of all those days we spent planning vacations together, fantasy vacations that involved everything from island resorts, villas, and infinity pools to reef explorations, surfing, and para-sailing. This was always our little thing, the thing we did together. Planning vacations—real or imagined.

We would get together and chart out every detail—from arrival to departure, accommodations to excursions, and everything else in between. Like that time we had extensively planned our little vacation to the Maldives and picked water villas at an island resort for our 'stay'. Striding atop wooden stilts dug into the shallows of the ocean, and reached by a wooden jetty, the water villa is a small hut that looks entirely temporary: hanging over the ocean, with the waves lapping beneath the floor and steps leading right into the water. But that is not all. The villa comes complete with a Jacuzzi enclosed by wooden walls on three sides with the fourth side opening to the sea. So you could make slow, bubbling, vapour-veiled love as you watched the dance of the sea.

We even picked out all the activities we would do there. Going down to the ocean floor in a submarine. Visiting an uninhabited island. Snorkelling. Parasailing. He would text me intermittently from office about the things we could do together. Like the perfect dinner date: a gorgeous fairytale tent lit by candles standing right on the beach; the waves caressing our feet. What dreamers we were!

That it might not materialise any time soon was inconsequential. What mattered more was the exhilaration of planning those holidays together. What mattered was the satisfaction of knowing we would, one day, experience and explore the universe with our fingers intertwined. The image alone was heady enough.

But that was then, when we literally, physically had each other, to talk, to touch and hold. The images now are held together by the tiny string of a promise, fragile and frayed, far too delicate for the combined weight of all the expectations banking upon it.

May 1, 2014

It was bound to happen. Another promise caves in on itself. Well, not really—it just keeps hanging in the air like all the others, neither here nor there.

'What's the update, when do we go?' I ask, for the tenth time perhaps.

'The visit visa is still pending . . .' he replies briefly. 'Sweetheart, I'm fed up of waiting, too. Believe me, I'm trying,' his voice floats over the phone—weary, frustrated.

I sigh in exasperation. My faith is, at long last, beginning to wane my unshaking belief that things are exactly as I am being told. Of all the terrible things to happen to a relationship, the worst is the waning of trust. The slow, serpentine dance of doubt.

I say nothing, but my mind hardens into a resolve to find out the truth. I decide to text the only other person I know in Oman. Yawar. He is the one who had first floated this offer to Salman, the offer of a new sugar-coated life.

I tell him, in plain words, that I need to know what exactly is going on there.

'Just tell me the truth, okay?' I text him. 'Is the visit visa pending for approval still?'

'No. It's not pending. It hasn't been applied yet.'

I draw in a sharp breath—of anger, outrage. Calm down, I tell myself. Give the man some credit. He did give you the undiluted truth.

'Oh,' I text back. 'Why?'

'We've suffered major losses in business. A partner committed major fraud and made away with several crores from the coffers.' That wasn't a surprise to me. I already knew about it. But that was a while ago, hadn't they recovered from those losses yet, I wonder. Moreover, the promise for the visit visa was made to me *after* this whole fiasco, not before. I am perplexed.

'House rents have gone up majorly in the past two years,' comes another text, before I can respond. But this wasn't something you said two years ago when you invited us, I think. Another text hits me before I can reply. 'And anyway, even if you were here, you'd be alone at home all day, wouldn't you.'

Anger billows in me like an ashen cloud looming ominously over a volcano. These were a far cry from the things he said two years ago. My mind clouds over with rage and I think of a hundred stinging things to say. But I keep shut, for my husband's sake. My confrontation-avoiding, conflict-hating husband.

One more text pops up: 'Plus, think of all those women 10-15 years ago, whose husbands lived abroad. Just think how they coped.'

Now, this is just a text. But I can almost hear a righteous smirk.

This, from the man who promised my husband a gap of barely 2-4 months before bringing his family over permanently. This, from the man who knew that Salman's first and most important condition was that his family would accompany him abroad, take it or leave it.

This is too much.

'Please don't talk to me about what happened 15 years ago. 15 years ago you didn't have a laptop or a cell phone. I dare you to spend 15 days without them right now,' I snap back, cuttingly enough, I hope.

Yawar backs off, then. 'We're working on it. Just a little more time.'

I fling my phone on the bed. I don't want any more platitudes from this hypocrite.

When Salman calls me next, I come straight to the point and tell him I spoke to the guy. I give him a word-by-word recap of the entire conversation. 'There's no visa pending,' I almost growl. 'It hasn't been applied at all.'

Silence.

'But he told me it had been applied for.'

'Well, he lied to you,' I bark out.

Either that or he is lying to you now . . . the serpent raises its hood, venom dripping maliciously, drop by drop. *You can't really tell, can you?*

I cup my head in my hands. My jaw hardens. My gaze falls upon the list lying on one corner of the bed—the list of things I was supposed to be taking on my two-month trip to Muscat. I snatch it up and rend it to pieces, strip by strip, square by square. Gather up the pieces and chuck them into the dustbin.

Not for the first time, I wonder when this will end.

Chapter 21

IN-LAWS AND OUTLAWS

May 1, 2014

Life continues as usual. Usual being, in the Indian context, amid the hot and spicy curry of relatives, social gatherings and, not to be forgotten, constant social scrutiny.

Right now, I am in a small village in western UP—the ancestral home of my husband's grandparents. My existence after marriage has been a strange crossover between extremes—my urban, English-speaking family and my husband's *desi* and robust, village-dwelling extended *khandaan*. Trapped between the two is me, the journalist and blogger who feels happiest in the metro city of Delhi. An interesting mix, if a tad unmixable.

Despite my immediate in-laws—Salman's parents—being educated, polite, sensible town-dwellers, the domino effect of the extended rustic family always clatters down towards us, in some way or the other. But never had that effect felt as glaringly obvious as when little Hamza appeared on the scene.

The birth of my son has, literally, landed me in the midst of raging crossfire, a never-ending, tragi-comic tug of war. This has, in fact, led me to conclude that *all* relatives—regardless of whether they are yours or your husband's—should *always* be referred to as in-laws. For they are the ones always laying down the laws. In-*laws*.

It is a fairly normal occurrence in life, no matter how unpleasant, that mothers get shot down all the time for their alleged incorrect parenting. The child might be hyperactive, not active enough, too polite (hence, a pushover), not polite enough, too fat, too thin, too addicted to books, not interested in books, too talkative, not talkative enough—there is an entire gamut of parenting flaws that relatives will only be too happy to point out. This is irritating enough in the normal course of things, but the impact of being constantly belittled is magnified manifold when you are the only one at the receiving end, with no partner to defend you or even to share the blame. To make matters worse, people from both sides of the fence are having a go at you.

To my family, my boy is a *junglee*, a wild child bordering on the uncontrollable. Exposed to a baby after almost two decades, they have completely forgotten what children are usually like.

'What an atrocious kid he's turning into! Throwing things around and running wild. Can't you keep him in check!'

At the other extreme are my husband's extended village relatives, who brand Hamza a pushover. A whining mouse of a boy. They have a house absolutely teeming with kids who create a racket all day long.

'What! Is this what you have turned him into? You have a "*mard bachcha*", a male child, and *this* is what you've made him? He ought to be able to hold his own, he must be able to fight and run and kick and punch! Make him a man, not a mouse!'

The worst part is, both sides are correct.

My one-and-a-half-year-old boy is a regular monarch when he is in familiar territory surrounded by folks he can lord over. But as soon as he is out of his den, he clutches at his mom in terror, howls at the slightest provocation, and cowers in fear when faced with a bully.

So what? Let's not forget that Hamza is barely 19 months old. It is perfectly normal for a little boy to be scared of the outside world, to be wary of strangers, and to be intimidated by bullies. Except for one little thing: my boy is exceedingly possessed by stranger anxiety, and a little too unused to rough-and-tumble play. Which isn't surprising, considering that he is growing up in the absence of his father with no 'manly' activities to speak of. What is worse, my mother has always had the chicken-soup syndrome: too much protection and too little independence. I am nearly always overruled when it comes to letting him play a little rough and venture out to explore. There is always a set of arms nearby to either haul him up or haul him out. This constant additional hovering has made Hamza more uncoordinated than kids his age—walking and running only on his toes. Naturally, he keeps tripping and falling over.

Now, this becomes particularly terrible when you are visiting a joint family (with not one but *multiple* joints) boasting over two dozen members, plus an incessant stream of guests. Every time someone tries to pick Hamza up, he bawls. Add to that the village courtyard with uneven flooring and his uncoordinated gait, and you have a kid that falls flat on his face every half an hour. Lips cut and gums bleeding each time.

A sure-shot recipe for disaster.

A recipe for day-long allegations of over-parenting, which is ironic, since back home I am subjected to day-long allegations of under-parenting. The constant whining, of both the boy and the relatives combined, is getting far too much on my easily frayed nerves. In case you didn't notice, though, there is a major difference between being heckled by your husband's relatives, and being heckled by your own: with your own people, you can snap back and tell them to back off. No such liberty with the husband's people—not by a long mile.

Grin-and-bear-it gets a whole new definition, only in my case, it is weep and bear it. Every time someone heckles me for my 'insufficient parenting', I go back into my own room and weep it out.

I hate and curse my son for being such a cry baby and a pipsqueak. I hate my mom for being such an overprotective, hovering drone. And I hate and curse the father of my son for leaving me alone to face this onslaught. He ought to be here. He ought to be the one fielding these questions, he ought to be the one teaching his son to be a '*mard*'. He ought to be sharing this responsibility with me instead of exiling himself in another country like an escaped fugitive, an outlaw. How I hate him.

More than anything, though, I hate myself for being incapable of properly rearing my child. For being incapable of handling my own life and doing something about it. Wretched, contemptible, loathsome woman.

I feel it. I feel it again.

The rage that underlines my very being, the magma that bubbles inside. Chokes me with its fiery flow, but finds no escape.

A village is a hive of glass, where nothing unobserved can pass.

— Charles H. Spurgeon

May 4, 2014

Before I was married, I had no idea what village life was like. Even my grandparents on both sides were city dwellers. And never had I glamorised country life either, the way many people do—for its simplicity, slow pace, close-knit family atmosphere, fresh organic produce, and so on. I was a town girl through and through.

To be honest, I never actually had to *live* in the village after marriage. It was just the ancestral home and the extended family that we used to visit in the village—only on festivals, weddings, and special occasions. And to be fair, my husband's ancestral home is a far cry from the typical village homes in India.

A sprawling *khandaani* house spread across 10 acres, flanked by the family's mango orchards on one side and a small lake on the other, and partitioned into separate, independent wings for each of the six families that make up the home. Like a private colony with interconnected doors that are forever open to each other. The rooms all come equipped with most of the amenities you would find in an urban, middle-class home. My bedroom is a large, well-ventilated room with a sparkling bathroom that I particularly like. A large rain-shower-head was fitted especially upon my arrival. But the thing that most delighted me when I first arrived as a bride was the courtyard facing my room—all abloom with pink bougainvillea and the *madhumalti* or rangoon creeper. The adjacent courtyard boasts a flowering pomegranate tree and a grand old neem, another one has a flowering peach tree while yet another boasts red chilli plants. A veritable organic heaven of sorts.

And yet, what struck me hard right from the beginning was the huge cultural chasm. Within the beautifully painted walls and blooming courtyards, the lives and mindsets are quintessentially representative of Indian villages. The values I have lived and sworn by all my life are alien here, drawing blank astonished looks if I so much as utter the phrase 'women's rights' or 'gender equality'—unfortunately/fortunately my favourite phrases in any conversation. Women are expected to know their place here, quite literally.

But then again, this isn't something odd or astonishing, considering that I have met some of the most deep-rooted patriarchal mindsets in swanky urban settings as well. It is not like my own relatives are immune to it. But the effects of patriarchy are never as strongly manifested as when you become a mother.

In truth, I am aware that I am here only for a few days. I am aware that their statements spring merely from a place of love for the kid, I am aware that all their advice can be taken calmly. But with everything going wrong in my life right now—dashed hopes, frayed trust, and unreliable business partners—calm is the one thing I cannot be.

What I am is desolate, suffocated, and utterly trapped.

Chapter 22

Letters and Notes to My 60-year-old Self

Relationships that come as appendices to the main wedding clause are perhaps the trickiest ones on earth. Granted, professional relationships are equally difficult, but if your boss turns insufferable, no matter how cushy the job, you can stick your tongue out at him/her one day and call it quits. No such exit clause available here.

When a daughter is born to a couple, very frequently their minds wander to that time in the future when she would be taken from them by people who would claim her forever. They wonder how that new world would treat her, and hence the extremely common blessing for girls: *Allah naseeb achha kare. Saubhagyavati bhava*. May you be blessed with good fortune forever.

And though it is meant to be a blessing, it is a profoundly sad one. Ever wonder why we do not bless boys this way? Because everyone expects boys to be able to *create* their destiny. A woman, feeble creature that she is, is bound to her destiny forever. And so, perhaps, if I had a daughter, I would have blessed her thus: '*Allah tumhein apna naseeb banane ki quwwat de*.' May you be blessed forever with the strength to *carve* your own fortune.

I don't remember *ever* hearing my father bless me with a prayer for '*achha naseeb*'. On the contrary, what he repeatedly quoted to us, me and my sister, were these immortal lines from an Urdu couplet:

'Khudi ko kar buland itna
Ki har taqdeer se pehle
Khuda bande se khud puche
Bata teri raza kya hai.'

(Elevate thyself to such great height
That before thy destiny is inscribed
The Lord himself would ask thee, his slave,
'What would thou wish to have me write?')

He would repeat this couplet day and night to hammer into us one single thought: we are the masters of our own destinies.

Nevertheless, he was a rare Indian father, because the norm requires parents to wring their hands in despair at the destiny of their daughter the moment she is born.

But I wonder, when a son is born to a couple, does their mind ever wander to the time he would be taken from them by another? A woman, a rival for his affections, an idol he will worship, much to the parents' chagrin? I am betting, no. Indian moms especially are so attached to their sons that they place them at the pedestal as the 'man in my life'. No, I am not indicating some sort of Oedipus complex. I am talking of this, which was more prevalent in the previous generation but exists even now:

Husbands were supposed to act superior to their wives—for that was '*mardon ki shaan*'. They never showed their emotional side or the wives 'would get too big for their boots'. One of my male relatives had a habit of telling his wife, 'If I don't criticise the dish you've cooked, it means you've cooked well.' Criticism or silence. Compliments be damned.

The woman, emotionally parched, unable to quench her thirst for approval and admiration, unable to express her physical desires for fear of being considered wanton, unable to find solace in the mere fulfilment of obligations, lives an unspeakable life of bottled frustration. And then, along comes the son. He *loves* what she cooks. Every son does. (Mine does, too.) And she finds herself showered with compliments. He is a child. Children express their love unhindered. Slowly, as he grows up, he starts caring for her. For her happiness and her health. Sees his mother being verbally, emotionally, or even physically abused, either by her husband or her in-laws, and becomes that Man—the wall of support she always sought. He becomes the mainstay of her life.

Then, of course, enters the other woman. His wife. But he is not the husband his father was.

He compliments his *wife's* cooking, gazes at her with love, supports her dreams and ambitions, cares about her well-being, and also cooks for the wife, much to the astonishment of his mother. And, one day, he confronts his mom, defending his wife—much like he had defended his mother not so long ago. And this woman, who had spent a major portion of her life fussing over her son, considering him her sole accomplishment in the absence of all other avenues, feels cheated. Betrayed. For her to grudge the daughter-in-law's happiness, then, is quite natural.

All of this is rather dramatic, though, and not everyone had a life like that. But to varying degrees, most couples—small town, middle class, 'Indian values' type—fell within this range. My father was an exceedingly romantic, mostly liberal guy who fed milk from bottles to his kids, changed their nappies, and combed their hair for lice. He was that husband who frequently massaged his wife's legs and back—something unheard of in his generation—because she suffered from a slipped disc. The husband who wanted his wife to loosen her hair because he loved to watch it cascading down her back, and who asked his wife to keep her hands henna-painted at all times because he loved to hold up her palms and inhale the heady fragrance. He would take her out for a stroll by the river and hire a cameraman to follow them and record their movements like a personalised romantic movie, while a *chapraasi* trailed them at a distance, holding me, then a one-year-old. That was 1988.

But even then, my mother remembers being fairly intimidated by his quick temper in the early days of marriage, and watching, fascinated and thankful, as his temper mellowed after I arrived:

'He would leave for office in a huff, angry over something, and ignore me when he returned. But when you were born, and he came back still angry, he took one look at you and his anger evaporated. I was so thankful for this angel in my life.'

Now this is a loaded statement, but I think this provided a major motivation for women to long for children. I remember when I was pregnant and not very happy about it, my mum-in-law would reassure me saying, 'Just wait till your son is born (the unborn baby is always a son for the in-laws all over India). You will have a great pillar of support!'

What she could not understand was that I already *had* a pillar of support in my husband. Relationship dynamics had changed drastically over the previous generation. I already had a complete, fulfilling relationship; I didn't necessarily need a baby to soften it. And more, far more importantly, I didn't necessarily need a pillar of support. I was quite capable of supporting and standing up for my own self, if the situation ever arose.

But now, now that I am a mother, I often find myself sitting at the fence, wondering what lies at the far end of the rainbow. The time when I will be the dreaded law. Because, to twist that line immortalised by Ekta Kapoor, the queen of soap operas: *Kyunki bahu bhi kabhi saas hogi.*

The daughter-in-law, too, will be a mom-in-law someday.

'Perhaps the world progresses not by maturing, but by being in a permanent state of adolescence, of thrilled discovery.'

—Julian Barnes, *Levels of Life*

When Richard Branson turned 65, he took on 65 challenges given by fans. Those challenges included writing a letter each to his 10, 25, 50, and 65-year-old selves. Interestingly, not one of those challengers asked him to write a letter to his *older* self. None went beyond 65, his age at the time. But why not? Wouldn't it be far more fruitful to pen a letter to your older self, than to pen one to a younger you?

Writing to your younger self is like baking a cake for a dead person on their birthday—they can't actually enjoy it (though you might feel good about doing it). In effect, it is just an exercise in self-congratulation. You will never be 25 again, or 10, or 15, so there is absolutely no point in giving advice to a non-existing person. In truth, these letters are written purely for the benefit of others—younger people, newer generation—so they may benefit from the wisdom of older people and their accumulated experience, which is particularly pertinent when you are a swashbuckling entrepreneur like Branson.

For your own self, though, the exercise is completely futile. What would be more meaningful, I suppose, is to write a letter to your older self. Assuming that you stay alive till the date, it would be quite a revelation to know how your younger self saw the world, what she or he thought and experienced. Memory is a fickle lover—it plays tricks with your consciousness; it shows you past events coloured in the light that you would like to see them in right now. But it would be infinitely interesting to know your real experience of that moment, as and when it happened. A few months ago, I happened to come across an old email conversation with a friend from college, and I could neither recognise my own voice, nor did she recognise hers when I sent it to her. We had both forgotten so much of our younger selves from barely 10 years ago. How much, then, would we actually remember from 30 years ago?

That is actually what a diary or a journal is for—recording one's former self. But a journal is a record, not advice per se. Giving advice to one's older self might open up a whole new perspective. Perhaps, once we reach that age, it might enable us to see things from our children's perspective, and lessen the inevitable generation gap. The acuity of youth is so badly discounted, and then we let it all slip away, turning into an exact replica of our forefathers and foremothers.

Which brings me back to the fence where I sit, peering into the unknown future, thinking, 'Someday, I'll be a mom-in-law, too.' And though there are numerous reasons for writing a letter to my older self, this one is as good as any. Here, then, is my strategy for the future. It may turn out to be completely unusable advice by the time I actually reach the age, but it is worth a shot anyway.

Dear 60-year-old me,

If you are reading this, you have managed to stay alive for six decades, which is no mean feat in itself. I am sure you are far wiser than me; you have experienced the vicissitudes of life in far greater measure. But I am also quite sure that your memories of me have faded to a point where you see me only in sepia tint.

You are standing at a great height now and can see a greater expanse. But since I am standing lower than you, closer to the ground, I can see small things in much greater detail, with a lot more colourful vibrancy. And I want you to never, ever lose the colours in your life. I don't want you, 60-year-old me, to find your colours fading into grey like your hair would be for sure. Grey in the hair is a good thing, actually: it means you have got dual-toned hair without spending a dime at the salon. But I am hoping you would still be visiting the salon when you are 60—don't let yourself slide into dreary 'sainthood' just because your kid is all grown up.

The reason I am writing to you now is to remind you of how you were 30 years ago and to remind you of what youth is like. So you can understand those who would be 'new' then, even as you are slowly entering the 'old'. Now, here is my little secret to remaining close to your child, and especially to the woman that falls in love with your child: Don't Grow Old. You heard that right. Stay New.

Don't you have heirlooms and jewellery and chandeliers and so on, which never degenerate no matter how 'old' they technically get? They remain classy—vintage, so to speak. Good as new. But being vintage and remaining 'good as new' requires a lot of effort. And no, I am not just talking about the trips to the salon—although those won't hurt either.

The most important thing that needs to be kept as good as new is your mind, through careful maintenance and refurbishment. If you are to understand the 'new' people of your time, you will have to read and watch carefully the thoughts and ideas prevalent among the youth at the time, you would need to be aware of the things they find entertaining and the things they find enthralling—as well as the evolving thought process—without being dismissive and judgemental of them. I can tell you for certain that they would be miles away from your own value system and interpretation of the world, but being dismissive or disparaging won't help. In fact, you would need to keep an open mind, for it may well be that the things you considered acceptable turn out to be truly outrageous. Don't forget that there was a time when slavery, sati, and domestic violence, all were considered acceptable. It won't harm you either to try and understand where your generation went wrong.

You would need to read as much contemporary literature of the time as you can, and watch contemporary movies and read/watch the news and be aware of the events around you. You would need, beyond anything, to listen to what your children are saying, analyse the things they say, and discuss them along with your own ideas. Discuss your ideas with them based on reason and sensibility, without resorting to the clichéd appeal of 'in our times, my son . . .' or 'when I was your age . . .'

I know for a fact that I absolutely resent these lines, and your son will resent them, too—to say nothing of the woman he will share his life with. The best approach is to find a middle ground, but only when absolutely necessary. In most cases, children that have grown into adults can and should be able to take their own decisions, and the best approach for you as a parent is a hands-off policy. You raised your son to be an independent boy, so let him exercise that independence now, and let him take decisions together with his partner. If at all you need to proffer advice, offer it in a positive manner, and preferably to the boy you raised, not to the girl raised in another family with possibly an entirely different set of ideas, values, and lifestyles. At first, you may not understand her at all, so it would be best to let the man she chose to live with handle all the sticky ends.

How else do you remain new? By adopting the gadgets and technology of the age you live in. I understand it wouldn't be easy at all, for I can't imagine what the technology would look like 30 years from now. But I need you to recall now, how difficult it was to first learn to cook. To first learn to drive. To first learn to bring up a baby. To first learn to manage in a big city all alone, after living your overprotected life in a small town. Everything is difficult for the first time, but you have mastered bigger things than a NewAge gadget, so I am expecting you to be interested in and using New Age gadgets even now, when you are 60. New Age inventions will let you into the fresh world and you won't feel left out. That is going to be important, I think, as you get grey in the hair.

What is going to be even more important, dear 60-year-old-me, is to have other achievements, involvements, and sources of joy than just your kids and grandkids. Believe me, it is going to be crucial for your happiness. That is one of the reasons I find so much joy and pride in my writing—both personal and professional—in my books and in travel. If I were to centre my entire life around my son and make him my only achievement in life, you would be the biggest sufferer. For, that achievement would no longer need mothering at 30 and find solace in another woman instead. I want you to be prepared for that and to not make your son the focus of your life.

I don't want you to base your *entire* happiness on events in his life either because the core of that happiness belongs to him; to you belongs only the periphery. If you will draw your *entire* happiness from his marriage and his kids or his professional achievements, you will find yourself trying to control all those decisions in a way that makes *you* happy. If, for instance, he chooses a profession or a girl that doesn't fit your ideal you will feel betrayed because that was your only source of happiness. If he chooses to have/not have kids against your wishes, you will feel betrayed for you would have concentrated your happiness only on them. For the sake of your sanity, your happiness, and especially that of your son's, draw your joy from things in your *own life*.

Set goals for your *own self*, goals unrelated to family. Goals for your own achievements, professional or otherwise. Don't let your only skill be taking care of others, for then you will never be able to let your son behave like a grown-up. Worse, you will even begin expecting your daughter-in-law to act like a 'mom' to your son—a fatal mistake.

Construct your happiness around you. Stay in touch with friends and visit them. Join a book club or some such community where you have other people to share your days with. Don't make family the only focus of your life. Make a list of books you would like to read now, make a bucket list of places you would like to travel. Just because elderly people in India aren't expected to travel anywhere except for pilgrimages doesn't mean that elderly people from other countries don't pack up their bags and become globetrotters once they have retired!

In fact, just imagine how big of an opportunity this is, for travel as well as for romance.

Your son is all grown up and has a family of his own. You finally have the house all to yourself and your man. Isn't that a tantalising thought? You could just take your cue from the grey in your hair: grey is sexy. Don't believe me? Just ask all those screaming fans of *Fifty Shades of Grey*.

So, go all out and plan vacations, explore the world, try new things, and have fun. Age is no bar for adventure, and young people would always like more enthusiastic elders around! Plus, when you are having fun in your own life, you won't grudge all the fun that your daughter-in-law would be having in hers.

Yes, you heard me. That is what generally causes a lot of heartburn to mums-in-law: '*Humne toh kabhi aisa nahi kiya!*'

'We never used to do this, tsk tsk.'

When, in truth, what they are really thinking is: '*Kaash humne bhi aisa kiya hota!*'

'Wish we could have done this, too!'

You better believe it.

And, yes, when your son becomes a father himself, try and understand that it is his turn to parent. You have had yours when you were bringing him up. So, you let his wife and him bring up their kid their own way. Suggestions are good, but be careful that they are worded positively and don't turn into taunts of incompetency or laments of '*aaj kal ki maaein*!' If you want people to benefit from your experiences, try and be helpful instead of judgemental.

Of course, I understand that when you are 60, you will be possessed by a fair bit of nostalgia for the world as you knew it, the life that you have lived. It is only natural, and you are only human. And it is perfectly okay to be nostalgic, because youngsters like listening to stories of an age past, stories of a time they never knew. It offers them a doorway into a wondrous ancient world—ancient to them, at least. It fascinates them, just as the 16-year-old me was fascinated by the stories of her mother's father who watched the coronation of Queen Elizabeth on a large screen in a London street, or the story of how he defeated King Zahir Shah of Afghanistan in a clay pigeon shooting competition aboard the ship that took him to England.

Remember him, the gentleman that he was, how he quoted Ghalib and Meer and Dard and Iqbal with aplomb, but dearly loved Simba from *The Lion King* as well! Remember the things he stood for, always ready with kind advice but never dismissive of the new world. I hope you will learn from your fierce grandmother how to stand up for and defend the ones you love, how to be super-energetic, alive and pulsating at 75 and managing to look incredibly gorgeous, too!

And yes, there will be so many times your kids will still need you, times when they will be at their most vulnerable. In those times, I hope you will be like your own mother-in-law—in the way she stood by the 24-year-old you when you were pregnant and a complete mess, how she took care of you when you were struggling with a newborn, how she taught you things you never knew, especially how she never once gloated on all these favours upon you.

And, I also hope that you will possess some fraction of the steel that shows through your mother's nerves, in how she coped with a devastating personal tragedy, how she single-handedly brought up two headstrong girls and retained her infinite kindness, humanity, and generosity.

Dear 60-year-old me, I am quite sure you will rise to meet all the challenges and responsibilities life brings your way, but I am also hoping you will have fun in the process—finding moments to bathe in the rain, to explore a new land, to steal a kiss.

I am hoping you will stay new forever.

With love,

Your inexperienced, short-tempered, impatient, naïve, idealistic 27-year-old self

Chapter 23
THE MELTDOWN

'You put together two people who have not been put together before. Sometimes it is like that first attempt to harness a hydrogen balloon to a fire balloon: do you prefer crash and burn, or burn and crash? But sometimes it works, and something new is made, and the world is changed. Then, at some point, sooner or later, for this reason or that, one of them is taken away. And what is taken away is greater than the sum of what was there. This may not be mathematically possible; but it is emotionally possible.'

— Julian Barnes, *Levels of Life*

May 8, 2014

There are separations, other than death, that might sometimes induce the same kind of grief.

One of the supposed golden rules of parenting that the older generation steadfastly adhered to was 'spare the rod and spoil the child'. Though now, paediatricians, child psychologists, and New Age writers might gasp in horror at this, culturally, the previous generation was inclined towards not sparing the rod. Like many others, I was also smacked as a kid, but I was never even scarred on the skin, let alone scarred for life. I remember the spankings more as a joke from the past, like the childhood mischiefs that you jokingly recall. Of course, not everyone would remember their own spankings the same way.

I remember my father always kept a cane atop his almirah, and the cane was named 'S.S. Verma' short for *Samjhavan Singh Verma*. Loosely translated as Mr Make-it-clear Jones. The cane never got an opportunity to be taken down, it was more of a psychological rod than a physical one. The mere mention of it was enough to get me to behave! Almost a decade later, when we happened to get hold of it, there was much oohing and aahing between me and my sister, like we just discovered an old haunted relic.

Times have changed now and everyone strictly reprimands you for beating children, even the older generation who dished it out with no second thought in their day. But even their dishing had been sparse and far between.

Nothing like the violence that has grabbed hold of me now.

My son is just about 19 months old and I have begun hitting him. Shaking him. Slapping him. My mother whisks him away immediately when these violent fits come upon me. 'She will kill him!' she wails and laments, a tad dramatically, and what I really want to do is kill myself.

I want to be killed for slapping my baby. I want to scream in agony, to scratch my own hands. I hate myself. Had this been another country, perhaps I would be behind bars, which would be justified. I am turning into a potential danger to my offspring.

At my in-laws' place: Late into the night, I am trying in vain to talk to Salman on the phone—our calls are always so few and far between—but Hamza just won't let me, grabbing the phone or making a fuss. I yank him up in my arms and almost dump him in his walker, in the other room. He is shocked for a second and then starts wailing. Salman's mom rushes to pick him up and soothe him.

At my mother's house: I am trying to write—my refuge from the world—and Hamza is playing happily, toys all strewn around the floor. Grandma Bazooka barges in.

Grandma Bazooka, like I have said before, is an Amazonian Woman species, the kind who is the best ally to have in a war. Her sense of justice, straight as an arrow, causes her to draw out her bow every time she gets so much as a whiff of unfairness, particularly to her loved ones. The downside of this battle-readiness, of course, is the excessive emphasis on discipline and things being just right all the time, like an army commander.

She enters the room hollering.

'Oh, this girl is useless! She can't handle anything! She can't handle her own child! All the toys are strewn around the floor! For heaven's sake why can't you keep the room clean?'

No big deal. Yelling at your kids and grandkids is a routine occurrence in Indian homes, nobody bats an eyelid. Nobody who is in their normal frame of mind. And that is not me right now.

I fly into a rage and shake the child, and shake him, and shake him. 'Why! Why can't you stop throwing toys around! Why!' I yell and shake with anger. My mom rushes in from the other room and sweeps him away from my wrath.

I hide my face between my knees, rocking back and forth, sobbing uncontrollably.

At night in bed: Hamza goes to sleep at 8 p.m. Relief is short-lived. Exactly at 9 p.m., he wakes up. Fresh as a daisy. At 11 p.m. my eyes are heavy with sleep, and he is pushing his little fingers all the way up my nose, poking them into my eyes, doing his best to keep me awake. I am dying of exhaustion, having been at his beck and call all day. I sing him a lullaby, desperate to be free. Doesn't work. I pat him again and again on the back, trying to induce sleep. I try and try and try for another half an hour. Nothing.

And then I imagine smashing his head into the wall.

Then I do slap him.

For some reason, this works like a charm. He cries at first and then nods off.

And then I lie awake in bed, watching the revolving blades of the fan. Round and round and round and round. And I see me.

Hair strewn over the face, neck in a looped rope, feet dangling limp.

I see myself hanging from the fan, eyes blank and bulging with the stare of death. Round and round and round and round and round.

I cannot sleep.

Daytime on my rooftop: Gulmohar, neem, and ashok trees sway in the cool breeze blowing across the colony's park, eagles soaring above them, their keening echoing down below. Parakeets whoosh into the air out of nowhere, squawking noisily and settling into the peepal tree at my neighbour's. A solitary purple sunbird flits busily in my garden, from the night jasmine to the chameli, sipping nectar. I stand on the rooftop, breathing deep, trying to relax. To unwind the knot inside that never seems to loosen up. Nature is always such a refuge.

I look down casually from the third floor.

And I see me there, down below.

My body, skull cracked open. Fallen from the top, plastered on the earth.

Blood oozing in a puddle.

Slowly I turn back from the edge, and climb down heavily.

There is no refuge.

May 13, 2014

10:00 a.m.

I am sitting quietly in the verandah, eating a bowl of home-set curd. My mom's special home-set curd is one of my top ten favourite foods on earth. Suddenly, Hamza comes pattering to my seat, spies the pot of boiled milk sitting on the table to be cooled before putting in the fridge, and with all the naughtiness of a little boy, smacks the entire pot to the ground.

It is nothing, really. Children do these things all the time. A potful of spilt milk actually means little, except for our belief that all food and drink is sacred sustenance from Allah and must never be wasted. I am mostly unperturbed and ask the help to mop it up.

And then who should come barging in but Grandma Bazooka.

'*Arrey*! All the milk! The whole *bhagona*! *Yeh ladki ek minute bhi apna bachcha nahi dekh sakti!*'

This chit of a girl can't mind her child for even a single minute!

The hollering continues.

My mind goes numb.

Each sound, each sentence passes dully through my brain like a buzz of background sounds. White noise rings in my ears. And then, one by one, every vein in my brain snaps, gushing blood in the insides of my skull.

My lips don't move. My eyes don't cloud over. I see everything move in slow motion.

My hand hurls down the bowl of curd with all the force it can muster, spilling the curd all over the floor.

Without a word, I get up, put on my abaya, grab my purse and laptop, and leave. Leaving my bawling child and the hollering grandma behind.

There is no place I want to go to. No friends left in Aligarh. No refuge.

Soon I find myself facing a popular café. I get in there, switch on my laptop, and get a coffee.

Then another. And then another.

I shut down my laptop at some point. Go out on the road. And walk. Just walk. Several kilometres at a stretch.

'*The other half of the day I walked all over town,*' I e-mail a close friend later. '*I'm not a walker. I never walk. Hardly ever. I prefer being driven around. But I had so much rage that day. I walked and walked and walked . . .*'

It is then that I see it: a nameplate on the metal gates of a beautiful house.

Dr Priya, Psychologist/Counsellor.

And I know. This is what I have to do. This is what I need. I can't end up killing myself. Or my son.

I go right up to the door. Locked. Just my luck.

I walk around some more, unsure of where to go. Home doesn't seem like home anymore.

And then I see the sun casting heavily slanting rays, and realise that I haven't offered my namaz. Faith is such a funny thing. Some people kill for it. How accursed they are. Faith is meant to save you.

'*Namaz saved me,*' I write in my e-mail to the friend. '*I suppose faith saves one from doing a lot of horrible stuff . . . but I find no peace in prayers these days. I just pray because I can't stop believing in God. It's not a habit. It's just something you have in your heart.*'

I go back home then, to offer namaz. But cry all through the evening, deep into the night. My eyes hurt for a long time.

'*Every day I make an agenda to keep myself from destroying myself. A hundred times I sit and imagine different ways of killing myself. Though I know I won't. Some days are better, some are worse. Some days I wake up angry. Some days I wake up crying.*'

'*I guess I liked* Levels of Life *so much for two reasons: One, I can feel the self-centred dark grief in there, the same grief that consumes me now. That makes me contemplate suicide all the time. He didn't do it, though. And neither will I. But I like it because I can understand how it feels to be lonely and hollow all the time.*'

To be in the darkest levels of life.

Chapter 24
The Happily Married Divorcee

May 15, 2014

Every time the thought of killing myself comes to me, I ask myself these questions. Who would be the one most affected by my death? No, not my child, but my mother. She had already lived half her life grieving her love's untimely demise. I couldn't gift her another lifetime worth of grief.

And then, I tell myself, there is always an alternative to ending your life: End the source of your misery. If it is a relationship that makes you feel helpless, end it.

Divorce is one of the f-words of small-town culture, especially if mentioned by a woman. But what is the point of being in a relationship that foists all of its disadvantages upon you without manifesting the delightful advantages? It makes you deal with unmanageable kids, endless parenting duties, heckling relatives, and everything else that comes with marriage, but it provides no love, no care, no moments of laughter and tenderness, no moments of passion and lovemaking, no moments of exploring the world together, no moments of pouring your heart out to each other. It is a travesty of a marriage that provides no companionship.

Why should I let myself be encumbered with a marriage that has become a farce of itself?

Marriage isn't something beautiful in its own, beauty in life and in death. It isn't a rose, beautiful in withering—fragrance inseparable from dried petals that grace the coffee table in a potpourri. Marriage is a living animal of flesh and blood, a human being. Beauty and trust when it is born; healthy and strong and purposeful when nurtured, slowly growing strong enough to withstand the inevitable blows and cuffs of life. But withering makes it ugly. Neglect and abuse deform it, much like the perishable human self. And when it dies, it becomes a rotting, decaying carcass. No matter how much you love someone, you can't keep their corpse with you forever.

Why should the corpse of a marriage remain?

A successful marriage isn't one that lasts many decades, as our grandmothers have lectured us forever. It isn't one that trudges on unhappily, with one partner oblivious of the agony of the other. A successful marriage is one where the *love* lasts. A loveless marriage is no marriage at all. It is a bitter separation cloaked in the hypocrisy of dutifulness.

The irony of my situation then, is almost laughable. To want to end a marriage that was beloved, cared for, and cherished like a chubby little pampered child.

Only, where was the marriage now? Where was that *man* now? Meeting him periodically for exactly six days after five months. Is that a marriage? Bringing up a baby alone, with your mother or your mother-in-law for help. Is that a marriage? Staying with your parents and working on your job. Is that a marriage? What does it mean to be married? Is marriage just an institution for producing kids?

Marriage is a partnership. It is friendship. It is a pledge of love. It is the brick and mortar of the walls you live in. Would you still call it home if you could live in it for only two weeks a year? Would you still be owning a home if, for the rest of the entire year, you would be sleeping out on the pavement?

Homeless homeowner. Partner-less marriage.

On the subject of divorce, we are rather fond of patting our backs. We look at the much higher divorce rates in other countries, and flaunt our 60-year-long marriages with all the pride of the champion. Not all 60-year-long marriages really are marriages, though.

Divorce is a difficult, painful thing. It is neither easy nor joyous to experience a relationship, which was supposed to be beautiful, turn sour and rot. Most of all, family elders try to talk you out of divorce by pointing out the pain that your children will undergo, if they are subjected to the hurts of a 'broken home'. The idea is that parents living together give the child a nurturing environment that is his or her right, and they get to learn the dynamics of a healthy, respectful man-woman relationship. (Although that is possible only if the marriage really is a healthy and respectful relationship.) A divorce, they tell you, breaks a home into jagged shards. The father and the mother living separately from each other can lead to trauma for children.

But then, how is that any different from the kind of marriage where the husband comes to visit his family once a year or even less? Where the woman stays with other family members and takes care of the children like a single parent? How does that not qualify for a broken home? A family in which the child only meets his father once or maximum twice in the span of 12 months, and is left wanting for attention, for there is neither that fatherly love nor the fatherly discipline for the rest of those fatherless days. How, then, does it qualify to be better?

Only on paper, only in your mind. Only in the lessons you have been taught about your purpose in life, to serve quietly and never demand. Only in being able to escape the word 'divorcee' that would stick to you like a crown of thorns for the rest of your life. But in truth, your plight is worse.

There ain't no divorcee like a 'happily married' divorcee.

Chapter 25
Labyrinths of the Mind

'There is a German word, Sehnsucht, which has no English equivalent; it means 'the longing for something'. It has romantic and mystical connotations; C.S. Lewis defined it as the 'inconsolable longing' in the human heart for 'we know not what'. It seems rather German to be able to specify the unspecifiable. The longing for something - or, in our case, for someone.'

—Julian Barnes, *Levels of Life*

May 18, 2014

'I've made my decision. I'm coming back,' Salman's voice reaches me over the phone. 'I can see there's no future for us here. I've tried my best and yet, I've failed to fulfil my promise to you . . .' His voice is tinged with deep sadness.

'In any case, I had set a one-year limit for myself when I left for Oman. I'd given myself a year to make things fall into place, and if they didn't work out, I would return,' he continues. 'We both know they didn't work out, so I'll be back in a couple of months, around July.'

In the normal course of things, I would probably have felt relieved, even joyful to hear that. But the last two years have shown me endless two-month-waits that never materialised into anything concrete; endless false starts and repeatedly risen hopes ruthlessly dashed to the ground.

'He is LYING!' the serpent rises, hissing into my ear. *'He is just placating you to buy more time. It is just as hollow a promise as all the others that have gone before.'*

Venom seeps through my brain. There has been a severe lack of communication between me and Salman for the past three months. He has taken over the management of one of their projects in Behla, a suburb which almost compares with the godforsaken suburbs in India, in the sense that there is very poor Internet connectivity and, in general, poor amenities. So the WhatsApp chats that had been sustaining us, in the absence of any communication through either telephone calls or Skype, Line, Viber, and what-have-you, have also dried up. He is immersed in work day and night, and that is all I know.

What I also know is that he had, till now, been trying to work harder and restructure everything for his friend to get the company back on track, and that is what makes me furious. I am sure he won't be back before he has finished this task that he had taken upon himself. Trust Mr Goody-two-shoes to put gratitude and friendship and other people's problems before his family.

'You have never been his priority anyway,' more venom trickles in. *'You are the least important person in his life. His own family comes first, then his friends, then anyone with any kind of problem or suffering in life that he can do something about, and you? You come last. You've always been last. Why do you want to believe him and be fooled yet again?'*

I gnash my teeth and shut out the serpent.

To Salman, I say, 'Hmm.'

That is all.

This used to be his line, not mine. But I am not myself any more. I am not even a shadow of the person I was, the person I had been all my life.

True, I had been declared crazy by people, but a euphoric crazy. Not a depressed crazy, not a ranting grieving crazy. On an official trip to Jordan, I had spotted a rainbow across the sky against the ruins of Jerash, and was so overjoyed that I had caught hold of the kids walking nearby and showed it to them enthusiastically—'Look! A rainbow! A rainbow!'

My colleague, amused beyond words, had then asked me, 'How old are you again?' Over the course of the next six days of the trip, she observed my antics and declared, 'Well, you certainly are an enthu! Enjoying life and all, huh?'

I was that person, who, in the early days of our marriage, would zoom around on a motorbike with my husband at midnight, and on the deserted roads of Delhi shout out with complete Bollywood style: 'I LOVE YOUUU, SALMAAAN!'

The man in question would chuckle quietly and enjoy.

That was the crazy me. Filmi crazy. Enthu crazy. High-on-life crazy.

Not this, not death-like crazy.

May 19, 2014

Midnight

I lie in bed watching myself hanging from the fan yet again. Feet dangling, neck broken, and eyes bulging like a ghost's.

Every night now, I see myself hanging there.

Every time I step out onto the road, I see my body—mangled and spurting blood—beneath the wheels of a passing car. I see them everywhere. Corpses of myself.

I see strange things and images inside words. The word slaughter suddenly reveals to me the word 'laughter' hidden inside it, flashing visions of a pile of dead, bloodied bodies and a killer with a dripping butcher's knife laughing hysterically over them.

I am a woman possessed.

Possessed by the idea of murder, of killing, of suicide.

Possessed by the idea of death, the idea of escape.

And now, possessed by a vile thought. Why should I carry on like this? Why should I bring up this baby on my own? Why should I sacrifice the life I want for this—this marriage which had become a zero sum transaction?

I will not bring up this kid. I won't. I will not stay here; I will leave this burning hell of loneliness and infinite waiting once and for all. When this boy can have an absentee father he can have an absentee mother as well. I will leave him and leave this city and go away on my own.

I will leave him to his other family members to love and to raise. I will not give him my life, my blood, and my flesh.

If I am destined to be alone, I will be alone on my own terms, alone with my work and my writing and my books and my life and my friends, alone and free—not alone and chained day and night, pledged to the service of this boy whose father didn't even care enough to be with him.

I—will—not.

I tell everyone—my own family and my husband's—that I am giving this boy up to them. I am leaving my son and I will leave them all. I will not take this anymore. I also tell them that I have another option lined up should they refuse: killing myself. (And though I don't say it, the third option is also fresh in my mind—the forbidden 'D' word.)

A tornado of horrified reactions breaks out since nobody quite knows what to make of this outburst. Their reactions range from disbelief and reasoning to scolding to reprimanding to invoking divine powers and then to placating, soothing, and showering words of solace.

The latter works.

I am soothed, temporarily, but my sanity hangs precariously on the edge. Deathly madness thrashes in my veins. The serpent in my heart pumps venom frenetically.

And yet, some sliver of logic, some sliver of resilience, some sliver of problem-solving still seems to remain in a tiny nook within me, for even as I am consumed by my frenzy, I realise the need to do something about it.

I see the solution in my mind.

A white bungalow with iron gates and the nameplate fixed on it:

Dr Priya, Psychologist and Counsellor

I will not kill myself. I will not desert my son. I will not be a woman possessed.

May 25, 2018

Dr Priya is a gentle, middle-aged woman with a patient demeanour.

'Hello,' she smiles kindly. 'What is your name?'

'Zehra.'

'Okay, Zehra, tell me. How can I help you?'

I take a deep breath and, perhaps, a gulp.

I have never had stage fright. On my wedding day, a close friend had remarked, 'The girl who never remained silent on stage all through school and college couldn't be expected to sit silently on the grandest stage of her life!' I hadn't been the blushing bride by a long mile, but the talking, laughing bride, an absolute anomaly for a traditional Muslim wedding. (The guests would comment, scandalised, on how 'contented' and 'assured' I looked.)

But now my tongue is stuck to my palate and I have no idea where to begin.

'Uh . . .' I stammer. 'I'm having problems with my marriage.'

'Okay. What kind of problems?'

'Ever since my son was born, my husband and I have not been able to live together.' I bite my lip, take a deep breath, and launch into my tale. She hears me out, everything, my story of being uprooted and exiled, the endless wait to get back with my man, and everything I have been going through since, at which point my voice cracks and tears start streaming down like an involuntary action—a blink or a sneeze. I continue, wiping them off intermittently with one hand.

'And in this entire year you've never been to Oman? Not even once?' she enquires.

'No.'

'I see,' she says. 'Do you trust your husband?'

'Well . . . I always did. But now with all these things happening . . .' my voice cracks again. 'I think he is not being entirely honest.'

'Hmm. Do you think he is faithful to you? Loyal?' she peers deeply at me.

For a second I blink. I don't get what she means. Then it hits.

'Oh!' I exclaim. 'Why, of course! Unless he could cheat on me with a car—which would be highly likely if it were possible.' I smile a little at the thought, despite myself. 'Nope. The only competition I have in his heart are superfast supercars.' I am sure of that, at least.

'Oh. Hmm. I see.' She is flummoxed. The ordinary response in this situation would have been to say yes and doubt one's partner's fidelity. But that is not what our relationship is like.

She probes further then, how we met, how long we have known each other and so on.

I describe exactly how much I pine for him. For the company of a person I could talk to all night long, spin dreams with, use like a punching bag. And everything else that he brought to this relationship. I tell her of the fires of desire that flare within, making my mind explode. Of the witch that claws me hollow, frenzied with the longing for blood.

She listens silently. And then asks more questions, about my childhood this time.

'Well, it was amazing as long as my father was alive,' I tell her. 'After that, it was mostly troubled.'

'And your father, when did he pass away? Were you married then?'

'Married? I was nine!' I tell her with a short dry laugh.

'Oh,' she nods. 'Hmm. And how was your relationship with him?'

'The best there can ever be. He was the one who goaded me to always take initiative—live life like it's nobody's business.'

She smiles. 'That's nice.' We discuss my father for a little while. Then she asks me about other members in my family. Mother, sister, grandmother.

'Grandfather?'

'He passed away, last year.' It makes me sad to think of that—of all the Urdu *shayari* evenings shared regularly, all the cricket matches watched together, sometimes all night long. The kind, gentle, humorous face.

'Sorry to hear that,' she frowns.

Then speaks slowly, carefully.

'I can see now, Zehra, where the problem lies. Everything here seems connected to your childhood. The lack of a father figure in life.'

I gaze at her, the furrow deepening between my brows.

'All of this is connected with the loss of your father. Your mind constantly seeks him out, and in your husband you have subconsciously placed all the love you held for your father. He has become the replacement for all the lost affections, all the childhood dreams cut short.'

My head feels woozy. Like someone just dumped me into a whizzing merry-go-round.

'And that is why,' she continues, 'you pine so terribly for him. It's not just your sorrow at separation from your husband, it is also the accumulation of all that sorrow you've held in your heart for your father.'

I gaze down at the mahogany table. My consciousness wanders deep into the labyrinths of my own mind.

Chapter 26

Picking New Fathers

'What the mind does after losing one's father isn't just to pick new fathers from the world, but pick new selves to love them with.'

—Helen Macdonald, *H is for Hawk*

For far too many years now, I have been picking fathers from the world.

The first man I met after my father died was the man who came to fill the official post left vacant by his passing: the new Additional District Magistrate. I had picked him to love, for he had the same booming voice and crackling laugh and was so gentle and kind. He was loving and witty and funny, cracking jokes and filling the heart of a nine-year-old with fuzzy, warm fatherly love.

Oh yes, I knew a thing or two about picking fathers from the world.

I had felt it most intensely, though, in the strange bond that formed itself between Salman and me, when I shared my deepest sorrow with him in some obscure moment of the night, in those times when free cell phone calls had just been introduced. The conversation itself is obscure in my mind, but I remember all too well how we had both cried with each other—me for my own grief, and he for mine, from a place of love only he could fathom. In a bizarre moment of searing grief dissolved in unfathomable love, he had called me his *beti*. His daughter. From then on, for many years, he would refer to me as his little one every time I was sad.

That was so, so long ago, very early into our relationship. We were both very young then, and I was still a teenager. I cannot recall with certainty the exact day or date, but the memory is sharp as a camera focused to precision. The strange emotion in that moment, though, is perhaps something no one else would understand.

However, more people understand the loss of a father than one would think, and more people try to exploit it than one would imagine. When I was in college, a boy had sent me a declaration of love in the following terms:

'I know how unprotected you must feel without your father and I want to protect you.'

I don't think I recall his exact words, but I do recall that offer of protection and support in my father's stead, and I remember recoiling from it in disgust and loathing. I remember hating him for his shallow, wretched gift of pity disguised as love, his offering of charity for the fatherless girl in need of support and protection. I didn't want anyone's pity. I had learnt to face the world and I could do it perfectly well, thank you. I wished to slap the boy's face. Though, of course, I was pointedly polite while rejecting his offer.

It was never this way with Salman. He loved me. Who I was. He loved the things he saw in me. When he professed his feelings, it was a simple declaration. He couldn't stay away from me. He wanted me forever. He was in love.

Simple. Like the man he is.

Like stupid youngsters in love, we created new e-mail IDs for each other like other teens give their sweethearts silly names. I created for him: incorrigible_salman@yahoo.com, for incorrigible is what I called him when I teased him. The ID he created for me: invincible_zehra@hotmail.com. *Invincible.*

There is nothing sweeter in the whole wide world than a man who calls you invincible. Powerful. He is not in love with you because he thinks you are a damsel in distress who needs to be saved. He is besotted with you because he finds you a wonder woman, an amazing person he would want to have in his life. And yet, neither of us really thought of all this, did we, when we chose each other?

Those other, deeper, crazier connections evolved naturally, with time. We discovered we weren't just sweethearts. We were everything to each other. I don't know how to put this without presenting an insanely strong Electra complex, but we realised we were each other's friend, lover, sibling, and parent. Or rather, he was my parent.

Just to put Freud in his place, there was nothing physical about this. It was a little girl's repressed psychological angst for a 'safe place'. A little girl running to a safe place from the imposing world and its confusions.

After so many years of fruitless wandering, with this man, I was home.

Hadn't I known it all along?

Hadn't I said this to my mother-in-law, just a couple of months after our wedding? She was talking to me on the phone and had asked me whether I was enjoying married life. I distinctly remember my answer:

'I have never been this happy since my father passed away. Never.'

Hadn't I dreamt this exact dream about a year after my wedding?

I had dreamt of my father—as I do every two-three months or so. It is a ritual over that corridor between life and death; it is how my father has met me all these eighteen years since that fateful night. Every few months, he appears in my dream and I, without fail, introduce him to my friends and tell him all the things I want to. He is always impeccably dressed—had never been otherwise—

handsome as ever and in strapping good health. Wearing the same shirts—navy blue, black, green, and brown—shirts that still hang in my mother's almirah and have not been removed in these eighteen years. Occasionally, he wears the dark blue tailored suit he had worn for his 10th wedding anniversary, the very last one that he and my mother were destined to celebrate. And in every dream—every single one of them—as soon as he appears in my sight, I run to him and he swings me up in his arms like he did every day on returning from work.

All of these dreams begin with us hugging each other. Sometimes he instructs me to do something, like the dream where he and I were having dinner and there was a beggar at the door, and my grandmother was about to shoo the poor man away when papa gravely asked me to give him a portion from ours. I had woken up that day and proceeded to give food to the first handful of destitute people I came across. Other times, we merely laugh and talk.

But this dream, it was strange. It wasn't like any other. I saw him, but I didn't run to him. I wasn't there. There was no me in the dream. Just him. He is there, and I have this faint ache in my heart, the consciousness of missing him and wanting him here. And his face is in a misty haze. Before my eyes, I watch his features shift, his face transform. His face transforms into that of another man dreaming simultaneously beside me—it is no longer the face of my father, it is the face of Salman.

This was the dream where, clearly and openly, the two men I love the most in this world merged into one.

I woke up and looked long and hard at the man asleep beside me. I knew what the dream meant. This man had filled the gaping hole in my frame. He had made me whole.

I didn't really need a psychologist to tell me that.

'You must involve your mind in other things. Go and meet people. Get a hobby. Get a full-time job . . .' the psychologist goes on.

I cannot tell her how I feel. I cannot tell her what it is like. I cannot tell her that I attend parties, I meet friends, and I meet relatives, and for the time that I am with them, it is alright. But the moment I am back, everything goes right back to where it was. There is no joy, no happiness, no relief. Just an empty feeling of going through the motions, living one day after another. Trudging through in blank, numb stupor.

As for getting a full-time job, I am absolutely not attracted to teaching; not because there is anything wrong with it, but because I have grown up hearing endlessly that 'teaching is the best profession for women.' My obstinate core refuses to give in to the stereotype. Besides, I am professionally already doing what I love the most: writing. I have my newspaper columns and articles, possibly the only place of refuge in my life. Words are my inebriation, I lose myself in them. The world ceases to exist. When I write, I am free. Which is a strange mirror for my relationship with Salman, and further back, with my father.

With both of them, I felt free. My father was the immensely encouraging champion of independence who never held me back, but pushed me toward things I might have been too scared to do.

The year is 1994. I am 7. We are sitting in a huge auditorium in Etawah—a small town in UP—watching a grand magic show by one of the most famous magicians in India at the time. My father being the Additional District Magistrate, we are sitting up front and centre in the VIP seats.

The magician suddenly calls out to the audience, asking for a kid of 7-8 years to come up to the stage and be the subject of an act. I look at my papa eagerly and ask him excitedly, 'Can I go? Can I go please?'

Mummy answers instead. 'No, no! Who knows what he might do?'

Grandma Bazooka, who happened to be visiting us at the time, chimes in, '*Nahi! Bilkul nahi!* Absolutely not!'

I glance at papa again. He winks broadly at me with both eyes and nods mischievously in the direction of the stage. Go!

I leap out of my seat without a moment's delay.

'Hello! Hello! Hello!' chants the magician. 'And what is your name!'

He thrusts the mic in my face.

'Zehra,' I say confidently. I was born to be on stage.

'Lovely!' he beams, all a part of his over-the-top act. 'How old are you, child?'

'Seven.'

'Wonderful! Wonderful!' And then he turns to the audience. 'Now, do you know what magic we are going to cast on Zehra? We will make her float IN THE AIR!' he booms.

I pretend like I am about to faint on the spot with excitement, and a ripple of laugher goes through the audience. I see my father's glowing face, chuckling, grinning, bursting with pride.

'Okay, Zehra! Now we will hypnotise you!' Very swiftly, unnoticeably, the magician comes by my side and says, 'When I make sounds of casting a spell, you have to sway back and forth like you are in a trance. Okay?'

'Okay!' I nod, a delirious thrill running down my spine. I am a magician's subject! I am going to float in the air!

The sorcerer's apprentice swiftly blindfolds me. I am plunged in darkness. Soon enough, I can make out sounds of eerie background music and the sorcerer chanting his spell. On cue, I start swaying back and forth like I have been doing this all my life—I am a pro!

'*Arrey*!' I hear my mother's astounded gasp. She actually thinks I have been hypnotised. I must be a darn good actor.

Now I can feel hands around me, picking me up and laying me down on something wooden, something flat. The top of a box or a table by the feel of it—as far as I can make out. The table only extends till my calves, so my legs feel like they are slightly inclined.

The eerie music deepens, growing louder and louder, as do the magician's chants.

'*Hosha hosha hosha hosha* . . .'

Suddenly, there is an enormous crash of wood falling to the ground and lo and behold, the auditorium reverberates with thunderous applause.

'Ladies and gentlemen! I give you, THE FLOATING CHILD!' the magician's voice booms with a flourish. I have no idea what he is going on about, because I am still lying on that table.

I can feel the table very clearly, of course, because I am not hypnotised! Whatever that man has done, the 400-strong audience is convinced that I am floating in the air on stage. Only I know I am not.

Later, when he removes the blindfold from my eyes, he thanks me with a wink, 'Thank you, Zehra! You've been very supportive!' (You bet I have.)

When I return, glowing triumphantly, I share a broad grin with my papa.

With my father, I learnt how to defeat fear. I was free.

For a brief period of time, in the year between the end of college and the beginning of the marriage, I had created my own freedom, with huge effort and rebellion, staying independently in Delhi and pursuing the ambition of my heart. My career, my friends, my books, and my life. Just the way I wanted it.

However, there is one thing you cannot create all on your own.

Romance. Passion. Desire. Call it what you will. It is a thirst that claws its way inside you, charging every pore and twisting the mind together with the body. Convoluted knots releasing steam into your system. Heating you up to the boiling point until you explode.

My marriage, therefore, was far too precious because it gave me both: independence layered with love, and romance without the fetters. Between the two of us, the standing joke was that our marriage was a live-in relationship—no fine print and no conditions apply. Just two people living independently any way they'd like to live.

With Salman, I had been free once again. Free of restrictions, of jails meant to guard against dangers, real or imagined. He never held me back from living my life. With him, I was safe and anchored, but with no locks, no chains, and no bars. I wasn't on a leash. I could fly wherever I wished, knowing that when I needed a refuge there would always be a home.

Wherever he was, was home.

And now there is no home.

And no wings to fly.

A princess locked in a tower. Trapped doubly with no escape hatch in the form of work in a different city. Trapped triply, bound to this little boy who is in the line of fire for no fault of his own.

Chapter 27

Conversations

June 28, 2014

The counselling sessions have perhaps been working because my heart feels lighter. But there may be another reason for it.

He has returned home.

Like a soldier from the battlefield, carrying the wounds and traumas of war.

You would think everything would be alright now. But the problem here is that we have both been in the thick of fire, each battling our own demons, each combating our nemesis. Getting out of the battlefield is easier than getting the war out of your head.

He is back and yet . . . we are not quite—how shall I put it—overjoyed at being together. The ghosts of quarrels, of unspoken tension, and bouts of desperate blame games hang heavy in the air, casting their deathly pallor all around.

This is not the reunion we had wanted; this is not the homecoming we had imagined. There are two tragedies in life: one is to lose your heart's desire, the other is to gain it, as George Bernard Shaw said. Always two tragedies.

His brooding and moroseness has grown to a point where it is unbearable. The strain that these past two years of forced separation have put on our marriage is tremendous. Gone is the easy laughter and graciousness of the initial years. Everything, but everything that has ever been important to us, lies in a state of disrepair, teetering precariously on the edge of collapse.

Little things provoke the onset of gloom.

'What's the matter . . . what are you thinking?' I keep asking now and then.

'Nothing.'

'You look upset. Something's wrong. What is it?'

'Nothing.'

After about 10 times of repeating the same questions, the actual reason comes out. The repetitive pattern drags us down like an iron ball chained to our legs.

We are here now, and yet . . .

I visit Dr Priya again.

She listens quietly to all of my complaints.

'Stop being a mood checker,' she declares finally.

'But I *know* when he's upset and he won't tell me *why*—untilI've asked him 20 times!' I protest.

'Then let him be upset. Let him take his time and come to you himself with whatever's bothering him.'

'He won't!' I insist. 'He'll keep being grouchy and morose.'

She sighs. 'Just try it. Don't be a mood checker, that's all.'

So I try. And it is not easy.

But the human body and mind have brilliant adaptive qualities. The more you practice, the more you perfect. And sure enough, Dr Priya proves right.

With the passage of days and weeks, and the stopping of those 'What are you thinking?' questions, the equation relaxes. I am not constantly looking for clues to his mood—what is making him sulky, what has happened this time—and when it does feel like he is sulking, I put on my best game-face, act perfectly normal, and soldier on as if everything is just peachy. Surprisingly, in the absence of being constantly pushed and cajoled, the man begins to offer information voluntarily. (Remember that nursery rhyme of Little Bo Peep? *Leave them alone and they will come home.*)

Slowly, the distance of half a continent is bridged and the dark clouds begin to drift away.

July 25, 2014

The man speaks. In the darkness of the night, darkness that is hushed and comforting, wrapping around us like a blanket of the finest fur.

We lay there quietly, arms tight around each other, our voices barely a whisper. Our little boy sleeps soundly, off to one side of the bed.

'This,' he says, indicating us, the two of us, ensconced in an invisible cocoon, 'is what makes my blood pressure normal. And my heart rate, too,' he chuckles.

I grin. This is the man I know. The man I fell in love with. Who talks of his love in terms of blood pressure and heart rate.

If only it were a metaphor, though. Since he returned from Oman, he has been constantly fatigued and sluggish. A complete body check-up revealed multiple deficiencies—vitamin D plunging to alarming levels and cholesterol spiralling in the opposite direction, equally alarming. Blood sugar is close to the danger levels as well. This past year has made a mess of my man. A mess that, ironically, mirrors the mess of my own body—equally low vitamin D levels, excruciating cervical spondylitis, and kidney problems to boot.

It is like our bodies are competing to show who has been hurting the most, inside.

'When I had that accident, remember? All I could think of for days on end was *what if . . .*' He trails off. I crush him to me because the very thought is unbearable. I could put a finger to his lips and say, 'Hush. Don't say such things.' But I won't. I want him to talk. Talk of his wounds and his heartbreaks, because all these months I have been the only one doing the talking. I want to listen now, now when the dam is broken and the words flow freely by.

'I couldn't stop thinking of you and Hamza,' he continues, swallowing the lump in his throat. 'I couldn't stop thinking of what would have happened if I … I left you both alone.'

Moisture clouds his eyes, and mine as well. The accident had occurred only a month after he had moved to Oman. A speeding SUV had rammed into their Lexus, sending it spinning wildly out of control, and the only thing that just about saved their lives were the seatbelts that held them in place and the airbags that deployed instantly. The Lexus was a complete wreck, and looking at it in that state was enough to make you shudder. All this time, I had avoided thinking about it. It was too much to deal with.

A car accident almost 20 years ago had taken away my father. That accident was the biggest turning point in our lives—the lives of my mother, sister, and me—and it hung forever over our family like a partial eclipse, dimming the light from whatever we found to brighten our days and nights. Tremors of this magnitude inflict permanent damage.

I say nothing.

'You know something strange?' he says. 'I became scared of flying, too. I developed a phobia of sitting in planes. Every time I had to take a flight, my heart would scrunch up inside me, persistently asking—what if I didn't make it? What if this flight became one of those episodes on *Air Crash Investigation*?' He smiles ruefully. I remain quiet, though his words are like fingernail scratches on my soul.

'But you're here now,' I say finally. 'And we'll all be okay.'

He takes a deep breath and smiles. 'I missed this,' he says. 'Talking softly into our pillows. Whispering the night away.' I grin at him and sigh yet again, contentedly this time.

He is right. This does lower the blood pressure and stress levels.

July 28, 2014

Men returning from far off lands come loaded with gifts galore. Expensive tokens of remembrance, assurances that you have never been far from mind. Symbols of the desire to bring you something from the lands that fascinate and entice; lands that they long to show you and fill you with delight. Unable to do that, they try to compensate by plucking out glimpses from that endless, incredible landscape.

From the gifts Salman brought home for his woman, the most beautiful and precious one was half a dozen curiously shaped seashells—handpicked from the ocean's lip that kissed the shore with every wave, leaving behind scattered shells like marks of love on sandy skin. Left behind by one lover, picked up by another.

Smooth, white as foam and just the right size to fit in my palm, this is by far the most beautiful gift he ever gave me, for they speak in the voice of the ocean and narrate a precious tale. They reveal everything that this quiet man finds difficult to express: how much attention he pays to things I enjoy and hold dear, how closely he listens even when he says nothing back. They speak of his longing to show me the ocean tinged with moonlight, his frustration at not keeping his family together, his suffocation at not being able to explain it all—the whole, unvarnished truth.

Who knew a handful of seashells had so much to say?

I run my index finger over their smooth curves and fine grooves, flip them over, and place them next to my ear. The ocean rushes inside.

'These are from the Shatti beach,' Salman tells me, gazing at them thoughtfully. 'I picked them from the shore myself. You would have loved the Shatti. It glows dazzling silver in the first light of dawn, before the sun rays arrive. You'd have been so thrilled.'

He looks into my eyes. 'You do so love the ocean. We'd

have spent every single weekend at the beach.' His gaze turns distant, wistful. 'That's what kept me going all this time, you know: the thought that you'd be here soon with me. That we'd explore all of this together. Every single place I went, every scene I set my eyes upon, made me long even more to show it all to you. And to think we came so close! That last time, when I was planning to get you there on a visit visa—I was so sure! I was sure I'd take you there and show you every single thing I knew you would have loved.' His voice grows very quiet. 'I can't believe I couldn't take you there even once.'

I take his hand. 'But you know it doesn't matter to me for even a single second, don't you?' I look into his eyes. 'You know that all I've ever wanted was to be with you, no matter where we are. Now you're here, and I don't care one bit about Oman.' I smile up at him and kiss his cheek. 'We'll have plenty of beaches to visit in our life. The entire universe to explore together. None of that matters really, now that you're here.'

'I know,' he says quietly. 'Still . . . I did picture us there together.'

Suddenly, he grins. 'And the food! Every time I tried a new dish I couldn't help but think of you—you with your penchant for *halabi kebabs*,' his eyes twinkle wickedly.

'You're never going to let me forget that, are you?' I smack his shoulder, grinning back. He pulls me into a huge hug, crushing me till I yelp.

'I love you so much you can't ever imagine,' he says softly, going all quiet again.

'I agree,' I chuckle, then look at his serious face. 'But neither can you. Life has nothing in it, absolutely nothing, without you. And that's the simple truth.'

The simple, unvarnished truth, like a handful of hand-picked seashells.

July 30, 2014

Some conversations are open-ended, punctuated merely with commas. They begin of their own accord and stretch on, intermittently, weaving in and out of the present, appearing and disappearing of their own free will, like the Cheshire cat and its standalone grin. We are in the middle of one such conversation, one that had been on hold for almost two years; a conversation that encompasses two concentric dialogues—between husband and wife; and between father, mother, and son.

Children understand far more than they let on. Far more than you would like to believe. Because to believe that, you would have to acknowledge you are not always the one teaching them—they are learning a lot more on their own. Hamza, whose lips grew comfortable with fully formed words merely 10 months after birth, has his own special conversation going on with his father.

'Baba?' he says, as if asking a question

'*Haan*, *beta*,' his father replies. Yes, my son.

Instead of a question there comes the sound of delighted tinkling laughter, with a huge slathering of mischief.

'Baba?' he asks again.

'*Haan*, *beta*.'

Bubbles of mirth plop again on a round, impish face. Over and over this goes, with all the merriment of self-invented games, until finally, the father falls into a conversation with me, the mother.

'Baba?' comes the question again, but he gets no response, for we are busy talking to each other.

'Baba?'

Yet again. No response. And suddenly we hear a '*Haan*, *beta*!' The little boy answers on his own, perfectly mimicking the tone of his father's replies, and promptly dissolves into peals of laughter at his own inventiveness. You can't help but laugh along.

There is something heartbreakingly beautiful in this impromptu game of monosyllabic responses repeated over and over, now that the little one has discovered how much fun it is. It is beautiful because it reveals a bond that has been carried over from the womb—the excited kicks in my belly at the sound of his father's baritone. And heartbreaking because it reveals the bottled emotions of a little boy unable to express in the language of grown-ups; unable to speak out exactly how much it hurt to not have his father with him every day.

A boy and his baba have so much to share, so much to bond over, so many games to play, so many pranks to chuckle about. They have a conversation to hold, an open-ended one that weaves in and out, in and out of each day and each night.

'Baba?'

'*Haan, beta.*'

Chapter 28
SURVIVAL AND SUSTENANCE

August 20, 2014

A family needs love to survive. But a little bit more to sustain.

We have known this for a while now, from the time we became parents. There is an F-word that has wreaked havoc in our lives. The word is Finance.

That is what drove us apart in the first place; the quest for better resources to keep our little nest warm. It is also what kept our family from being reunited in Oman. Granted, though, the separation was facilitated by false promises and precarious plans that settled upon us like condensed mist on a cold window, and by the time the glass was clear enough for us to see outside, the landscape had changed unimaginably. All this time I had been wondering what it was that prevented my husband from bringing his family over to Oman, and now he wants to tell me why.

In hindsight, it shouldn't have been so unusual, because you hear so many stories of this kind. But you never expect one of those stories to be yours.

Can't happen to me, you think. Your happy life is so far removed from all the horrible things that you could never be the victim in a tragic tale. A pity, for reality hits harder upon the delusional.

And so, Salman reveals to me—haltingly, with a lump in his throat—that a significant chunk of his annual financial dues were still unpaid, held up by the man who was once his closest friend, the man who invited him to Oman. I can see how difficult it is for him to say this, especially as an Indian male, for the men in our culture are brought up never to reveal weakness, never to reveal setbacks, especially to the woman in their life. It would expose a chink in their manly armour.

In truth, though, this was an act of far greater courage. An act that required the 'protector', the 'provider', the man of the family to set aside his ego, bare his soul, and lay his setbacks out in the open. And here he was, the man, the husband, the father, having the courage to reveal the truth.

The reason for all our strife over the past years lay inside the f-word.

'He has promised to transfer the entire amount in a month's time,' says Salman sombrely. 'So, just a few more days and it will all be sorted out.'

I have my doubts. But no point adding to our woes.

The more pressing concern right now is for us to start moving towards the future, beginning with him getting back into the Indian job market after a year's stint in Oman.

December 20, 2014

We had heard many stories and witnessed many examples first hand, of people returning to India from abroad and finding it difficult to find a footing back in the job of their choice. Choice is the key word here, because finding a job wasn't the problem. It was finding a job that matched your requirements, with a higher remuneration than what you earned abroad. It wasn't just about getting back; it was also about not having your worth slashed.

What we hadn't realised then, upon witnessing those examples, was how close an encounter we would have with such an experience ourselves. This, again, is not surprising, if not for the fact that you never expect the worst to happen to you.

The strange thing here is that I am not feeling it. I am not feeling the sting.

I am relaxed, which is rather bizarre. I am happy living in a bubble, an escapist's bubble, if you may. He is here with me, in the flesh—to talk to, to hold, to love. And nothing else matters.

Perhaps because his central place in my life has been that of a best friend, confidante, and lover rather than just a provider. Or perhaps because I didn't feel the need for a lot of 'things'. But it could also be because of the differences in the way that men and women view their roles.

He is worried about keeping us secure. He is the tree that fears its shade being insufficient for those in its care. Or maybe, he is hiding more than he is letting on. I can't really put my finger on it, but whatever the reason, right now we are both inhabiting parallel universes in our mental, emotional lives.

Chapter 29
Maktub

January 15, 2015

Another new year.

Two Januaries have passed since I moved to Aligarh, both of them cold, grey, and dull, in more ways than one. But this time, there is the hint of sunlight breaking through, a hint of warmth welcoming you out into the open. This time I have something to look forward to, something that had been all but forgotten amid the more pressing matter of sailing through the tempestuous waters of fate: the Jaipur Literature Festival, the extravaganza of literary delights which I had been forced to abandon three years ago on account of my problematic pregnancy. That time, three years ago, when I had been on a roll before the power cord of my carnival ride was yanked off abruptly, sending me flying across the field and crashing into the ground.

Three years later, it is that time of the year again, when bibliophiles flock to the Pink City for their annual feast.

I can't really say what reminded me of it—a newspaper advertisement? An e-mail notification? But the fact that I am able to focus on aspects other than my gnawing, pressing need for love, means only one thing—I feel whole again. Despite things not entirely being back on track, despite us still being in Aligarh and still looking for ways to get back on our feet and back to the Capital—despite all of it, there is that feeling of wellness, where you skim your fingers over your soul and it feels cool, polished, smooth—*healed*; unlike the cracks and shards that jabbed the skin each time and made you bleed.

Also, there are less romantic and more mundane reasons, too: I now have that person here who would love to travel with me for work assignments, who would look after the baby with pleasure while I worked, and who would always let me be me. By all standards of gender empowerment, I ought to be able to liberate myself. But not with a two-year-old in tow; I just can't do it on my own now. This man is my ticket to freedom. And an amazing, adorable, soothing, comforting ticket at that. Luxury ticket, so to speak.

So I dash off an e-mail to the editor of the newspaper where my literary columns appear, asking him if he would like me to cover the festival and send across interviews and reports. A few minutes later, just like that, it is done! I quickly register for the event and book us a room at the Clarks Amer—because quite a few of the authors and delegates will be staying there, and it should be that much easier to strike up a conversation and get into the flow of things. Everything falls so quickly into place that I can't believe my luck!

In truth, it isn't just the literature fest alone that means so much. This fest is like a symbol, a landmark that stands for all the things I had, the things I *was*; the things I had been forced to let go. This spectacular *literavaganza*, which was shot down by a senior journalist (along with other lit fests, in general) for being 'the fashion show of the last decade', and derided by one of my colleagues for being an 'intellectual farce', nevertheless means no less than the Statue of Liberty to me. A beacon marking the vast ocean I had crossed to finally get to this side. It is a leap out of a dreary, colourless existence with no glimmer, an existence of endless domestic drama. This is my 'Land-ho!' The exultant first cry of ships nearing shore.

In the great scheme of things, in the overwhelming

vastness of the universe, it is a tiny, inconsequential blip. But it is also a blip of life. A blip of heartbeat on a screen.

A sign of changing tides. As the Alchemist in Paulo Coelho's eponymous book would say: *Maktub.*

January 20, 2015

As Salman drops me off at the entrance to the venue hosting the Jaipur Literature Festival, I am filled with a gust of heady feeling I had all but forgotten—that feeling of wanting to smile for no reason at all. The brilliant colours, the milling crowds, an unspoken promise lingering on the winter wind, and crazy, happy me, with a journalist's ID around my neck and a notepad, pen, and recorder, all nestling within my beige cross-body sling bag. I try to suppress a broad grin as I walk past the security at the gate, the guard eyeing me suspiciously—an outlandish creature in a beige coat-abaya and dark sunshades, sporting oversized Nike sneakers. I have had many people exclaim in surprise over the pairing of oversized sneakers with abayas, but it is the most comfortable combination for me, especially on days that promise a lot of walking around. As for the abaya, it is the reason behind many people mistaking me for a foreigner, somewhere from the Middle East. This, funnily enough, works in my favour because it bestows upon me the air of a delegate and people seem to be nicer, somehow, to smart-looking foreigners!

So here I am, in the grounds of the Diggi Palace, taking in the sights and the sounds. Upturned umbrellas in the flashing hot colours of Jaipur strung together with puppet dolls form a canopy overhead while an art installation features a convertible as canvas—every inch of the open-topped car painted over with pictures of famous writers—even as performers break into traditional Rajasthani folk dance right beside me. For one long moment, I just stroll around the various venues, the Front Lawn, the Charbagh, the Mughal Tent, and so on, wallowing in sensuous pleasures. And then, it is time to get down to work.

Stacking up interviews with the numerous award-winning authors gathered in this star-studded carnival of books: Eleanor Catton, Man Booker Prize winner of 2014; Eimear McBride, winner of Bailey's Women's Prize the same year; Håkan Nesser, Swedish writer and king of crime fiction; Bilal Tanweer from Karachi, author of the hauntingly beautiful *The Scatter Here is Too Great.* Romesh Gunesekera, Sri Lankan author who stole my heart with *Noon Tide Toll*, a book of stark beauty; Samanth Subramanian who won the Shakti Bhatt First Book Prize, but bowled me over with his second book *This Divided Island,* on life in our southward neighbour, Sri Lanka, after 30 years of civil war.

These and a host of other literary stars from all around the globe. All of these authors I interview over the next three days of my stay in Jaipur. And with every interview, I feel *home.* Back where I belong, back in the middle of what I love. Having the most interesting conversations with the people I most wanted to meet—authors. I choose my favourite ones to talk to, ones whose books had moved me and created little spaces for themselves inside me. I ask them questions that I wanted to ask when I read what they had written, I speak to them to quell my own curiosity. Far from the cut and dried professional who is one among the pack of scribes, I feel completely solitary, in the most amazing way. Like Alice in Wonderland, for whom everything is a novelty, every moment a chance to be thrilled.

I feel like *me*, the me that had always been; the me who was filled with wonder at things that appear mundane to the ordinary eye, the me who had an infinite capacity to be delighted by life.

At the very end, in all my three days at Jaipur, days of stellar interactions, swiftly transcribed interviews, and deftly woven articles, when the others turn to partying and late-night revelry, I return to my room at the Clarks Amer, to the comforting warmth of my husband and son. The one and a half men in my life, who have been having a holiday of their own, watching TV, meeting relatives in the city, and savouring lunches in good company.

Downstairs, music blares out in full volume in the lawns, where JLF's after-hours entertainment takes place every night.

After we put our son to sleep, Salman and I have a late-night party of our own. Turning on the hot water in the bathtub, we lower ourselves into the snaking arms of steam, slowly slipping out of the dust and grime of the past two years fraught with endless complexities.

Sometimes, some days are so perfect that you just step back and marvel at them. Impeccably folded white roses on a silvery winter morn.

January 23, 2015

My last day in Jaipur.

I wrap up my conversation with performers from Azerbaijan's UNESCO International Prize-winners, the Alim Qasimov Ensemble, in the lobby of our hotel. As I bid them farewell and turn back to my room to give a final check for things left behind, a thought saunters into my mind. Three years ago, right about this time, I had imagined my life, my dreams, and my career to be done for. Dead. Over. Gone for good. I had been seized by the thought of being trussed up and boxed, seized by visions of a bleary, black-and-white existence sans the burst of colours that marked my very being. And yet, here I was. A little late, yes, but here nonetheless.

Had I killed myself in a fit of rage or under the sustained blows of circumstances, I might never have been able to get here, to the bright side. Never been able to step into this sphere of completeness, a sphere that holds not just my dreams but also love and motherhood. A picture so unbelievably perfect that it is almost a cliché. None of this, absolutely none, would I have seen had I hung myself from the ceiling fan or thrown myself under the wheels of a speeding car.

I would have vanished right there in the tunnel even as light waited for me to emerge.

Perhaps that is what I need to tell myself every time the darkness gets overwhelming. If I give up now, I never get to come out into the light. If I erase myself, the canvas remains blank. And I never get to see that moment when I ink my victory onto the pages of life.

That is what I need to tell myself from now on till the day I live.

Survivors get to tell their story. Survivors get to see what lies on the other side.

Chapter 30

The Man Factor

March 5, 2015

Finally.

Good fortune seems to be smiling down upon us. Salman has just had a call from a major American multinational company and they are offering him the right amount that he had been looking for.

This is huge. This is major. It means we can finally get back to a state of balance, of normalcy. A state of decidedness where life isn't just a haze that you keep walking into one step at a time, unsure of your direction, unclear about what lies ahead. You are just trusting the fog to lift at some point and reveal a promising blue sky that spells sunny days.

And suddenly, the fog lifts.

You can't believe your luck.

After months of repeated efforts, months of self-doubt and inner torment, Salman finally has his footing back. All this time he has been beset with doubts ripping his self-worth to shreds, sinking deeper and deeper within himself, doubly tormented by what he perceived to be his inability to get life back on track—not just for him but for all three of us.

A fresh wound upon the still-throbbing, deeper wound of betrayal by one of his closest friends.

The promised amount hasn't been sent from Oman yet—the amount that was Salman's by right; the remuneration not just for his blood, sweat, and tears, but also for his loyalty, honesty, and integrity. It was the sum total of his deepest, sincerest labour and toil, the repayment for his unflinching and unequivocal support. And it was denied to him. By a man who was among the handful that he trusted the most in his life.

This stab in the back claws at his heart incessantly, and that perhaps is the reason why we have been on such different emotional planes in the past few months. I have been on a high of having him here, having all the pieces of my heart together, while he has been silently, unsuccessfully, trying to push back the trauma of betrayal and that gnawing feeling of being insufficient for his family. Despite all my declarations of love, how could I have been oblivious to so much pain? How could I only worry about myself and my sorrows, and not pay attention to what was eating him up? Am I that selfish?

Boys don't cry, they say. And yet, as we whisper in the darkness of the night, I feel a little wetness trickle down his cheek onto my arm.

Boys do cry. But only where they feel loved and trusted, only where they can let their guard down.

For so long, I have fumed about and tried to stand against the cultural and social pressures on women. For so long, I have been acutely conscious of the capes we are forced to don and the roles we are forced to slip into. But never before this have I contemplated the tremendous socio-cultural pressure on men—as providers, protectors, and 'heads' of the family, responsible for the survival, sustenance, and betterment of all those within their shade. Responsible for putting on a strong, emotionless front in the face of turbulence and not 'burden' their families with the worries that hover over their minds. It is only now that I see it, in his creased forehead and lines around the eyes, the white hair sprouting secretively in his neatly trimmed stubble. Only now that he opens up, finally having a huge load lifted off his heart; now that he has a job again, a job of his preference and worth.

I see it now, the prolonged suffering of a man of deep silences.

All of this suffering has made us see each other more clearly—the warts, the scars, and the disfigurements; the glaring imperfections so difficult to imagine in the glazed-eyed raptures of love. But aren't we all just a little cracked in places? Scratched and chipped and faded along the edges?

Here we stand now, at the cusp of a new beginning, cracked and worn out but holding it together nevertheless; waiting to step into the light.

And yet, a tiny voice throbs in the back of my head, foreboding, whispering furtively from inside Pandora's box. The voice of doubt, the voice of dark clouds still hanging somewhere close to the horizon.

April 20, 2015

A month has passed since Salman moved to Delhi for his job. He is staying in a bachelor pad with friends, for now. By all means, we ought to be making plans for Hamza and me to move back to Delhi as well. And yet, we are not. An uneasiness hangs in the air, the kind we thought we had overcome by now. The uneasiness of secrets and gaps widening yet again.

We can't move back yet, and the reasons are unclear. There is *something*, definitely, but the 'something' gets lost amid non-committal sentences and winding hazy words spiralling one upon the other.

The pattern of the past years is repeating itself again. *One more month, another fortnight. I am looking at homes. It is happening, give it time.* All of it, repeating itself like a crazy nightmare put on loop. That terrible, terrible feeling of déjà vu.

Meanwhile, the little monarch is two and a half and feels far more than a dizzying handful. On second thoughts, when did he ever not feel like a handful? So much energy, so much exuberance, so much zest for life. That unending desire to explore and keep doing his thing, pushing away all human needs of sleep, food, and drink. He reminds me of someone I used to be, someone who has slunk into a shell, pushing out her alter ego instead. Angry, cursing, snapping. Teeth bared, hackles up, and claws out. Anger is exhausting. It wears you out faster than you would imagine.

Equally exhausting is a super exuberant kid who wakes up and declares decidedly, '*Baahar jaana hai.*' He wants to go out and play in the park just opposite our house, first thing in the morning. And he will not be comforted, cuddled, distracted, or moved an inch from his mission, which he tries to fulfil through screams and kicks and tears galore. He wants games and playmates and his rightful share of sunlight and air. But I cannot be out in the park with him all day, certainly not at the first crack of dawn, with our faces unwashed and teeth unbrushed and food not having passed our lips.

There are other, newer developments. Every time the school bus turns the corner into our government officers' colony, Hamza leaps up in excitement and climbs right into the broad-ledged window, eager for a peek at the huge yellow honking vehicle and the excited chatter of children getting on and off. He bounces and squeals in delight and exclaims, 'Want to get on the bus!' Buses are the love of his life, along with cars, trucks, tractors, trains, planes, helicopters, and absolutely any other form of transport—exactly like his father. Despite not having spent a lot of time with him, he has inherited his dad's torrid and unending affaire de coeur with everything that has wheels and can take you places. And the school bus, bright yellow and filled with kids, is such an appealing sight that it cannot be missed for a single day. On Sundays, there is a prolonged wait by the window, followed by questions like 'Mumma, where is the bus?' To which I reply patiently that today is the weekly holiday and the kids will be home, playing. The idea takes time to settle in his mind, accompanied by sulking and pouting and much ado about the truant bus. It is more than just the bus, then. It is also about the children inside it. Laughing, playing, chatting creatures. This little boy is all alone.

The idea of sending him to playschool begins to form in my mind, though I am conflicted. One part of me wishes desperately to believe Salman's assurances of 'two more months and we'll be in Delhi', but the other, more practical part reminds me of the pattern I have witnessed in the past two years. In the end, the latter half wins out. I put Hamza in playschool, thinking he would be delighted by the company and the school uniforms and the buses and the colourful classrooms and all the learning toys.

How wrong was I.

Like so many other instances in life, I completely misread the situation. What my boy liked was the *idea* of school. What he really liked were school *buses*. He wanted to board a bus and perhaps go all the way to school in it—but not, of course, to be separated from his beloved mumma and have to spend three hours every day in the company of strangers. This was my classic mom-mistake. Misreading my son and subconsciously projecting my own thoughts and needs upon him.

Mothers do it all the time.

Nevertheless, the school does prove to be good for Hamza in a number of ways, for it gets him into a routine, especially as far as sleeping and waking are concerned. Of course, it is another matter that he doesn't leave for playschool without howling his head off every single day. But there are other things, other ways in which I find him growing. My hitherto reticent-in-public boy, scared before strangers and extremely bashful in an unknown environment, is finally learning to deal with kids his own age, to make friends and hold his own in an argument or quarrel. I suppose one needs to go out into the world to learn how to deal with it at all.

May 1, 2015

Every day I drop Hamza off at 9 a.m. and pick him up at noon. Every day after school ends, he drags me to the large bird enclosure just 10 steps away from the nursery section, and talks and laughs with the screeching parakeets and cockatoos that hop from one branch to another. Then he runs to the aquarium in the left wing of the building, and gazes awestruck at the big black fish and small goldfish, trying to touch them through the glass. On the way to the big metal school gates, we pass the junior wing staffroom that houses another aquarium with four small turtles swimming in it, and we have to stop there as well. Hamza stands there, fascinated and mesmerised by the wobbling flippers, the patterned shells and the tiny heads popping out from under them. He tries to talk to them. He wants to know what they are saying. He wants to take them home.

I gently coax him out of the staffroom as the teachers chuckle, amused. He then spots the slides and jungle gym outside and spends a good 20 minutes climbing, sliding, swinging, while I click pictures on my phone, and record videos of him monkeying around.

This is perhaps the easiest time of the day for us, he and I, where we are away from everyone else. No shouts, no allegations, no demands, no reprimands, no ferocious disciplining requirements and no mean, snide remarks. We can be relaxed, joyous and, most importantly, we can be happy together. I like taking pictures of him, especially when he plays. Watching him grin, with those cuddly cheeks and sparkly eyes and still-crooked front teeth. And though he is still too young to express emotions verbally, I suspect that this is the happiest time of the day for him as well. He has grown to like school, but he likes it best when his mumma is around. He likes it best when I egg him on, calling out encouraging things and clapping when he makes it all the way to the top, assuring him when he is too scared to go on that bigger slide, and whooping and cheering when he finally zips down it with glee.

Every time he falls and picks himself up without my help, every time he climbs higher and chooses an even more difficult slide, picks up a new skill, and learns to be a little more independent, I feel a swell of pride and a puffing up of my chest. This is the time when I feel most like the celebrated 'mom'; the 'happy mom' that you see in TV advertisements and on magazine covers.

May 10, 2015

12:00 p.m.

Like all other days, I am here at Hamza's school to pick him up. I have the routine all mapped out in my mind: go to Hamza's class, watch him gather the toys, and watch him say bye to his teacher. Quite the teacher's pet he is.

'Hamza is such a dear!' says his teacher. 'He never throws toys around like the other kids. On the contrary, he helps put them all back in their right place,' she beams. I puff up a little more. I have made it a point to make Hamza help me every night putting his toys back on the rack before we go to bed. He replicates that in school.

Hamza seems happy. He has a safe, creative space to pour all that excessive energy into, friends his own age to play and fight with, and a teacher who is kind and sweet. I smile.

Still smiling, I pick up his bag and hold his hand, slowly moving out of the classroom amid the shrieks of other children leaving with their parents. It is then that Hamza tugs at my sleeve.

'Mumma,' he whispers to me.

'Yes?' I smile down at him.

He points to a child leaving the classroom holding his father's hand.

'*Iske baba lene aaye hain*,' he whispers again, a hint of confusion clouding his eyes. *His father has come to take him home.*

My son has just pointed out something very trivial, very commonplace, something I would never have paid any attention to. Many fathers come to pick and drop their kids, with many more fathers in the mornings than afternoons. I would have never given any thought to it, except now that my two-and-a-half-year-old boy has brought it to my notice.

Iske baba lene aaye hain.

A simple enough statement, and yet, there is something coiled inside it, folded within the limitations of a little boy's ability to express. His longing and his need.

His need for his father to come pick him up sometimes. His longing for the other half of him. *Baba? Haan, beta.*

Am I reading too much into a child's simple words? Am I perhaps projecting my own yearning onto him?

A pinprick in my heart. Two pinpricks. One for my own pain. The other for my son's.

I realise how the dull throbbing inside me sharpens every now and then—burning with the stench of helplessness, rage, and confusion stirred into an acidic mixture.

All of a sudden, the very act of having put my son in school here is like an ill omen. It seems to seal the fact that I am going to remain stuck in pause for a lot longer.

My heart throbs sharply with pin-pricks all over.

June 14, 2015

That which is false troubles the heart, but truth brings joyous tranquillity, says Rumi.

Not if it has been withheld repeatedly and for far too long.

How many times?

How many times must I come to know the truth, only to find out that it was just one piece of a much larger puzzle excruciatingly revealed bit by bit?

Almost a year has passed since Salman returned from Oman, and I have been getting only scraps of information here and there. And now, when three months have passed even since he moved back to Delhi and my restlessness is beginning to rise higher and higher, *now* I am administered another dose of the truth.

The amount that the employer in Oman still owes Salman is far, far larger than he had initially let on. It is huge and exceedingly worrying. And that is not all. The non-payment of all this burdensome money has led to something enormous and far more terrifying—an urban horror legend come true.

Credit Card Debt.

Mountains of it.

And all this, *all* of this, is spilling out only now—dragged out by the tail through ropes and ropes of determined interrogation. (I have had *some* experience in grilling people by now.)

I spread my palms over my face, rubbing myself out of disbelief. How did we get here? How?

Such a lot has been said about credit cards and the urban debt trap. Such a lot has been written about it. From the beginning of my career, I had sworn never to use a credit card ever, and to this day I have kept that promise. Buy now, pay now. Never buy now, pay later. If there is no money, save now and buy later, like our parents did. Our generation has this huge problem of instant gratification. Enjoy now, regret later.

In the very first year of our marriage, I had repeatedly insisted upon Salman not using credit cards at all; we had a good enough life without those, and everything else be damned. At that time he had given me a perfectly logical and sensible presentation of how he managed the credit card conundrum without running a debt of a single rupee—paying the due amount bang on time. And in my blind trustfulness, I had never bothered to ask him anything else ever again. Also, in my blind selfishness, I had never once tried to find out. Even if I did a couple of times speak to him about our finances, I was always assured that everything was peachy. Absolutely hunky-dory, nothing at all to worry about.

If only I had realised this was the man-factor playing itself out.

The man-factor which considers it best to keep the wife away from 'worries' even if that leads to her being bombarded with them later when the shit hits the fan.

And all our fans right now are literally splattered with smelly stuff.

All that money which the fraud from Oman has duped us of has led to this mountain of debt towering above us. Had the payments been coming on time, there would be no debt at all. Zero. Clean slate. But that is not all. The real disaster reveals itself when Salman tells me that paying off the debt will take almost one more year. Until then, I would have to be patient and bide my time in Aligarh.

ONE. MORE. YEAR.

As if two years and six months of all this had not been horrible enough.

Everything explodes.

Allegations and counter allegations flow thick and fast. Carefully woven, delicately embroidered relationships are ripped, shredded, and bloodied, blown to smithereens with an ear-splitting crash boom smash.

I am shocked and embittered. Not just by what has happened, but by the fact that after all these days, after all the hardships, after so much we had faced together, I hadn't been trusted enough to be told the truth in a single instalment.

Our conversations turn cold. Clipped. Broken pieces that were never truly fixed.

Truth revealed far too late brings anything but joyous tranquillity.

Chapter 31

Journeys of the Soul

June 27, 2015

Sometimes, the soul calls out for help and help comes silently, treading stealthily over the waves of time. Sometimes, it holds your hand and takes you to new lands, flying over barren, rocky mountains and treeless landscapes, into places of solace and miracle, places of history and healing.

Karbala, Iraq

In our times, the word Iraq throws up images of masked monsters launching bombs and gunfire, of screams and explosions and blood and chaos.

And yet, here I am.

With my mother and sister and a little boy in tow.

Okay, no false bravado. We are all here with a group. And no, this isn't a journalistic assignment. It is a spiritual journey. You could call it a pilgrimage.

A journey to the tomb of Imam Husain in Karbala.

And it is not going *quite* like I had imagined.

Four days ago

Indira Gandhi International Airport, New Delhi

An entire airport full of people is staring open-mouthed at me.

I have a bawling child perched on the luggage trolley and am wheeling him furiously around the entire place to make him stop crying. I now have a howling child hanging on from my arm while I get my luggage checked in. The child cradled in my arms continues to scream, even though I rock him frantically while waiting in yet another long queue at the immigration counter. The uncontrollable child thrashing his arms and refusing to keep quiet beckons the immigration officer to let me jump the queue, get my passport stamped ASAP, and take him inside (where he can damage other people's eardrums.)

The child is howling because we have left his father outside the airport. For one whole hour he has been screaming to go back to his baba, who is not coming with us on this trip because of work commitments.

This airport scene is a terrible start to our journey. I wonder how I am going to last 10 days!

June 24, 2015

Mashhad, Iran

Two days. We have two days in Iran to visit the two cities of Mashhad and Qom. The tomb of Imam Reza and that of his sister, Fatimah al-Masumah.

Imam Reza's tomb in Mashhad is among the holiest of places in the world for Shia Muslims, the topmost position being occupied, of course, by Mecca and Medina in Saudi Arabia, and Karbala and Najaf in Iraq. I had been to Mecca and Medina 5 years ago in 2010, the year that I got married. Half a decade later, here I am, in Iran.

But right now, in this land, I am facing a big problem: communicating with the Iranis. Generally, English works pretty well when you go abroad, but not in Iran. Come to think of it, communication was a problem in Malaysia, too, where Salman and I had gone for our honeymoon. But there it was more a question of understanding their accents and pronunciations. It had been baffling to talk to even the hotel staff at Genting, with very hilarious outcomes. 'Some problem' for instance sounded like 'so poem'. Needless to say, we couldn't fathom how poetry could be related to us waiting for 3 hours in the hotel lobby, just to check into our room.

In Iran, my son has made sure that I get acquainted with all the hardships that the word 'pilgrimage' seems to denote. Firstly, he refused to sleep during both the flights—from New Delhi to Dubai and Dubai to Mashhad—forcing me to stay awake throughout. He only slept at the airports where I couldn't. So I have been up for a full 24 hours when we finally reach Mashhad. To get to the hotel we have to lug our baggage for almost a kilometre. So I drag a 19 kg bag with my right hand, while propping a 14 kg baby on my left arm with an 8 kg bag of baby supplies slung on my right shoulder. That is a total load of 41 kg handled by me alone, and my own weight is about 56 kg. Talk about weightlifting!

I keep falling farther and farther behind the group until the group leader notices and offers to help, taking the trolley bag from me. (I would have appreciated it more had he offered to hold the baby instead, but what the heck, beggars can't be choosers.)

Needless to say, by the time we are in the hotel room I am dying of exhaustion, and when our roommate, a kind middle-aged lady, suggests going to the mausoleum right away, I burst into tears. I am in no position to move, let alone walk another 2 km. I let the others go on ahead, planning to go in the morning instead.

Around midnight, I realise we are out of milk. And Hamza, ever the world's biggest wonder, drinks milk only in his sleep. I tiptoe out of the room and down to the reception. Now this is no vacation, and this is no five-star hotel with a restaurant and room service. There is one man at the reception, and I ask him if he could get us some milk.

He stares at me blankly. 'Milk,' I repeat, and then, '*doodh*,' in Hindi, because I don't know what else to say. After a few more moments of gesticulation bordering on despair, I am hit by a brainwave. I rush upstairs to my room and bring down the baby's feeding bottle, saying again triumphantly: Milk!

Understanding dawns in the man's eyes. 'Ah, *sheer*!' he exclaims.

I slap my forehead. 'Sheer!' I recognised this Persian word because it was also used in Urdu! Such a common Urdu word for milk, why did I not think of it? Perhaps because Indians speak the less puritan version of Urdu—Hindustani, to be precise.

Again, the man asks me something else that leaves me stumped.

'*Buzurg*? *Sagheer*?'

After a moment's bafflement, I realise I am familiar with those words! *Buzurg* means an elderly person in Urdu, and *sagheer* means 'little one'! Yes, I get it—he is asking, perhaps, if I want the milk for an elderly person or a baby.

'Sagheer! Sagheer!' I exclaim excitedly, displaying the baby bottle and wondering simultaneously, what kind of an idiot would take this as a bottle for the elderly.

The man frowns and brings his hands together close to each other, reiterating, 'Buzurg? Sagheer?'

Suddenly I am hit by the realisation that he is asking me whether to bring a 'buzurg', meaning a *big* pack of milk or a 'sagheer', that is, a *small* one!

'Oh! Buzurg, buzurg!' I reply in relief, having accomplished this conversation.

The Irani doesn't know one word of English or Hindi and I don't know a word of Persian. But between the two of us we manage to get one 'buzurg' pack of milk.

June 25, 2015

Mashhad

Imam Reza's Tomb

The resting place of Imam Reza is a sprawling mausoleum complex with a huge golden dome and minaret in the centre, beckoning to pilgrims from all over the world. Every inch of the splendid arches and columns boasts intricate Islamic geometrical art surrounded by calligraphic representations of Quranic verses, with dazzling Iranian cut-glass work spread out magnificently over the ceilings and inner walls. A veritable feast for the eyes, and yet, the hundreds of thousands that flock to the shrine aren't there even remotely for its architectural splendour.

Imam Reza's tomb is a place for prayers to be heard and wishes to be fulfilled. But most of all it is the place for *ziyarat* of the holy Imam, a place where you 'meet' him spiritually. That is true of the tombs of all the twelve Imams, and the tombs of Prophet Mohammad and his daughter; they are places of spiritual upliftment, places of peace and of self-discovery.

The twelve Imams are the descendants of Prophet Mohammad's daughter, Fatima Zahra, and they, along with the lady herself, are revered as a continuing chain of guidance by the Twelver Shias. Which is why these tombs are the focal points of faith and healing, and people flock to them for spiritual solace. As do I, now.

Hamza is too small to remember this journey after he grows up. But in the depths of my heart, somewhere I hope that the experience touches his subconscious and leaves traces of the holy dust on the paths of his soul.

From here on to Nishapur, to Qom, and to Tehran.

Touching holy doors and floors, breathing in holy atmospheres, eating an Iranian meal now and then. Tomato-flavoured chicken with fragrant rice at one time, Iranian square *rotis* dipped in sweet cream *khameh* at another.

For Hamza, I buy dozens of chocolates to feed him at regular intervals, because the meals we get are sparse and far between.

It is at these chocolate shops that I encounter the Bollywood-*prem* of Iranis, their love for our song-and-dance cinematic melodramas.

'Indian, we're Indian,' I say by way of explanation about us not speaking Farsi.

Recognition glows in the shopkeeper's eyes.

'Ah! Hindi!' he says. Iranians refer to India as 'Hind' and therefore Indians are recognised as 'Hindis'.

'Yes, Hindi,' I nod, smiling. His enthusiasm knows no bounds.

'Ah! Amitabh Bachchan! Akshay Kumar! Salman Khan!' The man is positively glowing with bliss at being able to recount the names of some of my country's top actors. He beams at me while I laugh. Then, to my utter amazement, he bursts into an obscure Bollywood song and sings it all the way to the first stanza in Hindi! I laugh again, bemused.

'You know Hindi?' I ask him. He is one of those people who can somewhat understand English.

'Only sing,' he replies. The man has memorised the song without understanding a single word! I laugh some more.

He then slips an extra packet of chocolates into my bag and points to Hamza. I think he means they are a gift for him.

'*Shukran*!' I say, trying out the word which I had heard during my travels to Mecca and Medina.

'*Na, shukran neest*!' he shakes his head vigorously. '*Shukran, Arabi*! Farsi, *mamnoon*.' *Shukran* is Arabic for thanks. In Farsi, you say *mamnoon*.

'Ah, *mamnoon*!' I place my hand on my heart and thank him.

'Hindi? *Mamnoon* Hindi?' He wants to know the Hindi word for thanks.

'Well, there are two words actually. In Urdu, we say *shukriya* . . .' I pause, while he repeats 'shukriya' after me. 'In Hindi, the word is *dhanyavaad*.'

The man is stumped. He stares at me dumbfounded, trying his best to twist his tongue around the baffling word. 'Danaay . . .? Danba . . .?'

I grin and repeat. *Dhanyavaad*.

He whips out his cell phone, then, and hands it to me, grinning, like a brainwave just struck him. I understand. He is asking me to type the word in his phone so he can get the spelling just right! I do so, smiling, and we part cheerfully, each grinning at the experience.

And now, onward to Iraq.

June 27, 2015

1:00 p.m.

Iraq

After the spotless cleanliness and greenery of Iran, Iraq is quite a shock.

Tonnes of debris and broken vehicles lying at intervals by the roadside; withering, dry, blistering hot winds with the sun beating angrily down upon our heads like a resentful tyrant.

This land has been in the eye of the storm. The signs of war are all around for us to see.

3:00 p.m.

Karbala

The land of Karbala is legendary. It has many other names recorded in history: Nainava, Ghazariya, Shatte Furaat; the last one for being the land through which the river Euphrates flowed. This is where the famous battle took place between the family of Imam Husain, the grandson of Prophet Mohammad, and the armies of the tyrant ruler Yazid. Commemorated each year in the month of Muharram, this battle is the cornerstone of the clash between good and evil, the clash between truth and falsehood, between a pious man and an arrogant tyrant.

The climes of the place have been spoken about extensively in historical accounts: the hostile barrenness of the land, the scorching searing heat that threatens to split your skull. The heat gives me a warm, fearsome welcome on the first day as my nose begins to ooze blood.

The barrenness, though, has been replaced by the grand mausoleums—or rauzas, as they are called—of Imam Husain and his brother Abbas, and his small group of family members and companions. They are the martyrs of the battle of Karbala, the ones who stood against the oppressive practices of the ruler and lay down their lives to uphold the truth. Around these have sprung up myriad hotels for pilgrims, and bustling shops stocking everything that travellers might need or want. The blood of Husain has sprouted flowers in the desert, as we say.

4:00 p.m.

There are security checks at every point near the rauzas, even to get inside the area of the hotels and shops. That is understandable, considering the number of terrorist attacks on the pilgrims and the tombs of the Holy Imams in Iraq. But believers would rather risk their lives than abandon the land where their beloved martyrs rest.

Before we enter the rauza of Imam Husain, we first pay our homage at the rauza of Hazrat Abbas. It is customary to do *ziyarat* at the tomb of the younger brother before visiting the elder, because the fearless Abbas, whose name means the 'strongest lion of the pack' and whose tales of valour were spread far and wide, was given the foremost position among the martyrs by Imam Husain himself. Ironically, this honour was conferred upon him not for his battle bravery but for the fortitude he displayed in laying down his sword at the command of his brother, his leader, despite being the warrior who could have turned around the battle single-handedly. Why did Husain ask him to do that, when they could have won the war despite being immensely outnumbered?

Because he wanted to make the weakest, the commonest of people in the world remember that speaking out against oppression does not require one to be in a position of power and might. And that is also why he took the women and children of his family along when he set out from Medina to Karbala. To let the world know that he came not with the intention of fighting, but with the intention of reaching out and calling on Yazid's supporters to mend their unjust ways. And to let the women and children of the world know that they, too, have a role to play in the universal movement against tyranny and oppression.

Husain's mission was not battle, not domination through brute strength, but victory through martyrdom, through letting the world know that truth triumphs even in death. And that is a tale being told since a thousand years, a story of everlasting victory not through conquest but through *shahadat.* The literal meaning of the term *shahaadat* is 'to rise and bear witness'. And that is exactly what Husain and his companions did—they rose against tyranny and bore witness against injustice.

So it is that Abbas is the 'gateway' to the resting place of Husain; whosoever comes to meet Husain shall first meet his most trusted companion.

Hizabr e Dasht e Nainava Ameer e Lashkar e Husain . . .
Lion of the battle of Nainava, Commander of the forces of Husain . . .

Rauza, Imam Husain

To be inside the rauza of Husain is an otherworldly experience. In a strange, inexplicable way, it feels like a homecoming.

Like your roots calling out to you, like a place in a dream that kept beckoning to you, a twinge in the heart that you couldn't understand, and now, now that you are here, everything makes sense.

The stories of Karbala that you grew up listening to, all the *majlis* gatherings at your grandparents' home, commemorating the sacrifices of the martyrs, all these deep spiritual experiences from a tender age pulsate in every pore of your body. All those elegies you sang, lamenting how Husain's side was denied access to water for 3 days before the battle, how the severed heads of the martyrs were paraded in the markets, along with their families who were taken prisoner. Elegies of how the women and children were whipped mercilessly if they so much as cried for their loved ones. Every tear that escaped your eye, taught you compassion and empathy by experiencing a pain that wasn't yours; every shudder through your spine at the brutalities taught you to speak up against cruelty. Every tiny speck of love for humanity and the desire to fight for the oppressed, which made its way into your heart through these stories of sacrifice, culminated in this love for Husain.

Your soul pulled you all the way here. It is a homecoming. The culmination of your childhood, adolescence, and adulthood. The call of the blood in your veins.

To be here is to experience mindfulness, what you might call mind cleansing. Everything else falls away from your consciousness, and all you are aware of is being in the here and now. Being in the place that you have grown up hearing about, amid the names that have touched you and inspired you in ways unfathomable.

And when you join the line of pilgrims moving slowly towards the grave of Husain, his actual resting place, your heart is moved to tears. Here lies the defender of the oppressed whose head was severed from his body, who was denied a single drop of water. Towards his feet is buried his 18-year-old young boy, martyred in the battle. And on his chest is buried his 6-month-old baby, the infant whose neck was speared with a three-headed arrow for no fault of his own.

A place of great pathos.

The toddler on his father's chest reminds one of Husain's 4-year-old daughter Sakina who is buried in Syria, in an ancient prison where the ladies of Husain's family were kept as prisoners of war. The history of Karbala is incomplete without the stories of Sakina and her suffering.

Places of great suffering become places of great wish fulfilment, because of the cosmic power of goodness and selflessness. The sufferings endured by holy men and women bestow great gravity to the places of their rest, strength channelled through spiritual elevation. Great sacrifice transforms to great power.

I prop little Hamza securely on my hip and lift him up for a glimpse of Imam Husain's grave from afar. And now, as we reach the grave, he places his tiny hands on the *jaali* surrounding the tomb, and I ask him, gently, to offer his salaam to the Imam. For it is our belief that martyrs never die. They are forever alive, receiving sustenance from their Lord. So says the Quran.

As we head back from the rauza, for some inexplicable reason, my mind wanders to the time after my marriage when Salman and I visited my father's resting place in Allahabad.

Perhaps I remember this now because Allahabad is where my association with Karbala began. It is the place where, in my childhood, I observed the month of Muharram every year, the month of mourning for Husain. It is the city that is connected in my mind with two of my greatest heroes — Imam Husain, and my father.

It is natural perhaps, that as I exit the tomb of Husain, I begin to recall the last time I visited the grave of my other hero, my father.

I had clutched Salman's hand tightly, instinctively, as we entered the *qabristan.* He had clutched mine right back, reassuring me in his unspoken way that I wasn't alone in my grief.

The very first time I had been to my father's grave was a few months after his passing. I was 9 at the time and barely understood the gravity of death—except for what I had seen in movies. I don't think I really grieved for my father in the earlier years of his passing, not very consciously at least, for grieving requires comprehension and a depth of emotion usually not open to a 9-year-old. Since then, the older I have grown, the stronger my grief has been.

The chronology of grief is strangely fashioned. I have been mourning my father backwards for a long time now.

As I clutched Salman's hand in the *qabristan*, a knot tightened inside my throat, loosening itself slowly, pouring out grief through the ducts in my eyes. Tears streamed ceaselessly down as we walked soundlessly towards the cluster of five graves near a tree: my great grandmother, great grandfather, grandmother, grandfather, and him. My papa. Tiny purple flowers sprouting on the grave, like his booming laugh and cheerfulness had found a way to travel between worlds.

My mother, sister, and two cousins accompanied us to the grave, and we all prayed verses from the Quran for the deliverance of the departed. Grief kept pouring from my eyes even as I prayed. My cousin stared at my unceasing tears. It had been 15 years since he passed away.

After we had prayed and everyone stood up to leave, I found myself wanting to stay. Wanting to sit there with my palms on the earth, to speak to my father as I used to, and more than anything, to sit there and cry. Cry, cry, cry my heart out.

The need to cry was overpowering. And yet, I couldn't muster enough courage to ask the others to leave me there.

And now, today in Karbala, 5 years later, I think of Sayyeda Zainab, Husain's sister, who was not allowed to grieve for her brother, for her sons, her nephews, and all the 72 men martyred on that fateful day. I think of Sakina who was whipped and lashed, all because she wept for her father. None of Husain's imprisoned family members were allowed to cry and to grieve.

The denial of the right to grieve is that grave, dark form of oppression which only the grieving can understand.

To not have your suffering recognised is an almost unbearable form of violence, wrote Andrei Lankov. Even if that suffering is as outwardly insignificant as a forlorn woman raising a child alone.

Chapter 32
To Be a Hindi

June 28, 2015

Karbala

The most fascinating discovery in my journey to the resting place of Husain and his people is that this isn't just a place of grief. It is a place of joy as well, a place of love and shared happiness—of gifting joy to strangers. For the people living around the rauza, it is their place not just to cry, but also to smile, to take out their *iftaars* in the evening and spread the mats in the open areas and break their fast in the vicinity of where their *Maula* lies. For us, in the distant land of 'Hind', where Muharram is observed for two months a year, Karbala is a symbol of sacrifice and grief. But for these people, who live as neighbours to the Imam, Karbala is not merely a place of grief and sacrifice, but also of celebration of life lived with goodness and joy that is not dependent upon materialism and hedonism. So, when they need to share happiness, they walk to the door of their Imam. With Husain is their grief, with Husain is their joy.

In Karbala, we find many moments of joy and shared smiles with perfect strangers.

At one shop, we were purchasing souvenirs. 'Irani?' asks the owner. Everyone I meet in Iraq seems to think I am from Iran.

'Na Irani,' I smile. 'Hindi.'

'Ah, Hindi!' he breaks into a blinding smile. 'Hindi *habibi*! Hindi *habibi*!' He chants, hand on heart. *Indians, my friends! I love Indians!*

I smile broadly at him, delighted. It is positively enchanting how Iraqis love India. The mere mention of 'Hind' gets you free smiles everywhere. And other things as well. He dives beneath his counter and brings out tiny packets of *khaak e shifa* for us. The Dust of Healing. Earth in which the blood of Husain has been mixed, owing to his martyrdom. It is believed to have curative qualities.

'This is the real *khaak e shifa*, you know,' he says in English. 'It was taken directly from the grave of Imam Husain during renovations.' Iraqis speak English with ease.

I take the packets from him and ask how much he is to be paid.

'No, no!' he insists. 'This is a gift. You are Hindi. Hindi Habibi.'

I am touched and humbled by this gesture. Not because he gave us something free of cost, but because of his love for my country and her people.

Imam Husain, it is believed, spoke highly of 'Hind' and the peace-loving people that resided here.

> *'Bharat mein agar aa jata, hriday mein utaara jaata / Yun chaand Bani Hashim ka dhokey se na maara jaata.'*
>
> (Had he come to India, he would have been welcomed into our hearts / This glowing moon of the tribe of Bani Hashim would not have been killed through treachery.)

Thus goes an elegy dedicated to Husain by poet Naresh Pandit.

Perhaps that is the reason behind all this love for us among the Iraqis.

Later, in the afternoon, we are in the security check line and the security lady is patting me up to check for potential weapons before I enter the rauza. It is one of the many routine checks that happen around Karbala. Suddenly, the woman stops, looks directly at my face and asks me the question I have grown accustomed to by now.

'Irani?'

'Na Irani. Hindi,' I smile, expecting 'Hindi Habibi' to be showered upon me. Her response surprises me.

'*Jamila!*' she exclaims, appreciation writ large on her face. '*Jamila!*'

Beautiful! You're beautiful!

I am astonished and find myself blushing in surprise. The compliment is unexpected. As I move ahead, the woman beckons to her colleague at the other end of the room.

'Hindi!' she indicates towards me, informing her colleague.

'Ah, Jamila!' echoes the other woman admiringly, smiling at me as I move past her.

Self-conscious and blushing furiously now, I step out of the security check area. I would be lying, though, if I say that I am not absolutely delighted!

Iraqis are a genuinely warm, friendly lot. In so many ways they are like Indians—even the not-so-desirable ways where there is plenty of garbage visible at roadsides. But they are super welcoming and possess what we would refer to as *garm joshi* in our land. Warmth.

The women surprise me in their eagerness to help out a perfect stranger when she is struggling with her kid. And struggle I did plenty. Not that it was any fault of brave little Hamza, who walked far longer distances than his 2-year-old legs possessed the capacity to cover. And when that capacity was exhausted, I would swing him up in my arms and carry him all the way ahead, which was not a very easy thing for me to do either, given the extremities we were faced with: the distances we had to walk and the weather we had to endure.

One time, we spent all night at the rauza, offering multiple kinds of namaz and praying all night through to dawn. It is the night before Friday, a special time for prayers, holding even more significance for a traveller from far away who would be at the rauza for just a couple of days. Determined little Hamza stays up all night with me as I pray, sitting beside me and playing with my prayer beads and a couple of toy cars I brought to keep him entertained. As the night draws to a close and the sound of *Fajr azaan* breaks into the air, Hamza decides he has had enough. Just as the *azaan* begins, he lets out a long wail for his mom to take him into his arms. I am in a dilemma because everyone is rising for the pre-dawn prayers and I cannot pray with him in my arms.

All of a sudden, a toffee and a chocolate land upon Hamza's head, literally like *manna* from Heaven. I look around astonished, and spot an Iraqi mom smiling at me from five positions away to my left. She had heard my baby wail and had tossed the chocolates at me right from where she stood as she was too far to hand them out. One woman trying to help another.

Before I could even take in the beauty and kindness of her gesture, there is a nudge from behind and another woman hands me an apple. 'For your son,' she says. I smile warmly at her.

It is the kindness of perfect strangers perhaps which is the biggest takeaway of any pilgrimage. Where we are stripped of social status and cultural status, where we help each other without expectation, without transaction. Where we understand that the only way to serve God is through serving humans.

If this didn't permeate your core, it was merely a journey of the flesh. Not a journey of the soul.

July 2, 2015

Najaf, Iraq

The funniest part of this trip is that I am falling in love with Iraq, very unexpectedly, because of the food. It is flavourful yet non-spicy, a boon for a person like me who never had a good relationship with the trademark smoking hot spices of North Indian cuisine, particularly Mughlai.

My sister, here, purchases the spiciest snack labelled as 'hot', opens the packet, takes one bite, gets majorly disappointed, and hands it over to me.

'You have it, it's your type,' she adds wryly. What is 'spicy' in Iraq is bland to my sister and just perfect for me. Chicken-flavoured cheese balls. Now that is a first!

In fact, the iftaars served regularly from the Rauza of Imam Ali now seem pretty bland for me, too, for we are now in Najaf. And yet, this bland food agrees with me far better than the make-your-eyes-water dishes that I have to battle with so frequently back home. It is the month of Ramzan and quite like Karbala, the people living in the vicinity of the rauza at Najaf bring out their families with their iftaars, and after offering namaz spread out bedsheets on the ground, lay their food upon them, and have iftaar all around the rauza. Today I am alone, for my mother and sister and Hamza have all gone back to the hotel, dead tired after a day of walking long distances. I have stayed back just to taste the *iftaari* handed out from the rauza, like an Indian *langar*. A small aluminium packet of Iraqi food in hand, I sit down outside the gates of the rauza, among the crowd of Iraqis breaking their day-long fast.

Unexpectedly, the Iraqi family next to me offers me fruits from their spread. I refuse vehemently, but they insist with great fervour.

Do they think I am a lonely, homeless, broke pilgrim? Have I been eyeing their food inadvertently? Or are they just plain generous, for no specific reason? Never before in my life have I had iftaar with perfect strangers. And it is a sweet, fruity kind of feeling. The Iraqis are jovial and warm. And yet, you only have to look around to know what they have been through.

Yesterday, our group was taken to Kadhimiya—the northern neighbourhood of Baghdad, home to the rauzas of the seventh and ninth Imams—and to the city of Samarra, home to the rauzas of the tenth and eleventh Imams along with his mother and sister. A world heritage site as declared by UNESCO, Samarra has been in the thick of violence and sectarian attacks, holding witness to it in the ghost town around the rauza. Eerie empty houses pockmarked with bullet holes line both sides of the road that leads to the tomb. No less haunting are the twice-bombed minarets and domes, now being reconstructed even as we move around in the building.

My friends wonder how I could have agreed to travel to Iraq, a war-ravaged country very much in the thick of violence. And yet, despite the harsh weather, the long distances in the most savage heat, despite holding back tears of frustration when my son would straddle my neck as I prostrated in prayer, and worse, despite the threat of gunfire looming over our heads—despite all of it, in this turbulent land I have found peace.

Peace is not silence. It is not stillness. It is not found merely within buildings and holy lands. Peace is hidden within the patterns of our mind, the images constructed for years which suddenly come to life. Peace is contained in the heart, in its responses to the universe around us, in the love we hold that enables us to experience everything more fully. Hardened hearts, emptied of love and mercy, can never experience peace.

Chapter 33

Boats Ashore

July 4, 2015

Aligarh, India

The humdrum safety of small-town life in India feels surreal after the incredible journey we just undertook. For a long time, we bask in the healing glow, discussing every detail amongst us.

Slowly, the glitter fades and reality comes back into the frame. There is still that little issue of my family living a split life for almost three years now and the need to get our resources on track to get it all back together. And the other little issue which is that my relationship with my husband has gone for a toss, all tangled up like a mess of high voltage wires, crackling with tension.

August 5, 2015

Salman calls me up to inform that he is scouting for an apartment to rent. Finally!

'What about the credit card debt?'

'We'll deal with it.'

We discuss distances, localities, societies, floors, bedrooms, balconies, and rentals. He has shortlisted several options on his intra-office website that enables employees to let out homes to colleagues. There is one 3BHK on offer for a pretty decent amount but there is no woodwork. Cross out. There is another 3 BHK but it comes with a pretty steep rental. Cross out. And then there is one 3 BHK right on the ground floor and with a reasonable rental. That's the one.

There is a catch, though. Of course. There had to be. The flat has been rented out to relatives of the owner and they will be vacating it in a fortnight from now.

Oh. Okay. Another fortnight. That is . . . not so bad, I suppose. What is another fortnight compared to three years of waiting?

August 25, 2015

I knew it. We are jinxed. Someone has put a hex on us. The same pattern keeps repeating over and over again in our lives and for the life of us, we are not able to break the curse.

It has been twenty days now. The owner of the flat we are trying to rent asks us to wait another week and that is when he will get the flat vacated for sure.

I am angry. Very, very angry. Just let this flat go, I tell Salman. There are hundreds of other flats in Delhi/NCR. This isn't the only one, is it?

Sept 2, 2015

Letting go isn't one of Salman's strong points. (I ought to have known that by now, considering how committed he has always been to me.)

Another fortnight has passed since then and it is quite obvious that the previous tenants are in no mood to vacate the flat. Salman finally gives up and begins his search all over again.

Sept 15, 2015

Finally. A 2BHK flat in a good neighbourhood with all the amenities and facilities of modern life. We get it through the intra-company site, and the owner tells us that we can shift in right at the beginning of next month. The rent agreement would be finalised in a week.

The beginning of next month. Two more weeks to go.

What is the catch? What is the fine-print? Where is the 'T&C apply'? Where? What? How?

It can't be that smooth. Not when it comes to us.

Could it be that the curse is drawing to an end? Are we jinxed no more?

Only time will tell.

Chapter 34

HOME

October 3, 2015

3:00 p.m.

Home.

A two-bedroom flat in a high-rise building of a nice residential society within a beautiful township in the National Capital Region.

Two hours' drive from Aligarh, three days of packing and preparation. Kitchenware shopping on the insistence of my mother.

No lists made.

No dreams spun.

No hopes attached that could be dashed to the ground at the last minute.

A strange culmination.

Salman unlocks the door of our tenth floor flat and I walk slowly through the hall and the bedrooms, blank and numb in an alien surrounding.

The culmination of three years of agony, right to the date.

A happy ending. If happy endings exist.

Salman glances at me several times, anxious to see if he has finally made things right. Anxious to know if the house he chose has won my heart. And I do not know how to tell him that I cannot feel my heart at all. Like the swimmer in bone-chilling waters who cannot feel his legs for a long time after, I have been swimming for far too long in the cold, dark ocean of illusions. In an inward spiralling, *Inception*-like dream consciousness, I have lived far too long in a world where everything turns out to be . . . unreal. The icy currents have numbed my heart. I don't feel anything.

Looking at the house over and over again, I try to miraculously *induce* the missing joy. But these aren't modern-day labour pains—you can't induce them and get them over with.

I force a smile and feign enthusiasm that I don't feel in the slightest bit.

9:00 p.m.

I look at the cream-coloured walls of the room and the dark mahogany furniture outlined against it, trying to imagine what curtains would look best here, and what I should adorn the walls with. I try to pull out long-held fantasies and dreams of having my own cosy space, to beautify it my way. I skim my fingers over the fresh sheets on the bed and wonder where all the feeling has gone.

After so much anger, hurt, rising hopes, falling hopes, enthusiasm, determination, shock, resentment, frowns, smiles, tears—so much emotion, such blistering extremes of it, I have perhaps been emptied to the gut. Tipped over and drained.

I try feebly, yet again, to make myself *feel.* Anything. Not necessarily euphoria or joy, just *feel.*

Nothing.

All that emerges are wisps of doubt and disbelief. Smoky remnants of hope charred over and over.

Is this it? Is it finally over? Are we here, well and truly?

Despite myself, I keep expecting the house to vanish in a minute, and the man lying down beside me to grow large red eyes and change shape into a devilish creature while the ground beneath us slips away, wobbling like jelly, before I wake up panting and break into cold sweat. Any minute now, I keep expecting to wake up.

My mind has grown so accustomed to mirages it refuses to believe that the desert has fallen behind. It has blindfolded itself, refusing to acknowledge that something major has happened, that this spells an end to a seemingly never-ending ordeal.

Like the refugee boats in the ocean reaching shore when all hope has died quietly.

October 30, 2015

'All language is a longing for home.'

—Rumi

Earlier this year, at the Jaipur Litfest, I had interviewed journalist and author Samanth Subramanian on his shocking and thought-provoking book *This Divided Island*. The book has now made it to the shortlist of the Samuel Johnson Prize and I have been asked to interview him again by the newspaper that I write for.

As I am digging up the Internet for more background research, I come across an article on the launch of Samanth's book. A person in the audience had asked him a question: 'Can people who have moved to a new land claim that the place they live on is theirs simply because they have lived there for many years?'

Samanth responded with another question: 'How long do you have to live in a place before you can call it a homeland?'

It is a very pertinent question, especially in the context of his book, which documents the ground reality of Sri Lanka after the end of a 30-year-long civil war between the Tamils and the Sinhalas. These problems aren't exactly region-specific, though. It is a global phenomenon, one that is increasingly visible now. You see it all the time in news reports—he is an immigrant, she is a foreigner, these people came as conquerors, those came as refugees, these people are outsiders, those are minorities that hailed from so and so country. And now, even though they have been living here for decades—if not centuries—you still refuse to acknowledge that this is their home, too.

'How much land does a man need?' wrote Tolstoy in 1886.

How many years does a man need for a land to be his homeland?

How long, indeed?

It has been about three weeks since I moved to my new apartment, of which Hamza and I spent just ten days there as we went back to Aligarh for the remaining time to observe the month of Muharram. Yesterday, as I returned and switched on the lights of my apartment, I felt . . . home.

Which is not how I had felt when we had first moved in.

What has changed?

Being away from this place, I could view it from the perspective that distance brings. Going back to where I had come from, I could see what I had wanted to escape. From that height, I could see home.

Home, sweet new home.

How did this new place that had felt cold and alien suddenly acquire the air of home?

Perhaps because I found peace in it.

Perhaps because I could fashion it the way I wanted. Because I had invested my time and effort in it and could invest freely, going ahead. I was responsible for this place, involved in it, and could make it what I wanted. More significantly, in here I could be who I was, and who I wanted to be.

And that is what is home.

Or even, homeland.

You are responsible for it. It is your concern. You make it what you want it to be, you nurture it like a child, like an image of your own self, of all the selves that live in it. Its problems are yours, and so are its joys and celebrations. More than anything, it is home because it gives you freedom.

But along with freedom, there is responsibility. Together they make a place a home. Until each person, each group, and community finds a share in the freedom and the responsibility, it cannot be a real home. Each person dwelling in there needs to feel that they have invested something in it and that they can harvest the joys and benefits that accrue from that investment. They need to know they have a say in the direction their home takes, and their contribution to it will be acknowledged. They need to feel free, and also to feel secure. Because it is just not a home if you can't feel safe within it, if you can't live in peace.

One might wonder though, don't love and care embody the spirit of home? Yes, they do. Without love, without care, without concern for each other, there can be no home. But various kinds of love exist in this world, and not all are the kinds you would want to have.

Love can be smothering, stifling, strangling. So can care. You might be loved by someone, and yet not *feel* loved. Because the way they choose to give you their love might not be the way you wish to receive it. And that makes all the difference. If, in my great desire to treat you to a delicious meal, I cook three varieties of chicken and seekh kebabs, without bothering to remember that you are an avowed vegetarian, what sort of love would that be? Ill-informed, biased, assumption-based love, as opposed to the love that seeks out ways to give actual joy to the beloved, keeping in mind the preferences of the loved one. Then again, what if I knew you were a vegetarian, and yet cooked all those dishes for you, because I thought I knew what was best for you, because I wanted you to adopt my way, the 'best' way? What kind of love would it be then? Bossy, controlling, selfish love, which dismissed your preferences and desires and made me foist my own wishes upon you. That is not to say I don't actually love you—but it is definitely not the kind of love you would want to receive.

There is also a disabling kind of love, reflected in over-protectiveness and bordering on pity, which all but destroys the self-esteem of the loved one. The kind of love where you do everything for those you love and not let them do a thing on their own—no matter how much they may want to do it. Where you constantly shower the object of your affection with pity for their weaknesses, without enabling them to overcome those. The love that leaves you almost disabled and crushes your independence.

Those are the kinds of love that make it impossible for a home to be home. So, yes, love is of great significance but freedom to be loved in the way you would *want* to be loved makes all the difference. And that is why freedom comes first.

But freedom without responsibility wouldn't make it your home, it would make it a temporary dwelling instead—a hotel, if you will, or a guest house perhaps. You are just there to have a good time and reap the rewards of its success, but unwilling to brave the pains taken to get there. You do not wish to invest in it. But until you do so, it will never be home—for a home's needs must be fashioned with your blood, sweat, and tears.

Home is the echo of the body's longings to put down roots and belong to the earth, for earth is the element that our bones and our flesh were first fashioned from.

November 1, 2015

Home.

Where you do things together, where you grieve and you smile and you bicker and you make up, several times over.

Hamza is a lot calmer now that his parents are living together. Despite my attempts to understand the longings of his tiny heart, I hadn't anticipated how much of a difference this would make. There are significantly less tantrums, significantly less anger. Not just on his part but on mine as well. For one, whenever I am exhausted and at my wit's end on how to deal with his three-year-old stubbornness and meltdowns, Salman steps in. He takes over from me—he soothes, he reasons, distracts, or scolds—as the situation may be. I am no longer the sole person taking on this huge responsibility, no longer the single parent.

For what it's worth, these three years have taught me some major lessons. They have made me empathise with and see more clearly the extreme struggles of my mother. Despite all the love and the strong bond that we share, I have harboured some secret grudges against her—against her parenting style, against the things she said and did, or did not say and did not do. And it is only now, after three years of virtually being a single parent, that I have finally understood how difficult it has been for her, being a single parent for two whole decades.

Twenty years. Only now do I grasp the gravity of it.

Right now, for me, a mountain has been lifted off my chest. Once again, the Russian fairytale comes to mind, where the heroine is pushed down to the bottom of the lake with a mammoth rock crushing her chest, keeping her down, down in the depths, unable to breathe, unable to come up, unable to be rescued.

But I am safe now.

Have I been rescued by my knight in shining armour?
Have I rescued my own self a little bit, just a little?
Or have we been rescued by fate?

November 5, 2015

I find friends.

I find scattered around me, in the various high-rise buildings, women that I can call friends. A surprising community of like-minded people. Through the boon of technology, I find women who are cheerful, educated, compassionate, and empathetic. Not all of them have careers, but all of them are good people who appreciate each other and pull each other up. I find this scattered community of people who are not constantly peering and poking into each other's lives, not gossiping about each other but going about their own sweet business, living their own interesting lives, a blessing to have around me. I have escaped the small-town viciousness of constant interference in one's personal life, constant scrutiny, commentary, and mockery of one's personal choices, constant pressure to toe the line. And yet, most amazingly, I have also evaded the big city malaise of people who are so disjointed from each other that they have nothing to do with each other's joys and sorrows, and no one to help them out. These women seek help from each other, invite each other to celebrate joys and share grief, and extend a family-like helping hand whenever the other needs them.

It fills my heart with joy to have these people around.

November 16, 2015

Majlis at my place.

I had made a solemn vow, an oath to myself when I returned from Karbala, that the moment Salman and I finally find a house, the moment we move into it and be together as a family, I will hold a majlis at my place—a spiritual gathering to commemorate the martyrs of Karbala.

I have longed to hold this commemoration at a place I can call my own for a long time now. Perhaps, a leftover longing from my childhood, from my father's ancestral home where these commemorations were carried out with much fervour. I have no family here, but I do not feel the slightest need to call my family over for help. This new-found group of scattered friends is my new family.

They purchase the cloth of the *alam* on my behalf—a replica of the flag carried by the martyr Abbas in Karbala, which is kept symbolically in these gatherings. They stitch the *patka* or the accompanying cloth behind the main *alam*, they volunteer to come and help me out with the preparations, they stand by me through everything. They are angels sent down from heaven. They show me that inside all of us there is an angel waiting to spread wings, if we but allow it to fly.

I make food with my own hands for all the 60 guests—assisted by my domestic helps, who are another group of angels in disguise. If it were not for the helps at our homes, seriously, I wonder how we would keep our careers together or even our marriages. The fact that I can write all my articles in peace, or even spend some quiet romantic moments with Salman, is almost entirely dependent on the tonnes of work managed by my helps, which affords me many a quiet moment of contemplation and love. They are also, thus, the mainstay of all this food I make—grinding the *masalas*, making the *paranthas*, washing the utensils, and so on and so forth.

Kebabs, *paranthas*, *chhole*, *dahi-phulki*, and *gajar ka halwa*. Sounds like a feast, but it is not a celebration. It is soul food. A token of gratitude. Thanking the guests for arriving at your place and not sending them back with empty stomachs, and thanking the Lord for the honour of hosting a sacred commemoration. That food can be sacred is a thought that is all pervasive in Indian culture, in any religion you could think of.

There is a lot of work to be done, but it is indescribably fulfilling. It is the act of fashioning my home. Blood, sweat, and tears.

December 25, 2015

An unexpected Christmas gift.

I get a call from a former colleague who offers me a position in a luxury magazine, a job where I do the maximum work from home and go out only to interview eminent personalities. This is a very significant development, for there is no family back-up to care for my son if I take up a full-time position, and I am loath to put my son in the care of people who are not family. Yes, career moms do it all the time, and it works out just fine. But we all have our little fears and demons hiding in the closet, don't we? This offer is like the best of both worlds, where I balance my professional passion with my pressing urge to be a hands-on mother, and also create a dream home, now that I am here in it.

My heart suddenly feels full and I wonder at how perfectly the pieces have begun to fall in place, etching out a pretty, sanguine little landscape.

Once again, I hear the echo of that little word.

Maktub.

Chapter 35
HEALING

When I interviewed Booker Prize Winner Eleanor Catton at the Litfest in January last year, I asked her to define for me the one biggest thing she had learnt on her journey of discovery as a writer. She took a moment to consider.

'I learnt,' she said contemplatively, 'that all great stories are love stories.'

December 28, 2015

As the months roll by, I realise that in the time we were apart I had romanticised my husband far beyond the truth. I had turned him into the prince of my fairy tale dreams—so many things that he wasn't. So many annoying, aggravating traits, so many exasperating and incorrigible habits that I had forgotten. But I had also forgotten so many things that he was—sweet, beautiful things that hold within them the capacity for solace and peace; things that matter in the mundane, commonplace affair called life.

What one really needs, I suppose, is not a knight or a prince, but a simple, sensible, compassionate human being who treats you with the respect deserved by a fellow human, encourages you to be the fullest version of yourself, and stands by you throughout the vicissitudes of life.

Salman and I, we have so many things to discover about each other with our coming together again, things that we have to relearn in an almost new beginning of married life.

It is as if the first two years had been a beautiful but distant dream and the next three horrible ones a nightmare, and we have only just woken up to finally live with each other. Everything needs to be pieced together afresh.

I can't help but ponder over the fact that all heroes in fairy tales and mushy Mills & Boons are dripping rich princes and Rolls Royce-owning billionaires. But that is not always the case in real life, is it? Real love doesn't come with diamond studs and gold bands attached. Real love goes through real ups and downs. Real-life heroes handle real-life responsibilities such as jobs, families, credit cards, and parenting, and they handle them with grit. Real-life heroines don't have fairy godmothers and magic wands. Real heroines do a lot of rescuing themselves.

Real lovers rescue each other. And real love stories don't end with a kiss and a happily ever after. They begin at 'ever after' and you have to keep putting the 'happily' back in them. Again and again and again.

January 10, 2016

The best new year in forever.

Now that Salman and I are together, we function as a team. Perhaps not as smoothly as we would like to believe, but as a team nonetheless.

We pay off that dreadful credit card debt. We shop together for home décor and own our living space. We look up recipes on YouTube and experiment together. We buy plants for the balcony, flowering and non-flowering ones, but especially the fragrant jasmine. That is my favourite. We play hide and seek with Hamza and pretend not to see the bulge hidden behind the curtain. We take him down to the park where all three of us proceed to race each other. We watch movies in the other room on the laptop when Hamza is fast asleep, and we stay up all night talking.

We sit together at the dining table long past dinner, holding each other's hands and speaking quietly of the years that just went by, putting into words that emotion, which in Urdu one might call *shikva*: a deep, intimate, lovingly pleading complaint; of things that were and were not. Slowly we unwrap our emotional baggage and lay it at each other's feet, picking out broken bits and pieces, and attempt, haltingly, to heal.

It doesn't happen overnight.

There is a lot that needs to be done. We need to forgive. Forgive each other and forgive our own selves.

It is not easy.

There is so much residual hurt, so much leftover pain, it throbs and pinches periodically. Wounds take painstakingly long to heal. But we sit here, face to face, eyes to eyes, grief to grief, and joy to joy, with a little boy playing on the floor to our right, oblivious to all the tumult he has been through from the moment he was born.

'Baba, look I am a circus boy!' he says, getting down on his hands and knees and raising one leg gymnastically back in the air. 'Ta-da-da Da-da!'

His audience applauds appreciatively. He then brings out his menagerie of animals—lions, elephants, horses, parrots—all set to perform their respective acts. 'Baba, I will be a zookeeper when I'm big!' He beams at us.

Hamza is little. He remembers no sorrow, only the joy of the moment. The fulfilment of having his family together, the delight of limitless imagination.

Childhood heals fast. Adulthood takes longer.

Hamza is healed and whole.

Salman and I? We are still somewhere on the meandering path to the snow-covered slopes of healing.

But we are getting there.

Epilogue

When You Read This, Hamza

Unplanned.

I read an article a few days ago, in which the writer emphasised that her baby had not been unplanned, or an 'afterthought', or an 'obligation fulfilled'.

And I didn't want you to ever, even for a moment, label yourself as 'unplanned', without understanding what it might mean.

There are countless things in life that occur unplanned. Love is one of those.

Falling in love with your father wasn't something I had planned either. Not in a million years could I have fathomed that he would be the man I would share my life with.

For as long as I can remember, I was very decided about the things I wanted from life. Because the Indian society is so shaped that girls as young as 8 or 9 are made conscious of their impending marriage, I had formed very clear thoughts about who I would marry and how. At the age of 12, I had decided I would not change my last name when I married. At the age of 13, I decided I would never marry a man whose family asks for dowry. In fact, I would never let my mother give me any dowry at all. (Both of these promises I proceeded to fulfil.) And when I was 14, in standard X, I had decided I would name my daughter Zainab. I was in love with that name. (I had no idea, of course, that it would be a son arriving instead.)

And so, too, I had very fixed ideas of what kind of man I would like. Witty, funny, smart, open-minded, adventure-loving—and with a preference for dancing. And romantic, don't forget romantic. (I suppose I had based that description on my greatest crush of those times: Hrithik Roshan.) But most importantly, over and above all those, it had to be a man who wasn't egoistic or overbearing, a man who treated me as his equal, and who didn't park himself as an obstacle in my career path.

It was around this time that I first met your father. No, it wasn't love at first sight for me (though for your dad it was, he claims). I wasn't interested at all 'in a guy like him'. I didn't like the serious, religious, sermonising types. I probably hated him, and all the more because my family kept telling me, 'Look at him, what a good man he is, so responsible. Learn something from him.'

Yeah, right.

To cut a long tale short, my falling in love with him came several years later.

And over all these years of marriage, he has delighted me by being witty, funny, charming, smart, adventure-loving, and (with much training) romantic, as well. And he certainly isn't egoistic or overbearing.

But the thing, dear heart, is this: I loved him not *because* he was all that I had dreamt of. I loved him just *because.*

I fell in love with him for his honesty, his integrity, his genuineness of character. For being a man I could respect, and even find guidance with. A man I would never actually have imagined loving. And *this,* my son, is what I want you to remember: unplanned doesn't mean unloved.

They often compare us women to flowers. It is not because we are fragile or ornamental. It is because we have layers. We are composed of a multitude of petals in so many different shapes and sizes. A woman is a daughter, a sister, a wife, a mother—and a doctor, lawyer, engineer, teacher, journalist, or what have you. She is all of those, and they are not pitted against each other. They are what make her who she is, each of those petals combined. Like a brilliant multifaceted diamond, we are all of those at the same time. We don't have to pick one over another. And that is where the problem arises.

Society forces you to choose. It forces you to declare that you are one thing above all others. And mostly, it expects you to declare that above everything else you are a mother. Well, I am not.

I'm not a mother *above* everything else. I am a mother *along with* everything else that I am. It is an integral part of me. And I shouldn't have to denounce all other parts to acknowledge this one.

This, my son, is something I hope you would understand one day, particularly for the sake of the woman you shall share your life with. Someday, I hope you both share a love greater than the one your father and I have. And that day, you will know that loving her doesn't mean we are less important, or vice versa. In the same way that loving you doesn't detract from my love for your father, nor does his love detract from my love for you. You are both inseparable parts of my life.

But here is the difference, love. And I hope you would appreciate it someday. He is the man in my life. Just as for you would be the woman you love. And that is not me—though the world would again force you to acknowledge that your mother is the most important. That is when I hope you will tell the world: they are both different facets of me, and they are not pitted against each other.

She would be the one who completes you. And yet, that wouldn't mean you were incomplete with us. It just means she makes you a fuller, better version of who you were—that is how God intends it to be. And so it is with us; your father and I were blissfully complete with each other. But when you came along, you made us better, fuller version of ourselves—that is how God intends it to be.

I pray that you would understand the many diverse loves that our being is composed of, that they are all different and meant to coexist, without competing with each other. That I don't love you *as much* as I love your father, and I don't love him *as much* as I love my father. I just love you. I just love your father. And I just love my father. Simple. No levels, no greater than or less than. No one is 'the best'. You are all me.

I hope one day you will understand this.

Or maybe, one day you will come up with your own theories and ideas about the way we love and the way we live. I would love to hear them and be contradicted.

Until then,

With as much love as a mother's heart can hold,

Mumma

Acknowledgements

I am grateful, first and foremost, to my editor Ruchita Ahuja who understood this book and the complex emotions emanating from it, and with the lightest of touch, chiselled and sculpted the edges into shape.

Many thanks to Mr Shubhrangshu Roy for the effort he put into reading the first draft and going through it with his editor's pen—and for believing in this book, always. Thanks to Sana Zehra for her patience and support and her very important comments about the first draft.

Special thanks to Kathi Ostrom Gowsell, who was the first person to suggest that this story must be given the shape of a book. Despite living on separate continents and never having met each other, we are connected in indefinable ways.

I am grateful to Rana Safvi Apa whom I always turned to for guidance and for answers to my numerous questions. Hanadi Falki, Dipali Taneja, Kiranjeet Chaturvedi, and Piyusha Vir for their readily offered suggestions.

My closest friends Reema Ahmad and Jyoti Singh for their invaluable inputs and unflinching support not just during the writing of this book, but during my tumultuous journey of early parenthood. You had my back in the worst of times, and reassured me that I was a good mother after all. My dear friend Nadeem Kazmi who was and is always my 'guru', who takes it upon himself to keep reminding me of who I am and why I need to believe in myself.

Many thanks to all the readers of my blog who showered me with love and sent me heartfelt messages, telling me that I must keep going, for I was their voice, too.

Thank you to my amazing parents, who share a deep love for literature. My mother, for narrating the short stories of Tolstoy and Chekhov at bedtime, and for keeping in her almirah every little scrap of childish poetry I ever wrote. My father, for being the one who taught me to never stop dreaming no matter how impossible the dream—and to always speak the truth. For guiding me, unfailingly, from the other dimension.

Thank you to my sister—always my baby—for loving me to bits, for being fiercely loyal and always egging me on to be the best version of myself.

Most of all, I want to thank my partner, for putting up with my tempestuous streak, holding my hand through the most devastating storms, and taking the utmost pride in my work. For pulling me out of the black holes of self-doubt, and for personifying everything that is good and pure in this Universe.

Last of all, because you are the youngest of all, I thank you little son, for peeking into my notepad and reading the words 'failing as a mother', and coming to tell me, 'You will not fail, mummy. You will pass. You never fail at anything, I know.'